Strike Eagle

Also by William L. Smallwood

Warthog: Flying the A-10 in the Gulf War

The Air Force Academy Candidate Book

The Naval Academy Candidate Book

The West Point Candidate Book

Strike Eagle

Flying the F-15E in the Gulf War

William L. Smallwood

BRASSEY'S INC.
Washington   London

Brassey's Inc.

Editorial Offices
Brassey's Inc.
8000 Westpark Drive
First Floor
McLean, Virginia 22102

Order Department
Brassey's Book Orders
c/o Macmillan Publishing Co.
100 Front Street, Box 500
Riverside, New Jersey 08075

Brassey's Inc. books are available at special discounts for bulk purchases for sales promotions, premiums, fund-raising, or educational use through the Special Sales Director, Macmillan Publishing Company, 866 Third Avenue, New York, New York 10022

ISBN 0-02-881058-9

Printed in the United States of America

TO FOUR WHO GAVE IT ALL:

LT. COL. DONNIE HOLLAND
MAJ. TOM KORITZ
MAJ. PETE HOOK
CAPT. JIM POULET

ACKNOWLEDGMENTS

In May 1990, before Saddam Hussein invaded Kuwait, my friend Lt. Col. Harold "Skip" Bennett talked me into visiting his squadron, the 461st Deadly Jesters, at Luke Air Force Base, Arizona. "We've got an awesome new airplane and I would like to show it to you," he said. I made the visit, did a walk-around on the flightline with Skip, then went to the squadron and watched a video taken during a night flight. I could hardly believe what I was seeing. As if in daylight, the pilot flew the airplane through a winding mountain pass, then attacked a truck in the desert. "There had to be a full moon when this video was made," I said to Skip. He just smiled. "Nope, it was pitch black that night. I know because I was flying the airplane." Then we went to the squadron bar—it was Friday afternoon—and I was regaled with F-15E stories by enthusiastic crewmen who were in the process of transitioning to the airplane. It was a memorable afternoon, and ultimately the reason I became interested in writing about the adventures of the Strike Eagles after the Gulf War. So, thank you, Skip, and thanks to all you guys in the bar that afternoon. You hooked me good.

Before embarking on my research at the different air bases where the Strike Eagles were stationed, I visited the McDonnell-Douglas factory, where I interviewed test pilots and engineers and toured the assembly line where the Strike Eagles were being assembled. Thanks to Lee Whitney who organized the visit, and to Gary Jennings, Paul Nelson, Dave Thompson, and Irv Burrows, who gave me long, informative interviews.

Thanks also to Lt. Col. Mike Gannon at Air Force Public Affairs, who arranged support for me at all the air bases I visited. Thanks to this support I was able to track down and interview 106 of the crewmen who flew the 48 Strike Eagles that fought in the Gulf War.

I started my research at Luke Air Force Base, Arizona, where all Strike Eagle crews are trained. (As this book went to press, the training unit was moving to Seymour Johnson Air Force Base.) Capt. Joe Davis in the Public Affairs Office at Luke was very helpful. In addition, Lt. Col. Terry Branson, who was one of the first operational pilots to fly the F-15E, instructed me about flying the airplane as if it were a single-seater and I were about to go out and fly it. He spent several hours teaching me everything I would have needed to know to take off, climb to altitude, descend, and land. After that, I was passed on to Maj. Tim Malone, who took me to the simulator and patiently endured while I went through the motions of being first a pilot, then a WSO. Also helpful during my visit to Luke were Col. Bron Burke, Lt. Col. T. J. Wyatt, Lt. Col. Steve Spencer, Lt. Col. Ron Heyden, Capt. Jim Gilstrap, and Capt. Bob Schwarze.

At Seymour Johnson Air Force Base, Mr. Jay Barber at the Public Affairs Office went out of his way to help me during a two-week visit. Thanks also to those who provided background interviews or other assistance related to my research, including Lt. Col. Patricia O'Connell, Lt. Col. Mike Gegg, Lt. Col. James Ruttler, Maj. Rick Jones, Capt. Kent Johnson, Capt. Laura Warn Berry, Capt. Robert Del Toro, Lt. Jay Chafin, Mrs. Betty Jane Turner, Mrs. Char Gruver, M. Sgt. Danny Brown, M. Sgt. Steve Neufeld, Tech. Sgt. Stephan Lackey, Staff Sgt. Karl Bowlby, Sgt. Lloyd Sample, and Sgt. Herbert Parrish.

Several of the crewmen read parts or all of the manuscript and patiently replied to multiple requests for information beyond their initial interviews. For their help I would like to acknowledge Col. Mike "Slammer" Decuir, Col. Steve "Steep" Turner, Col. Dave Eberly, Maj. Tom Griffith, Maj. Jim "Boomer" Henry, Capt. Mark "Yogi" Alred, Joel Strabala, Maj. Jack Ingari, Chris Hill, Capt. Merrick Krause, Maj. Rich Crandall, Maj. Larry "Hammer" Coleman, Col. Scotty Scott, Capt. Larry Bowers, Maj. Joe Seidl, Capt. Greg "Moose" Barlow, Rick Henson, John Pavlock, Capt. Chuck Robinson, Capt. Rich Horan, Capt. Steve Kwast, Capt. Bill Mullins, Capt. Jeff Latas, Lt. Col. John "Taco" Martinez, Maj. Dan Bakke, and Capt. James "Chainsaw" McCullough.

Col. Ray Davies, despite a heavy schedule, took time to describe in detail how Al Kharj was transformed from bare desert into a working U.S. Air Force base in less than one month. He also furnished helpful videos and reviewed chapter 5 of this manuscript.

The following crewmen were interviewed at least once during the inquiry, and several responded numerous times to follow-up telephone calls. Thanks to all of the following: Brig. Gen. Hal Hornburg (Maj. Gen. select), Col. (Brig. Gen. select) Dave "Bull" Baker, Capt. David "Hammer" Castillo, Capt. Jay "K-9" Kreighbaum, Maj. Jerry "One-Y" Oney, Capt. Darryl "OBD" Roberson, Maj. Gary Cole, Col. Dick Hoey, Capt. Norman "Abbe" Reese, Maj. Brian "BJ" Dillon, Capt. Tom "Two Dogs" McIntyre, Capt. Bill Schaal, Capt. Ken Garrison, Capt. Jim "Cubes" Grahn, Capt. Tom Plumb, Garrett Lacey, Capt. Al Botine, Capt. Ned Rudd, Maj. Lee Lewis, Capt. Jim "Bear" Hayden, Maj. Bill "Frenchie" Chamblee, Col. Bob Ruth, Ray Smith, Capt. Mike Duvall, Capt. Dwayne Smith, Col. Stoney Sloan, Lt. Col. Paul "PB" Burns, Capt. Brian Allen, Capt. Nick Sandwick,

Brian Shipman, Capt. Brad Freels, Col. Bob Gruver, Capt. Matt Riehl, Capt. Randy "R-2" Roberts, Capt. Mark "Bones" Wetzel, Capt. Mark Stevens, Maj. Steve Chilton, Maj. Mike Cloutier, Capt. Joe Manion, Capt. Joe Justice, Lt. Col. Charlie Heald, Capt. Kevin Mertens, Capt. John Flanagan, Capt. Brian Killough, Maj. Dan Wise, Lt. Jeff Mase, Capt. Karl Von Luhrte, Capt. Murray Roberts, Lt. Col. Mark Ordess, Capt. Kerry Phelan, Capt. Mark Mouw, Capt. Bill "Bruno" Millonig, John Norbeck, Capt. Houstoun Waring, Lt. Col. Keith Trumbull, Capt. Rick McGivern, Maj. Gary "Greeno" Green, Capt. Gary Klett, Mike Smyth, Capt. Ansel Mangrum, Capt. Keith "Spitter" Johnson, Capt. Charlie Bowman, Capt. Greg Johnson, Maj. Randy Garrett, Maj. Al Gale, Maj. Bill Polowitzer, Maj. Craig Wilcox, Capt. Reno Pelletier, Capt. Chris DiNenna, Bart Pfautz, Maj. Baxter Sosebee, Capt. Mark Waid, Capt. Greg Torba, Capt. Russ Mack, Capt. Tom "Radar" O'Reilly, Capt. Tim Bennett, and Capt. Kevin Thompson.

Special thanks are due to "Tanker Dan" Wise for copying several hundred of his slide photos for me.

In addition, Lt. Col. Mike Hoyes at F-15E Fighter Weapons School gave me special insight on F-15E tasking during the Gulf War.

As always, I want to thank the field guys at Silver and McGraw— they know whom and for what—and my son, William M., for his ever-critical input to my thinking.

I also want to thank my editor, Don McKeon, for his stalwart support, and my wife, Patricia, for her special sustenance.

Contents

Strike Eagle

F-15E
Desert Storm
Operations

F-15E Bases

0   50 100   200
         miles

1

The Dubious Warriors

"When word came down that we were definitely not going, I turned to the guys I was with and said, 'Go pack your bags; when they say you are definitely not going to do something, you are going to do it.'"

Capt. Rick McGivern

They had been flying for ten straight days, averaging more than two sorties per day. Their butts were sore—the seat in the F-15E "Strike Eagle" was much harder than the seat in the F-4, from which most of the crews had recently transitioned. And they were tired. Most had flown three missions yesterday, and this morning they had been up since 0300 hours getting ready for the biggest mission of all, a twenty-four-ship gaggle of Strike Eagles flying deep into Iraq to attack four strategic highway bridges.

In preparation for the mission they had first gone to the intel shack where they had signed out their Escape and Evasion (E&E) Kits—kits containing maps and procedures for escaping the enemy if they are shot down. They also signed out a Communication Security Card (COMSEC), which listed secret radio frequencies and authentication procedures for identifying friend from foe in the combat area. In addition, each crewman had reviewed his own Isolated Personnel Report (ISOPREP), which listed personal information that would be on board the AWACS planes coordinating the mission. That information would be used to authenticate them should they end up on the ground calling for help on the hand-held emergency radios they carried in their survival vests.

Now it was 0500 and they were sitting in the main briefing room of the Chiefs—the 335th Tactical Fighter Squadron (TFS)—because Lt. Col. Steve Pingel, the Chiefs' commander, was leading the mission. Most of the crewmen, however, were from one of the sister squadrons in the 4th Tactical Fighter Wing. They were Rocketeers, but more commonly called "Rockets," of the 336 TFS. This morning it would have bothered the Rockets taking their briefing in their rival squadron's territory had it not been that mission commander Steve Pingel, a Vietnam veteran, was so highly respected. Many of the Rockets had lost respect for their own commander, but they would have followed old "Bald Eagle," as Steve Pingel was known to the young guys, through hell and back.

The mass briefing began with the traditional time hack—they synchronized their watches. That was followed by the weather briefing, which informed them that the target area would be covered by a heavy, broken cloud deck with only five miles of visibility in the haze below it. Upon hearing this, the weapons system officers, or WSOs (pronounced "wizzos"),[1] who flew in the backseat and whose job was to find the target and tell the computers how to bomb it, grimaced. The bridges they were going after were in mountain valleys, which made them difficult to map on their radars—the first step necessary for accurately targeting their bombs. In addition, the bridges were known to be guarded by heavy concentrations of antiaircraft guns (triple-A) and by numerous surface-to-air missiles (SAMs). SAMs, the more feared threats, could be avoided if they were observed in flight with sufficient time to pull the airplane around in abrupt evasive maneuvers. However, with the thick cloud deck over the target area and SAMs popping up through the undercast, only quick visual acquisition and split-second reactions on the controls would save them from the deadly missiles.

After the weather briefing, 1st Lt. Robert Del Toro, the Rockets' intel officer, stood up and looked over the forty-eight crewmen who were about to embark on the mission. What he saw bothered him. A few of their heads were drooping and several others were looking up at him through glazed eyes. He launched into the briefing vigorously and with authority, for he had been up most of the night working in the mission planning cell. He reviewed the E&E and COMSEC procedures; then on a large map of the target area he pointed out known triple-A and SAM sites. Some of the SAM "rings," or areas of

---

[1]Mostly the WSO is called a "wizzo"; however, the same person may also be called a "pitter" because he rides in the backseat or "pit" or, simply, the "backseater." WSOs are not trained as pilots, although they must learn at least the rudimentary skills of flying while on the job. All WSOs were initially trained as navigators.

effectiveness, could be avoided by flying carefully selected ingress and egress routes. But certain other SAM rings enclosed the targets and there was no way to avoid them. For some missions the "Wild Weasels," F-4Gs with antiradiation HARM missiles, would accompany the Strike Eagles, ready to destroy SAM radars should they became active. Also, the Strike Eagles were sometimes accompanied by EF-111 "Sparkvarks," which carried electronic jamming equipment to help neutralize the effectiveness of SAM radars. However, on this day the Strike Eagles were going it alone, without either of these supporting assets.

Then Lieutenant Del Toro launched into a discussion of the air-to-air threats that could be expected on the mission. In the Iraqis' awesome fighter inventory were two of the Soviet Union's best fighters, the MiG-23 Flogger and the MiG-29 Fulcrum. In addition, they had numerous F-1 French Mirages, which were flown by Iraq's elite pilots. The bridges targeted by the Strike Eagles were within relatively short range of several Iraqi fighter bases, and Del Toro explained that the crews would very likely encounter these air-to-air threats and would probably have to fight their way into and out of the target areas.

Del Toro then hesitated, and according to those who remembered that early morning briefing, his facial expression became much more serious when he said, "And, oh, by the way, I think you should know that in the real world Saddam Hussein just invaded Kuwait. It happened during the night and it looks like he might overrun the country."

So it was at Seymour Johnson AFB in North Carolina on the morning of August 2, 1990, where the Rockets and a few of the Chiefs (those who were trained to fly the new Strike Eagle) were completing the last day of an Operational Readiness Exercise (ORE). The twenty-four-ship "rainbow" mission—so called because it included both Rockets and Chiefs—was the grand finale and the first test of the "large package" concept where massive amounts of ordnance would be delivered on targets within a very short space of time. But they were going to Virginia to simulate attacks on bridges, not into Iraq. And the fact that the whole training exercise was based upon the theoretical scenario that Saddam Hussein had invaded Kuwait and was threatening Saudi Arabian oil fields was purely coincidental. Those on the 4th Wing Intelligence Staff who dreamed up the scenario[2] have never tried to claim any special prescience; they all admit that the remarkable coincidence between their manu-

---

[2]Credit Capt. Scott Bethel for generating the original concept three months before the actual event occurred.

factured scenario and the real-time invasion of Kuwait at the time of the training exercise was just dumb, blind luck.

Those in the audience who remembered Del Toro's announcement about the Iraqi invasion say that it did not startle them. The idea of a bunch of Arabs fighting over an oil field didn't strike them as unusual. As the crews stood up and stretched, then filed out of the briefing room to get their helmets, oxygen masks, survival vests, and G-suits, two or three stopped to talk to Del Toro. "I explained that [Lt. Col.] Steep Turner, the wing weapons officer, and I just happened to be watching CNN in the intel shack," said Del Toro. "Nothing had come down through our intel channels at that time so I couldn't give them any more information."

The forty-eight crewmen went out and flew as six four-ship elements at 500 feet up low-level route VR-1751 through West Virginia and Virginia. It was the first time that many F-15Es had flown in a strike package and on the way home the leaders slowed up so that all the aircraft could get together and arrive at the same time. As they approached Seymour Johnson all twenty-four planes were in a line-abreast formation, with two-ship elements about a mile apart. Said Capt. Mike Duvall, who was in one of the leading elements, "It was one of the neatest sights I'd ever seen. When we landed and turned on to the taxiway some guys were on TAC initial, pitching out, and behind them for several miles was this big gaggle of planes still coming in. It was awesome."

There was a lot of excitement in the debriefing, with many suggestions offered on how to improve their tactics when using such a package. Then, said Captain Duvall, "After all of us had announced that we had gotten direct hits with our simulated bombs, Colonel Pingel stood up and admitted that his simulated bombs missed their target. He admitted that he didn't know how they screwed up. But that's one of the things that made us respect him as a commander. He wasn't afraid to stand up in front of us and admit that he made a mistake."

They were in good spirits when they hit the squadron bar. They had had eleven days of good flying, their airplanes had performed as advertised, and they were getting Friday and Monday off because they had worked through the previous weekend. However, the news they were watching on CNN slowly began to dampen their enthusiasm. By midafternoon of August 2 it looked like Saddam Hussein was after more than the disputed oil field that was on the Iraq-Kuwait border. Now, along with the newscasters, those in the bar were talking about the invasion and speculating on what might happen if Saddam overran all of Kuwait. Would he stop there, when the lucrative and massive Saudi oil fields were just a few more miles down the coast? And would the Strike Eagles, the newest and most potent combat aircraft in the U.S. Air Force inventory, be sent over there in an effort to stop him? At that time there were thirty-six

Strike Eagles at Luke AFB in Arizona where crews were being trained, but almost all the others that had come off the McDonnell-Douglas assembly line were at Seymour Johnson. So if the Strike Eagles were called into action, the crewmen gathered in the bar knew that they were the ones who would have to go.

Maj. Paul Burns was one of the crewmen who remembers the discussion in the bar. "We talked a lot about it," he said, "but, personally, I didn't think there was a chance we would go. At the time most of us thought Iran would be the country to create problems over there. If CNN had said that Iran invaded Kuwait or Saudi Arabia, we wouldn't have been all that surprised."

Capt. Randy Garrett, the plans officer for the 4th Wing, was in the group with Paul Burns when they were speculating on their own potential involvement. "I was pretty negative about the possibility of us going over there," said Garrett. "I mentioned the fact that Jimmy Carter had sent some F-15s over during the Iranian crisis and I reminded everybody that as they were halfway across the ocean it was announced that, 'Oh, by the way, they are unarmed.' That was real effective, right? Anyway, we were all about convinced that the only thing that might happen was for some airplanes to be sent over there as a show of force—just as a bluff—but not to go into action against Iraq.

"Then Colonel Hornburg [the wing commander] came in and joined us for a beer. Since I was scheduled to go on leave, and since I was plans officer for the wing and would be needed for a potential deployment, I asked Hornburg what I should do. He was pretty laid back at the time. He said to go on and take my leave because we were a wing in transition. We had been an F-4 wing, and at that time we only had one squadron of F-15Es fully mission ready—the Rockets—and we were about one-third of the way through the transition with the second squadron—the Chiefs. In addition, our airplanes were not completely ready for combat. We didn't have the internal countermeasures systems installed, we didn't have targeting pods, and we were certified to carry only two types of bombs. Hornburg didn't explain all that, of course—we knew about the deficiencies of the airplanes. He did say, strictly as speculation, that if anybody deployed it would probably be the Albinos[3] from Langley [AFB] and that they would go just as a show of force."

---

[3]The air-to-air models of the F-15 (A and C) are officially designated "Eagles" and are painted light gray. The F-15E Strike Eagles are painted dark gray and at night they look black. Because the air-to-air models are so much lighter in color, they are known throughout the F-15E community as "Albinos." The Albino pilots also have names for the Strike Eagle. Because the Strike Eagles fly low, they are sometimes called "Mud Eagles" or "Mud Hens." They have also been called "Beagles" because they are "bombing Eagles."

Lt. Col. Patricia O'Connell, the feisty and demanding 4th Wing intelligence officer (IN), had other ideas. Being a Vietnam veteran, she was acutely aware of the target imagery and threat information needed by combat pilots and, according to a junior officer who worked with her, "Didn't give a damn which tree she had to shake to get information for her pilots. She could ruffle a lot of feathers but she didn't care." Friday, August 3, was a down day at the base but not at wing intel. O'Connell had all the intel personnel there, initially to evaluate the just completed ORE, but also to start getting ready for a possible deployment. "At that time," said another junior officer, "on her own initiative she went directly to the Defense Mapping Agency and ordered maps that the crews would need if they deployed. They were FedExed to us immediately."

There was a wing picnic Friday afternoon—a tradition after an ORE, and lots of hot dogs and beer. Over the weekend most personnel on the base scattered to the winds for a three-day August holiday. But not Patricia O'Connell. Said she, "I had a feeling that we should be getting ready . . . my wheels were turning and I felt that the situation in Kuwait was serious. I knew the awesome capabilities of our airplanes and could not imagine them not being used. I called TAC [Tactical Air Command Headquarters] and asked, 'What's going on?' I was told to back off—the words were, 'Don't lean too far forward.' What they were concerned about, of course, was that precipitous action by us could get someone thinking that the United States was going to do something that we weren't going to do.

"I was concerned. The weekend was coming up and I was uneasy. I let my people go, but the next day, after a night of worrying about all this, I called my chief of targets—she probably won't speak to me even to this day—and had her come in that Saturday and take total inventory of maps and charts that we guesstimated would be used in a Southwest Asia theater of operations. I also made a lot of calls and everybody kept telling me to quit worrying—that the F-15E wasn't fully operational and wouldn't be going. But I knew General Horner who was head of Ninth Air Force, and I knew he was intrigued with the potential of the Strike Eagle. I just knew we were going to go, and we were not prepared! We did not have the kind of imagery those aircrews would need to fight in that theater. With that in mind I finally called the deputy IN at TAC and said, 'Listen, if you hear anybody thinking about sending the Strike Eagles, tell them that we are not ready to support them.' After that conversation I went ahead and placed an order with the Defense Mapping Agency for the maps we might need.

"We lacked a lot of things needed to support a combat squadron but one of our worst deficiencies was the lack of filmstrips for the moving map display in the cockpit.[4] I immediately went to work on that. After a lot of calls to defense contractors, which included tracking down people who were on vacation, I discovered that our filmstrips weren't ready but that those used in the U.S. Navy's F/A-18 could be modified and that they could get them to us right away.

"And yes, by being aggressive we were able to solve some of our problems, but we were still very unprepared. For example, we couldn't even give those crews E&E kits for that region—we didn't have any up-to-date maps to give them should they have to bail out. We had no precise targeting information, and our photo, radar, and infrared imagery, which the Strike Eagles are extremely dependent upon—much more so than other strike aircraft—was totally inadequate. As I told the Deputy IN at TAC, we were definitely unprepared and I meant it!"

The Rockets had a golf tournament on Monday. It was one of their famous "Rocket Opens" with two golf carts loaded with beer and the captains trying to beat the colonels and the "ringers" they brought in from the other squadrons. A good time was had by all and by Tuesday morning they were ready for business as usual, which began with an aircrew meeting in the Rockets' main briefing room.

The squadron commander was late for the meeting, having been detained at the wing command post, and when he arrived he added to the discussion already underway on lessons learned during the ORE. At the end of the meeting he was asked what he knew about a potential deployment. While admitting that there was a good possibility the Albinos from Langley would be going, adding credence to a rumor that had been making the rounds, he tried to assure them that the Strike Eagles would be way down on anybody's list for deployment. Then he repeated the same rationale they had heard before: That the wing was in transition and the planes were not fully ready for combat. Leaving that meeting, Capt. Tom "Two Dogs" McIntyre said, "I think it was the impression of about everyone in the squadron that the Rockets would not be sent over unless a real food fight started over there."

---

[4]On each of the cathode ray tube multipurpose displays (MPDs) in the cockpit—the pilot has three MPDs and the WSO, four—a moving map display can be called up. (Aircrews call it the TSD—tactical situation display.) This is a very detailed map, in brilliant colors, that shows the area the airplane is flying over. The exact position and movement of the airplane is indicated by a small, white airplane on the map. If the airplane's radar is locked on an enemy airplane, or "bandit," the enemy will appear on the map as a small red airplane, and its exact position and direction of flight can be observed.

Two Dogs McIntyre wasn't scheduled to fly that Tuesday so he went to wing headquarters to work on a publication that he had been assigned to prepare. "Late that morning," said McIntyre, "I was collating some pages spread out on four desks when I saw some colonels walk by the office. None of them said anything as they went by, which was unusual; normally, at least one of them would have stuck his head in and said something. I just assumed from the look on their faces that they had gotten a good chewing over something we did wrong during the ORE. Then Colonel Bob Ruth and Major Donnie Holland came by and saw me working. They said, 'Hey, you're not going to need that,' referring to the local flight guide I was assembling. I said, 'Why not?' and Ruth said, 'Go home. Get in crew rest. We're on alert to deploy. Don't say anything to anybody. Just stay by the phone.'"

About that same time Capt. Mark "Ironman" Waid was debriefing the morning mission he had flown with the Rockets' squadron commander. "We were just getting the debrief underway when he was called away," said Waid. It was a two-ship mission and the three of us sat and waited for a while until it was apparent that he wasn't coming back. We went to the ops [operations] desk and that's when we got the word that we were on alert to deploy. They said to go home and start packing."

Capt. James "Chainsaw" McCullough was the scheduling officer for the Chiefs and he remembers how the rumors were flying around that Tuesday morning. Because only about one-third of the Chiefs' crews were mission ready (MR) in the new plane, he knew there wasn't a chance that they would be going. He and some of the Chiefs who were MR were depressed about this—they wanted to go, too. "Then, sometime in the early afternoon," said McCullough, "Lieutenant Colonel Pingel came in from a stand-up [wing staff meeting] looking pretty serious. When I saw his expression, I said, 'Sir, is there anything going on that you can tell us?' He looked at me and said, 'Yes, there is. Call a meeting of the squadron.' I made the announcement and all those in the building came down to the main briefing room. Colonel Pingel told us that the Rockets were on alert to deploy and that since several of them were on leave, six crews from the Chiefs would have to augment them. Then he told Taco [Maj. John Martinez] and me to make him a list of crews but not to include any IPs [instructor pilots] or I-WSOs [instructor weapons system officers]—that we needed to keep them working to get the rest of the Chiefs MR. We went to Taco's office and went right to work on the list. And since I wasn't an IP, I made sure I was at the head of the list."

"I went home then, and I was excited. I couldn't tell my wife anything so I went over to [Capt.] Joel Strabala's house—he was one of the Chiefs on the list to go—and we got in his den and started talking about it. Then we turned on Channel 32, the Weather Channel, and watched until they gave the weather for Iraq and Saudi Arabia. At that time I wasn't even sure where Kuwait was so we were paying real close attention to the map when they showed it."

Lt. Col. Steve "Steep" Turner was the wing weapons officer and had known about the deployment from the time the wing was alerted. But now he had a gut-wrenching problem. He had a crushing amount of work to do to get ready for the deployment, and in addition, he was to lead one of the six-ship elements that would be leaving. But this was also his wedding anniversary, an occasion that both he and his wife, Betty Jane, observed religiously. "Finally," said Turner, "I got away and went home to face my wife. She was just getting ready to take our son to Bible school. I said, 'Maybe you might let somebody else take him; we need to talk.' She did that and I said, 'Oh, by the way, I'm going to have to leave.' At the time she had no idea that I would have to go—and a few hours before that I had had no idea I would be going. We just didn't think it was going to happen to us."

Lots of wives and husbands were receiving the shocking news the late afternoon of Tuesday, August 7, 1990. And while support personnel worked all night palletizing supplies and equipment that would be needed to support combat operations, the crewmen on alert to deploy dutifully tried to get as much sleep as they could.

The next morning the alert crews were notified that the "execute" order had come down. They were going for sure, but not immediately because all the tankers needed to support them were tied up escorting Albinos from Langley and Vipers (F-16s) from Shaw AFB that were already on their way. They soon got the definite word; they would go tomorrow afternoon in four six-ship elements, departing at thirty-minute intervals. The destination? And for how long? The only thing they knew for sure was that they were going someplace in Southwest Asia. And as for the length of time, they were told to pack for up to a one-month deployment.

With the stay-home spouses in varying degrees of shock and depression, those who were deploying tried to make the most of their last day home. Many of the crewmen, now thinking seriously about surviving in hostile territory if shot down, felt that the .38-caliber revolvers issued to them for combat missions were a potential hazard to their health because they held only six bullets, and were slow and clumsy to reload. Concerned crewmen had long ago decided that if they had to go into combat, they would rather spend their own money and buy a better weapon to carry.

So, that Wednesday, every sporting goods store and gun shop in Goldsboro, North Carolina, was selling out of 9mm automatic pistols. The Berettas (Model 92FS) went first, then the Model 19 Glocks, then the P-89 Rugers. All of these weapons used a fifteen-shot clip and were sold with an extra clip that could quickly be inserted if reloading was necessary. Hence, should there be a fight with an enemy, the downed crewman could fire thirty quick shots, five times the firepower of the standard-issue, .38-caliber revolver.

One other item was a high priority on their purchase lists that day. Chainsaw McCullough, one of many who made such a purchase, explains: "I have a two-hour butt. That means I can take about two hours on the hard seat of the Strike Eagle without getting sore; after that I really start to hurt. So after I went out and purchased my P-89 Ruger, my next stop was K-Mart, where I purchased one of those blow-up, rubber doughnut cushions. I knew I had a thirteen-hour flight coming up and even though there might be a little problem if I had to eject while sitting on that cushion, I figured that was a better alternative than bruises." (Chainsaw's rubber doughnut lasted until he popped it in combat doing a high-G turn.)

That night there were a lot of poignant moments in the environs of Goldsboro, with both men and women sitting down to have the last meal with their loved ones before departure. Wives, husbands, and children all experienced heavy anxiety not knowing where the departing spouse was going or the extent of the danger he or she might be facing. Everybody, of course, had their eyes glued on TV newscasts—mostly CNN—and the news from Kuwait was growing more ominous by the moment. Iraqi troops had easily overrun all of Kuwait and their huge armored forces were massing at the Saudi border. All the while, TV commentators and prognosticators were reminding everybody that the rich Saudi oil fields just down the coast from the Kuwait border were extremely attractive targets for the Iraqis, who were heavily debt-ridden after their long, costly war with Iran.

The mood was not as somber at Billy's Backstreet Bar where four bachelor friends met for their ritual Wednesday night dinner. "We were a regular foursome," said Capt. John Pavlock, "and two of us, Boo Boo [Capt. Jim Poulet] and myself, had been in Spain on a ten-day R&R just before the ORE and we had really lived it up. Boo Boo was a great companion, fun-loving, and we had had a super time in the clubs over there. We talked about that some, but mostly we talked and speculated about what we might get into over in the desert. [Capt.] Nick Sandwick was deploying with Boo Boo and me and he was pretty serious that night. [Capt.] Dwayne Smith, we called him 'Slam,' was the fourth person at the table and he was miserable because he was in the Chiefs and not scheduled to go. It was like being with a guy who was just as good as you but who didn't get picked for the starting team. I had a big steak that night, figuring it would be my last for awhile. We also drank a few beers but we didn't do anything wild; we didn't leave a table full of empty bottles like on a normal Wednesday night. And as I recall, we were fairly subdued when we left. We were heading into the unknown, and of course we didn't know it then, but one of us was not coming back."

Not everybody was having a last fling that night. Two Dogs McIntyre, Maj. Tom Griffith, and Lt. Col. Mike "Slammer" Decuir had been in the wing command post for many hours. "That afternoon," said Two Dogs, "I had been helping the movement control team with all the little things we had to do to get ready. Then, about 5:30, this courier drives in from TAC headquarters in Langley with the routes that we were going to take. These were extremely important, of course. We couldn't do any intelligent planning without them. But I remember that courier, with his spy case handcuffed to his wrist, just sitting there waiting until exactly 6:00 P.M. when his orders said he could break them out. We just had to stand there and wait."

They sent Two Dogs home later that evening to rest because he was going to fly the next day in one of the Strike Eagles. "But," said Slammer Decuir, "Griff and I had to work out the routes and get them in packages for the guys who were flying. We stayed there until about ten o'clock, then raced home and packed, and Griff picked me up about midnight so we could go back and catch a C-141 that was leaving at two o'clock. I was so busy I hardly had time to think, but it was hard on my wife and two teenagers. I tried to console them by saying that I would only be gone for two weeks—a month at the most. I really believed that; I thought we were going just as a show of force. I never dreamed I would end up staying over there for eleven months."

About eleven o'clock that night one of the pilots got a big surprise. Slam Smith, who had sat morosely through a farewell dinner with his three bachelor friends, had just hung up the phone after talking with his girlfriend, an airline attendant. "I had just started pacing the floor in frustration—I couldn't get it out of my mind that I was just as good as the guys who were going—when the phone rang again. It was a call from the wing; they had decided they needed another pilot and I was to report at midnight to go over on a C-141 leaving at two o'clock. I quickly called my girlfriend, then began to throw things in a bag. I felt just like a guy jumping off the bench, ripping off his warmups, and charging into the big game."

It rained most of the night, and the next morning low, ragged clouds were hanging over the base. Then it began raining again, a hard, torrential rain. The visibility was less than one-quarter mile and the cloud ceiling over the runway was ranging between 200 and

300 feet. On any other day all fighter flight operations would have been suspended, but the crews, peering out the windows that morning, knew that the inclement weather was not going to give them a reprieve. They were flying a fighter built for all-weather operations. It was designed to fly near the speed of sound at 200 feet above the ground, at night, in clouds, to drop bombs precisely on a target; then, if necessary, fight its way home and survive combat with any of the world's best air-to-air fighters that might attack it. Equipped with the latest and most sophisticated radars, sensors, and navigation equipment it was truly an awesome weapon, and, even though it was not 100 percent ready for combat, the generals had decided that it was better than anything else they had as an air-to-ground attack aircraft. The crews all knew that, of course, and despite the hammering of the rain on the roofs and windows, and the sharp, rumbling peals of nearby thunder, and the hopeful tears of wives and children clinging to them, they knew they were going today.

That was about the only thing they were sure about that morning of August 9, 1990.

2

Destination Unknown

"Go see the movie Bull Durham *and you'll catch the feeling of
our crews going over there. They were just like those minor
league baseball players wanting into the big leagues; they
wanted in the big show."*

Col. Dave Eberly

They were sad and emotionally tense when they said their good-byes to their families. But when the forty-eight crewmen who were
going to deploy to the Persian Gulf gathered in the Rockets' main
briefing room at 1000 hours for their mass briefing, there was
excitement in the air. These crewmen were the air force's elite; most
of them had been rigorously screened by a team led by a three-star
general before they transitioned to the Strike Eagle. They were the
U.S. Air Force's talented bonus players who had endured months of
practice just so they could get into the big game. Now it looked like
game time might be just days away.

But this was no ordinary road trip. Getting to their assigned base
in Southwest Asia, which they learned for the first time was Seeb,
Oman, required about a fifteen-hour nonstop flight. And their air-planes were loaded with three external fuel tanks, or "bags"; two
travel pods—empty napalm containers in which personal belongings
were carried; four AIM-9 heat-seeking air-to-air missiles; and two
AIM-7 radar-guided air-to-air missiles. This type of load had never
been carried before and official approval did not come down from
the air force engineering gurus until eleven o'clock—thirty minutes
before the first cell of six ships was to depart.

The briefing itself was routine. According to Capt. Rich Horan, "It was the same kinds of stuff we had heard many times before because we had done a ton of mobility exercises." What was new was the information about Seeb, Oman, which had been dropped off the night before by an F-111 from Cannon AFB. Various facts stuck in the minds of the crews; most remembered that it was near the water, that they would probably be living in a hotel, and that the Omani women were not allowed to drive cars.

After the briefing, around the ops desk and the television monitor depicting the weather, there was laughter and joking and Capt. Greg Torba said that several of them were munching from a bag of pork rinds because that was the last pork they would see for awhile. Also, about this time the crews picked up a box lunch from the stack in the hallway. However, when they were opened hours later over the Atlantic, the meat was missing from some of the sandwiches. One of the heavy eaters among the crewmen, who shall remain nameless, was accused but never convicted of the misdemeanor.

The aircrews got soaked getting into their airplanes, and as they taxied, rain battered their canopies; visibility was so low they could barely see the airplanes in line ahead of them. As the first cell of six arrived at the end of the taxiway and crews were running through final items on their checklists, they heard Colonel Hornburg's voice on the radio: "Sixty-sixteen is waived." Air Force Regulation 60-16, which controlled takeoff minimums, was set aside at the authority of the wing commander. The airplanes were now cleared to depart at the discretion of the tower and the pilots.

Memories of that departure remain vivid for many of the crewmen. Col. Dave Eberly, the wing deputy for operations (DO), who was in the first cell, will never forget the sight of Maj. Ray Hart, the wing chaplain, as he stood near the end of the taxiway, drenched by the rain, saying prayers for all of them.

Capt. Mark "Yogi" Alred remembers hearing a KC-10 tanker cleared for takeoff while he was on the taxiway, yet he wasn't able to see it until it was three thousand feet down the runway.

Chainsaw McCullough's mental picture of that departure is perhaps the most poignant and typical of many other crewmen. Said he, "I'll never ever forget seeing the crowd of wives huddled together out there as we taxied out. They were absolutely drenched but they were all waving and cheering for us. In the crowd I spotted my wife huddled down, trying to share an umbrella with Donna Strabala. That's a scene I carried in my mind all the way through the war. Unfortunately, by the time our cell [the fourth] departed, conditions were almost zero-zero and our wives didn't even get to see the airplanes take off."

Captains Nick Sandwick and Jay "K-9" Kreighbaum[1] were the first to encounter trouble on the flight. "After we were about 150 miles out over the Atlantic," said K-9, "we broke out of the weather at 18,000 feet. It was just perfect; our lead was in sight; our tanker was in sight; we were all in a nice trail formation—then we lost our left engine. Nick got it relit, but before he said anything to me, he told Lead what had happened. I knew it was over then. Lead came back and said, 'Understand you have restarted engine.' Nick says, 'Roger.' Lead comes back, 'Go home; turn back now; report when you have Seymour on the TACAN.'[2] We did and I went cold mike and had a temper tantrum. It was the one time in my life that I did that. I'm not proud of that but it indicates how badly I wanted to keep going."

Nick and K-9 arrived back at the base with no further engine problems, but were held up in the weather until all the Strike Eagles had departed. They then landed safely after shooting an instrument approach below normal minimums. This was about the time that their squadron commander was landing at Langley AFB.

The Rockets' commander was flying the lead ship in the first cell with Maj. Gary Cole. "Our problems began during the first refueling," said Cole. "We started leaking fuel out over the left wing, and it was pouring out faster than the tanker could pump it in. I thought for awhile that we were going to go swimming but we made it back to Langley. There we got an officer who was a former policeman to drive us to Seymour. Before leaving the base, he stopped by the security police office and got one of those portable emergency lights and put it on the top of his car. We made it to Seymour in record time."

A few hours later, as darkness fell, some of the other Strike Eagles began experiencing similar problems, which, they found out later, were caused by a faulty shutoff valve in the pylon that held the auxiliary fuel tanks to the wing. Under pressure from the tanker's refueling boom, some of the valves failed, causing fuel to siphon out of the auxiliary tanks. One of the planes with this problem diverted to Lajes in the Azores. Another landed in Rota, Spain. Still another had to divert to Sigonella in Sicily.

The others kept going, some nursing minor leaks, but determined

---

[1]Jay Kreighbaum got the nickname "K-9" when a scheduler, tired of spelling out the whole name, counted the nine letters after "K" and came up with the abbreviation.

[2]A VHF transmitter that pilots can use for navigational purposes; from it they obtain directional and distance information.

to stay up if they could. "Later that night," said Capt. Baxter Sosebee, "a huge big moon came up over the middle of the Atlantic. Then, when we hit the Portuguese and Spanish coasts there was a stream of airplanes going both ways across the Med—mostly tankers and cargo planes. It was like going into Dulles Airport in the busy part of the day; it was nonstop radio chatter."

The sun was coming up when they flew past Libya, and all the crews were alert, not knowing when that country's renegade leader might send aircraft out to attack them. Nothing happened, but soon those in the lead cell had another problem. The tanker they were following informed them that they were not going to their planned destination. "Where are we going?" asked Maj. Pete Hook, who had taken the lead when his squadron commander had to turn back. "We can't tell you," came the reply from the tanker. For security reasons they could not broadcast on open channels.

The crews talked to each other and passed the word back to the other cells that their destination would be changing. In the meantime, Pete Hook tried to get the tanker to encrypt the new airport's four-letter identifier and transmit it on secure radio. That failed; somehow the radios were incompatible. Then Hook suggested that they flash their director lights in Morse code. That did not work either; they could not distinguish the dots from the dashes. Finally, after what Two Dogs McIntyre described as a "real goat rope," it was deduced, after several possible destinations were mentioned, that Dhahran on the coast of Saudi Arabia was their destination. Hook passed the word back through the cells on secure radio and all the WSOs began plotting new courses, fuel needs, and estimated time of arrival (ETA).

Baxter Sosebee, who was in the third cell, said, "We got that information about the time we were coming up on Egypt and the news didn't affect me as much as what I was seeing out the canopy. I was looking at the most awesome desert I've ever seen—just miles and miles of sand broken by a ten-mile narrow band of green, which was the Valley of Kings—the Nile Valley. There were no roads anywhere in the desert—there was just that little narrow strip of green. Then, as we passed into Saudi Arabia, it became awesomely quiet."

Pete Hook passed the lead to Colonel Eberly because Eberly was the ranking officer in the formation. Dhahran was where the 1st Tactical Fighter Wing from Langley had deployed a few days earlier, and when Eberly landed and taxied into one of the shelters, he was met by Col. Stormy Summers, the 1st Wing DO. "And standing beside him," said Eberly, "was the Saudi wing commander, Col. Medh A. Al-Lihaibi, who, interestingly enough, I had met when we both attended a seminar at the War College. They were both standing there by the airplane in chem gear, with masks and stuff strapped on their hips. After opening the canopy and shutting down, the first thing Stormy said was, 'What are you guys doing here?'

"I climbed down, shook hands with Stormy, then renewed old acquaintances with Medh with the traditional Arab backslapping. About that time [Col. John 'Boomer'] McBroom [lst Wing commander] pulls up and he repeated Stormy's question: 'What are you doing here?'

"I said that I wasn't sure why we're here, but we're going to get these airplanes out of here as soon as we can get some gas. We started to get into his truck and he asked, 'Hey, where's your chem gear and your gas mask'—they were afraid of a Scud attack. I got my gas mask out of the cockpit, then we went to his office across the ramp and called General Olson in Riyadh. He agreed that we needed to get out of there—we were the first offensive airplanes in the theater and, together with the F-15Cs, were an attractive target. At the end of the conversation, Boomer hands me a yellow sticky and says, 'Here's your orders.' I looked at it; it said, 'Go to Thumrait.' I looked at Boomer, 'Where is Thumrait?' and he said, 'I don't know either.' We jumped back in his truck—by this time the last of our group is landing—and I had him take me down to the ramp. There I jogged around the ramp telling everybody to leave their stuff in the pods and to get their chem gear and come inside.

"Boomer and I then went inside and one of his guys found a map of the continent. With a sweeping motion, working clockwise, we covered the map until we found Thumrait at the bottom of Oman. Laying a piece of scrap paper on the map, we measured the distance, and with the map scale determined that we could make it to Thumrait on internal fuel. Then I had all the crews come into the main briefing room. We had to brief them for the flight, but more important, I wanted to look each of them in the eye to make sure they were in shape for the remaining one and one-half hour flight. We had just logged a little over fourteen hours coming from Seymour. In the briefing room we got an intel update, then I got called out and was told that I couldn't leave without the Saudi wing commander's approval. I asked to be taken to him.

"We headed across the base and down into an underground bunker, and there was my friend Medh. I explained that I had been wanting to come for a visit but unfortunately we couldn't stay. He's very gracious—he says that they have room for our planes and our crews—that we would be no problem. In the course of this conversation he is inquiring about my family and how things have gone since War College, but I can see that he is more concerned about the survival of the fighters on the field. I thanked him for his hospitality but explained that we must go, that we are sweetening Dhahran as a target. Then he agreed that maybe it would be better if we left and I

told him we had a place to go—that we were going south to
Thumrait and that we would go VMC [visual meteorological conditions—flying by eyeball, not on instruments] and wouldn't need any
help other than his clearance to leave."

Meanwhile, in the briefing room, Two Dogs—Eberly's WSO—was
trying to get the attention of the group so he could brief them on the
next leg of the flight. Said Two Dogs, "Earlier, while Eberly was
doing his colonel things at the command post, I went over to where
Langley was operating and talked some pilots into giving me a couple of maps. Then I talked to some Saudi pilots and they explained
that all we had to do was take off and fly a heading of 150 degrees to
get to Thumrait—that we didn't have to talk to anybody along the
way. After Eberly left the briefing, the guys were a little rowdy and
not listening too well. Finally, I told them to shut up and listen. That
was a little out of character for me, so they quieted right down. Then
I told them that we were not staying—that we were going to a place
called Thumrait, which was in Oman. After that, I went over the
routing with them, and explained what I had learned from the Saudi
pilots."

Capt. Jack Ingari was in that briefing but he was not one of the
crewmen. He was the flight surgeon assigned to the squadron and
he, along with the wing deputy for maintenance (DM), Col. Ray
Davies, had come over on a C-141 with some other support personnel. Said Ingari, "We left the night before and stopped at Torrejón
AFB outside Madrid. I have never seen so many planes in my life;
there were transport planes everywhere and they were saying that it
was going to be twenty-four hours before we could get refueled and
out of there. That didn't go over well with Colonel Davies; he wanted
to be at our destination when our planes arrived. We went to the big
hangar that was used as a transient facility and Colonel Davies just
happened to see the wing commander's car parked on the ramp with
the keys in it. Without saying anything to anybody, he gets in the car,
drives out to the ramp, finds some guys fueling a plane, and asks
them to do ours next. Now how could they turn down a colonel who
is driving the wing commander's car? So they fueled ours next and
we were on our way—to Dhahran, as it turned out, rather than Seeb,
Oman.

"When we landed at Dhahran, I ended up at the briefing because I
wanted to check on the guys and see what shape they were in after
fourteen hours of flying. They were okay. Most had taken one of the
'go' pills I had prescribed—dexadrine—and I told them to take
another if they felt the need. What I was most afraid of was that they
would start eating and relaxing and then it would be all over for
them. I warned them about that at the briefing."

Four of the airplanes that landed at Dhahran had fuel leaks and

Colonel Eberly ordered them to remain there until they were fixed. Then, because the airplane he had been flying was one of the four that had been leaking, he took the airplane that Capt. Ken Garrison and Capt. Brian Allen had been flying and headed to Thumrait.

Capt. Jeff Latas and 1st Lt. Russ Mack were among the first to take off from Dhahran. Said Latas, "We had no idea where Thumrait was; we just had coordinates that we punched in our INS [inertial navigation system]. Also, we had no idea what was there or who was there. As we flew south we were amazed at the desolation. There was nothing, absolutely nothing for hundreds of miles. Just sand, and not a living soul. About one hundred miles out I called the tower and made contact. But it must have been an Omani; I couldn't understand a thing he said. I tried again at about fifty miles and this time a British voice came up and cleared us to land. We both felt a little better after that—some of the guys only had partial fuel and I don't know what they would have done had they not landed.

"We touched down—it was a nice big runway—and taxied in to a ramp. But then what were we to do? There was no one there to shut us down except a few Omanis who were standing off in the distance just looking at us. But then this C-141 lands and pulls up near us. With its engines still running the door comes down and maintenance guys hop out and come over to shut us down."[3]

It was brutally hot and the wind was blowing so hard that when the crew opened their canopies, all their papers started to blow away. They were also tired, and those who had not taken a go pill were experiencing an adrenalin letdown that one pilot said turned some of them into a "chocolate mess."

Capt. John Norbeck was one of them feeling the letdown. "Like most of the guys, I was beat. On top of that there was the letdown coming into this isolated base out in the middle of nowhere—we had expected to be living in a hotel in the capital of Oman and near nice, sandy beaches. But at Thumrait there was no city or town anywhere near, no civilization of any kind anywhere near the base—it was just out in the sand.[4] We were feeling pretty melancholy after someone found a bus and drove us to where we were going to stay. It was a big hangar filled with vehicles—mostly fuel trucks—that had been

---

[3]Lt. Col. "Slammer" Decuir was on that C-141. "At Dhahran," said Decuir, "Eberly gives us that same yellow sticky and I took it to the crew. They had no idea where Thumrait was, but they were great. They said, `Okay, we don't know where it is, but if that is where you want to go, we'll figure out a way to get there.'"

[4]There were some masonry buildings within a few miles of the base but they were deserted. They had been built by the sultan for some of his Bedouins, but apparently they did not take to apartment living.

pre-positioned at the base for just this kind of emergency. Somebody brought some cots and some MREs [meal ready to eat—combat rations], then, when it was about dark, this old beat-up jeep drove up. A guy got out and introduced himself as Andy Kubin. He was a Brit Jaguar pilot working on contract with the Omanis. He said that he had just heard that we had arrived. Then he said, 'Hey, guys, you want a Heineken?' He showed us two cases of Heineken in the back of his jeep. It wasn't cold—they don't have much refrigeration over there. But it tasted great, and we went from being melancholy to being happy in a heartbeat."

Andy Kubin with his Heineken beer was like a visiting angel to the crewmen who shared his gift. And later, as the Americans got to know Kubin and his British colleagues better, their respect and appreciation deepened. But that was in the future. That evening of August 11, 1990, the bleary-eyed Strike Eagle crewmen were just trying to focus on their most immediate problem, which was: What the hell are we going to do next?

3

Waiting for Saddam

"If Saddam had any tactical sense at all, he would have come down the east coast and taken over all those oil fields. There is nothing we could have done about it. It was the general assumption that he would do that. I was amazed that he didn't."

Lt. Col. Keith Trumbull

"I knew that the Iraqis could overrun the Saudi oil region in a week."

Gen. H. Norman Schwarzkopf

Colonel Eberly hit the ground running in Thumrait. First he nego-tiated with the Omani commander to get his crews a meal in the Omani Officers' Club. After their meal, he held a short discussion with the crews in the lobby of the club on what they might do should their jets be called upon to fly an emergency mission during the night. After that, while the crews sacked out on cots placed amid fuel trucks in a storage hangar, he went to work and persuaded the Omani commander that the U.S. aircrews were entitled to use the base's new officers' quarters. That news was gratefully received, and during the night some of the crewmen overcame their fatigue long enough to move into the newly finished quarters.

At daybreak the next morning the crewmen were awakened by alien sounds coming from the loudspeakers outside their quarters. Half awake, struggling through the residue of fog left after their deep sleep, they listened. They heard wailing sounds, mixed with bizarre, rhythmic chanting. Most listened for another moment, decided the sounds represented no threat, and went back to sleep. A few of the curious peered out their windows and were greeted with a sight that would be a part of their daily routine in the months ahead. It was prayer time—one of several during the day when practicing Muslims roll out little carpets and get down on their hands and knees to face Mecca and pray. The sounds coming from the loud-speakers were from a mullah, a teacher of the Koran, praying.

Prayer was also on the minds of many of the crewmen that morning as they awoke and became fully aware of the gravity of their situation. Saddam Hussein had nine of his elite Republican Guards divisions poised on the Kuwaiti border with 1,200 tanks and 800 artillery pieces, ready at any moment, it appeared to intelligence analysts, to wheel southward toward the Saudi oil fields. The crewmen were briefed on this threat, and were advised that they were the only air-to-ground aircraft in the theater that could be thrown against the Iraqi forces should they come south.[1]

However, there were major problems for the Strike Eagles in assuming that responsibility. First, and most important, the Strike Eagles were never intended to be used against moving armor on the front line of a battlefield; that is for close air support (CAS) aircraft such as the A-10. The Strike Eagles were designed to fly behind enemy lines, at night, and with pinpoint bombing accuracy destroy key targets such as ammunition dumps, bridges, and communication centers. In addition, because they also possess the F-15's traditional capability as an air-to-air fighter, they could conduct their missions without a protective fighter escort. They were bombers, but they were capable of defeating any air-to-air fighter in the world, and it was intended that they should fight their way into and out of a target area if that were necessary.

So the crewmen, who were trained for the designed role of the Strike Eagle, looked at each other and shrugged when they heard about their potential assignment. "What the hell are we going to do against moving tanks?" they asked.

It was not only a question of how to hit moving tanks that concerned them. Their biggest concern was what weapons they could use. They did not carry infrared guided, air-to-ground missiles such as the Maverick that was carried by the A-10; they carried AIM-9s and AIM-

---

[1]Some F-16s from Shaw AFB had arrived in the theater but had no bombs. The Strike Eagles had a pre-positioned bomb dump nearby, which is why they were the only aircraft that would be tasked to attack the Iraqi armor. F-15 Albinos were also in theater, at Dhahran, but they were strictly air-to-air fighters.

7s, which were strictly for air-to-air combat. Nor was their 20mm Gatling gun of value as an antiarmor weapon; it, too, was intended primarily as an air-to-air weapon. So all they could use against the Iraqi armor was bombs, but even then there was a problem.

At the time the Strike Eagles had deployed, only two types of bombs had been certified on the airplane: Mark-82 500-pound bomb and Mark-84 2,000-pound bomb. However, these were general demolition bombs, designed to explode and create damage in a relatively large area from flying shrapnel. They were great weapons for blasting buildings and ammunition dumps, but against armored vehicles they were almost worthless unless there was a direct hit.

The antiarmor bomb of choice (at that time) was the Mark-20 "Rockeye," a canister with more than two hundred bomblets that are released over an area when the canister opens at a designated height above the ground. Each of the bomblets contains a "shaped charge," which, when it explodes, sends out a slug that can penetrate armor. When Rockeye bomb canisters open over tanks, two problems are solved. First, when hundreds of the bomblets are released, there is a much greater probability that the armored vehicles will be struck. Second, when the bomblets strike and explode, they are almost certain to cause debilitating damage.

For the crewmen, most of whom truly believed that Saddam Hussein was about to send his armor into Saudi Arabia, and that they would soon be sent to attack it, the Mark-20 Rockeye bomb was their main hope as they contemplated their potential effectiveness. But, in regard to the bomb itself, there was good news and bad news. The good news was that Thumrait had been designated earlier as a bomb dump for Southwestern Asia and there were tons of Mark-20s available—they just had to be assembled from component parts that were stored in the dump. The bad news was that the bomb had never been dropped from a Strike Eagle before and they had no assurance that it would release properly. And, although the software in their computers was supposed to include the necessary information to use the bomb, the crewmen were leery because it had never been tested.

It has become almost a cliche to say that the all-volunteer military forces are far more professional than forces made up largely of conscripts. But numerous examples of military professionalism were demonstrated during Operations Desert Shield and Desert Storm, and the action of M. Sgt. Danny Brown during the first days of the Strike Eagles' deployment to Thumrait, Oman, is one of the most outstanding. Without supervision, Sergeant Brown used his own initiative to find the bomb dump at Thumrait and, in sandstorms, in brutal August heat, and without protective goggles for himself or his crew, managed to get a bomb assembly line going the first day after

their arrival. Then, said Capt. Yogi Alred, the Rockets' weapons officer, "[Lt. Col.] Steep Turner, the wing weapons officer, and I went
out to the bomb dump right after we arrived on the field [they were
both delayed because of fuel-leakage problems] and we were amazed
at what was going on. Sergeant Brown already had his bomb assembly production line going, putting together 82s, 84s, and Rockeyes,
and they were producing bombs at the rate of one per minute! It was
an incredible achievement. In addition, one of his men had had the
foresight to put three cases of Kevlar lanyards on a pallet when we
deployed. These things stretch out to thirty inches after bomb release
and if we had had to use the old metal ones, they would have beat
our CFTs [conformal fuel tanks on which the bombs were hung] to
death before we got home. Those guys saved our bacon."

Of course the major questions facing the crewmen were where
and how they were going to use the Rockeye if they had to attack
Iraqi armor. Said Capt. Ken Garrison, who had just arrived from
Dhahran with one of the planes that had experienced fuel-leakage
problems, "Right after I got there I was assigned to do MPC work—
work in the mission planning cell. There were four of us: Rubbers
[Capt. Brian Allen], OBD [Capt. Darryl Roberson], Beak [Maj. Larry
Widner], and myself—two pilots and two WSOs. They said, 'You four
guys go to the squadron,' and I didn't even know there was such a
place. So we went into this building and found a bare room and
started taping black paper and black Hefty bags on the windows to
secure the place. Nothing had been unpacked from the pallets, so we
started doing that next, pulling books out of crates—the Dash Ones,
Thirty-fours, and the Three Dash Ones—the classified stuff. Then we
sat down on the bare concrete floor and began going through the
books taking down the numbers for Rockeye deliveries. Although
none had ever been dropped from our plane, we found numbers that
we thought we could use—numbers for doing levels [deliveries], 10-
degree, 20-degree, and 30-degree diving deliveries—we wrote down
every different delivery we could think of on a card, then we dupli-
cated it so if the planes on alert got the call, they would have a
choice. They could do a medium-altitude delivery if they could see a
big column of things moving, or if they had to get down low to
search for a column or whatever, they would have the numbers to do
that, too.

"We also found a map of Saudi Arabia and we began looking just
under Kuwait. The four of us were going, 'Let's see, what if they
push down here—it looks like there's a bunch of oil fields there and
that's probably where they'll go. Let's take the average terrain elevation there.' That's what we based all our attacks on. We picked a
number off the map and said, 'Here's the elevation you can expect
out there.' We sat on that bare concrete floor and worked all night

on that stuff, and by the next morning we had a packet ready for the crews going on alert."

By the next morning they had twelve airplanes on fifteen-minute alert. Lt. Col. Slammer Decuir, chief of standardization and evaluation for the 4th Wing, described how the alert system worked. "Things were pretty crude at the beginning. Those first days we sent the guys out to cock their airplanes, then they would come in the squadron building and lay around on the floor—we had no furniture for awhile. When they cocked their airplanes, they started the engines, aligned the INS [inertial navigation system], did the BIT [built-in test] checks, made sure the flight controls were working, stored the INS alignment, then shut down. Later, should they get scrambled, all they had to do was jump in, start the engines, take thirty seconds to let the ring-laser gyro spool up for INS alignment, select navigation mode, then taxi and go. Actually, most of the fifteen minutes in the alert period was time they needed to get to the jet, get strapped in, and taxi. It only took about one minute to start the jet and get it rolling after it had been cocked.

"As those first days went by, we also began to rethink our tactics. Basically our task was to go up there and do old-fashioned road recce [reconnaissance] just like the P-47s did in World War II. The young guys didn't know anything about that, but some of us had practiced road recce missions in F-4s under the guidance of the guys who had flown in Vietnam. So we sat down and pooled our knowledge, then tried to educate the young guys. Our main objective, of course, was to find an armor column and stop the front and back vehicles in order to bottle them up. We had practiced that with road recce missions in F-4s, doing big S-turns back and forth along highways. Our main concern, should we attack, was the ZSU-23-4 [a Soviet-designed, radar-guided, four-barrel machine gun], which could kill us if we were careless while attacking at low altitudes. One thing we stressed was that in reattacking we should swing out at least ten miles before returning so their gunners could not follow us.

"We thought we might be going to war any minute so all these strategy discussions were pretty impromptu. However, after a few days, we started refining our tactics to where we had formalized three different kinds of attacks. The first we called the 'How 'ya doin' attack' because that was the favorite expression of two of our guys—[Capt.] Mike Stansbury and [Capt.] Rich Catano. With this attack we would go in low, pop up and deliver ordnance, then go down low and get out.

"The second option we named the 'Hon-yocker' attack. We would go in at a medium altitude, drop our ordnance, then run out low. The third option, the 'Kit and Kaboodle,' turned out to be the one we used most often in Desert Storm. We ingressed to the target at medium altitude, mapped our target with radar, rolled in with a diving delivery, and pickled [released bombs] above the range of the bad triple-A and small shoulder-held SAMs. Generally, this meant that we pickled anywhere between 18,000 and 15,000 feet and tried to stay above 10,000 on the pullout. Then we would egress at medium altitude—18,000 or higher."

Ordnance and tactics were high on the list of topics that concerned the crews. But there were numerous other extenuating circumstances that complicated their mission. One was the great distance from their airfield to the potential invasion route. Their airplanes at Thumrait were almost nine hundred statute miles south of the Kuwait-Saudi border. In effect they were sitting west of Chicago worrying about how they were going to stop armored columns crossing the Connecticut border from attacking and overrunning New York City and the New Jersey shoreline.

Another problem was their lack of secure communications with Central Command Air Force Headquarters (CENTAF) in Riyadh, Saudi Arabia. In the building they had selected as squadron headquarters, which was actually a truck maintenance garage, there was one phone in what had been a big service bay. "That was a problem," said Capt. Baxter Sosebee, "because the dial of the phone had arabic numbers of a type that we couldn't read, and they start on the lower right and go up, which is the opposite of ours. I can still see our squadron commander trying to make calls to CENTAF. It was just a public line, and at the time, we didn't know that our calls were routed through Kuwait on the way to Riyadh. Finally, after several days trying to communicate on that phone, we were able to obtain secure faxes routed from Riyadh to Langley and then by satellite to us. It wasn't until several weeks later that we had secure comm lines via satellite to CENTAF."

They were also cut off from the rest of the world in other ways. There were no magazines or newspapers. There was no CNN, which provided intensive coverage of the emergency for many people of the world. In fact, there was no television at all, and it would be three to four weeks before any of them would even receive mail. Their only link with the outside world was through the BBC World Service— short-wave newscasts out of London—the same low-key radio news service that their grandfathers had listened to in their foxholes during World War II.

The days passed slowly. Dressed in their G-suits and survival vests, lying on the hard concrete floor and using their folded gloves as a pillow, the alert crews whiled away their twelve-hour shifts, sometimes talking, sometimes sleeping, always apprehensive, if not downright fearful, of the mission that they would be called upon to fly at any moment.

Said Capt. Rick Henson, "I figured we would lose 50 percent in a heartbeat. I figured we would lose 50 percent the first day doing CAS. I knew it. We would be very exposed. Everybody felt that way; we talked about it. There was a tremendous amount of openness and honesty among the guys—a lot of emotion—a tremendous amount of emotion—more than you ever see in a standard fighter squadron. Not much bravado. We were scared. I can't explain it any other way. Guys were sitting around going through their survival vests, saying, 'Now I use this for this and this for that.' We were serious. It is almost like you see your destiny. You see what you are up against and it doesn't look pretty because a dark gray jet against a tan desert—during the daytime . . . well, it's a big target. We all kind of felt like we were sacrificial out there—that we were to go out and sacrifice ourselves to slow them down so that somebody else could stop them."

They talked about a lot of other things as they whiled away the hours on the floor of their squadron. A recurrent topic was Saddam Hussein. What was he like? What was he planning? Was he coming south, or was he not? At that time most believed that he would. They believed that he would be a fool not to do so when there was little to stop him and when there was so much wealth within easy grasp.

Then, as the days passed, they had to think about threats other than Saddam Hussein's armored divisions poised on the Kuwait border. Oman, where they were located, shares a border with South Yemen, once a capricious Marxist state. Among the Omanis at Thumrait there was a fear that the Yemenis would show support for Saddam Hussein by attacking them. And while nothing official was seen in the way of contingency tasking for the Strike Eagles, they felt the weight of the Omani fears and believed that they would be ordered to defend the Omanis if they were attacked.

Then came the United Nations trade embargo placed on Iraq. In theory it was to be enforced by ships and aircraft of the Coalition naval forces. But in fact all aviation assets in the Persian Gulf area could be used if needed, and the Strike Eagles were officially placed on alert for embargo enforcement tasking.

Then time slowed down. The adrenaline boost that propelled them through the first few days, when they were frantically preparing for war at any moment, eventually petered out. As each hot August day passed, the hours grew longer, the days seemed interminable, and their once high energy levels were bludgeoned away by the three brutal truncheons of the desert—the heat, the raging winds, and the abject desolation. They were professionals, of course—as high a quality of professionals as could be found in any air force at any time in history—but they were also human. Out of touch with their families, worrying about pregnant wives and missing the laughter and warmth of their children, shadows of despair began to darken their quiet hours. And the inevitable, dreaded question crept into their minds. How long are they going to keep us here?

Neither their squadron commander, nor his commanders in Riyadh or Washington could answer that question. The only thing they were sure of was that the president of the United States had authorized the flow of massive reinforcements to the region. This mobilization was well publicized on CNN—Saddam Hussein's reported major source of intelligence. It was hoped that a growing deterrent force would cause him to falter rather than incite him to plunge southward while his window of opportunity was still there. The strategists who had studied his faltering ways during the Iran-Iraq War were betting heavily on the deterring action of the buildup. But they were a long way from Saudi Arabia and Oman. And besides, the commanders who would have to orchestrate an air interdiction campaign had to believe that Saddam was coming. In their war colleges they had studied and discussed the wishful thinking of the McClellans and Hookers, and the near-criminal nonchalance of the commanders at Pearl Harbor before the Japanese raid. Also, they had spent their entire careers practicing instantaneous responses to aggressor attacks that could have been launched at any moment by North Korea or the Warsaw Pact nations. "Readiness is our profession" was more than just a motto; being ready to stop enemy attacks had been their way of life. So, the commands that went down to the Strike Eagles had a hard metal edge to them. Forget about whether he is coming or not; assume that he is and you damn sure better be ready to stop him.

But what did being ready mean? To the crews it did not mean lounging around in flight gear on twelve-hour alert periods for two weeks. In their minds that was like putting cross-country runners in bed for a two-week period so they could rest up for a race. The highly demanding skills needed to fly and manage the weapons systems of the Strike Eagles required incessant practice, and those skills atrophied exponentially with time when they were not practiced. After two weeks of nothing but watching heat waves shimmering over their ramp, the crews were damned miserable. They knew that each day of inactivity significantly decreased their chances of fighting effectively with their airplanes.

"We were also pissed off, big time," said one of the crewmen. "The morale in the squadron was so low I think many were ready to revolt. We had the worst squadron commander I'd ever seen in my career and, frankly, we were sick of the whole mess. And none of it was because of us being over there and living with the uncertainties of going to war. We were ready for that; that was what we lived for. What pissed us off was the way he was trying to run the squadron."

Their problems with the squadron commander started shortly after he took over the 336th Squadron more than a year earlier. The 336th was one of the original "Eagle" squadrons, made up of Americans who had volunteered to fly for the RAF during the dark days of World War II. That was when it had looked like Hitler's Germany was going to overrun all of Europe, including Great Britain, before the United States got into the war. For nearly fifty years the 336th built on that proud heritage, and while much of its legacy was buried in squadron histories, some of it was outwardly manifested by the wealth of memorabilia that was displayed in the squadron building—on the walls in the form of pictures and murals, and in their highly unique squadron bar. But, according to numerous crewmen who insisted that the sad tale be told, the new squadron commander ordered all the walls to be stripped of pictures, the murals to be painted or papered over, and their unique squadron bar to be ripped out. Said one of the senior captains, "I had been in the squadron from 1984 to 1988, right after [Lt. Col.] Bristol Bill Burnett had been the commander. It was a great squadron at that time—he had really built up the morale and the pride. Then, when I came back to the squadron, the walls had been cleaned off and it looked like a hospital. Friends of mine would come in and immediately they'd say, 'What's wrong with your squadron?' Any outsider could see that he had cut the heart out of the squadron. People didn't want to be at work; they stayed in [the U.S. Air Force] only because they liked flying."

Another aspect of the problem was the squadron commander's background. "He was strictly an air-to-air guy," said another captain. "When he came into this squadron, he was afraid of the ground; you could tell it when you flew with him. And he never got comfortable in the air-to-ground role. That was one of the many reasons he was never accepted in this squadron.

"Another reason had to do with his personality. He was a nice enough guy—he'd reportedly been a real nice guy before he took over this squadron—but he was not a people person. He couldn't really communicate with his people, and when he tried, he wouldn't look them in the eye. I can still see him, standing before the squadron, trying to talk to the guys, with his head down, wringing his hands."

"His real problem," said one of the instructor WSOs who had been in the squadron under another commander, "was that he was totally afraid of his job. The F-15E was brand new in the air force and he was in a high-visibility job. He admitted to one of the guys that he was told not to lose an airplane—that that would be the end of him if he did. He was also told by a very high-ranking general not to do any of that air-to-air crap. So he was under lots of pressure that many of the guys didn't appreciate. But it was so bad that when I was a scheduler in the squadron, Shaw [AFB] or Langley [AFB] would call up and say, 'How about some air-to-air with your guys today?' and we weren't even allowed to talk about it. That pissed a lot of the guys off because we were supposed to be able to fight our way into and out of the target area but we were not allowed to practice what the airplane was designed to do. Some of us had an air-to-air background in F-4s and we got a little air-to-air at Luke [AFB] when we transitioned, but that was it. We went off to the war unprepared, and some guys were real nuggets—some guys that had transitioned from the F-111 and the A-10 hardly knew what they were doing in the air-to-air role."

At home in Goldsboro, North Carolina, the crews had numerous outlets for their frustrations. They golfed, they boated, they fished, they partied, and most were heavily involved with family activities. They had none of those outlets in Oman, plus they had all the negative factors associated with their isolated environment and with a squadron commander who was under even greater pressure than when they were at home.

Thanks to the efforts of Colonel Eberly, to whom the crewmen looked for real leadership, they finally started flying after two weeks and, as one major put it, "It was like a bunch of thoroughbreds being let out of the corral. There was more talent in that squadron than I had ever seen anywhere and when it was turned loose, the flying was awesome. There were hardly any restrictions in Oman—we flew when and where we wanted and it was a real treat compared to the way we had to tippy-toe around the ranges at home. The Omanis were great—they even let us attack our airfield. That was something we couldn't dream of doing in Germany or England or at home. It was the best flying I've ever experienced."

Oman flying soon became their major outlet and as the author heard their stories, the telling was always accompanied by smiles and that far-off, distant look in the eyes that all aviators get when they recall their dances with billowing clouds and their tail chases through canyons. One canyon in particular was most memorable for them. They called it the "Grand Canyon" but it was just one of the many dry gorges eroded into the Oman coastline. However, it was large enough for a pair of Strike Eagles to do a tail chase below terrain level and, in their terms, "practice" terrain masking and radar evasion techniques.

The wonderful Oman flying undoubtedly helped the morale of the crewmen, but one nagging problem remained. It was the proverbial burr under the saddle and it festered, erupted, and for awhile, threatened the stability of the squadron. It all had to do with their airplane and how it was designed to fly missions. The Strike Eagle

was designed to fly low and at night. It is equipped with terrain-following radar and a LANTIRN pod that uses infrared radiation to
give night-flying crews a near-daytime view of the terrain over
which they are flying.

They fly low for three reasons. First, radar detection by the enemy
is related to the altitude they are flying. For example, an airplane
attacking at an altitude of 1,000 feet might be picked up on enemy
radars when twenty-five to thirty miles from the target. At 500 knots
airspeed, that would give the enemy about three minutes to react
with defensive measures. However, when flying at 200 feet they
might not be seen until they are five miles from the target, which, at
the same airspeed, would give the enemy only thirty seconds to
react—a highly significant difference.

The second reason for going in low is to avoid attack by enemy
air-to-air fighters. When the attackers are low, it is very difficult,
even for the "look down" radars found in the latest Soviet-built fighters, to pick up and track low-flying airplanes. In addition, if the
attackers are detected, it is extremely difficult for enemy fighters to
get in a position where they can shoot down low-flying aircraft with
air-to-air missiles.

The third reason for going in low is to avoid enemy SAMs. At 200
feet it is nearly impossible for the guidance system of a SAM to lock
on and then make the missile turn sharply enough to track a fast-
moving airplane.

Now, consider what the crews in Oman were hearing every day
during their intelligence briefings. The Iraqis had one of the finest
early-warning radar systems of any country in the world. With a network of radar stations scattered throughout the country they could
pick up and track attacking aircraft invading their country from any
direction. They also had hundreds of first-rate French-built and
Soviet-built air-to-air fighters that could be scrambled in moments
should their early-warning radar detect invaders. In addition, they
had an inventory of thousands of SAMs, both radar- and infrared-
guided, that could be positioned and ready to shoot down aircraft
attacking any target in their country.

So the message was clear, at least to most of the Strike Eagle
crews: IF YOU ARE GOING TO ATTACK THE IRAQIS, YOU HAVE
TO FLY LOW! You have to fly low to be effective. You have to fly low
to stay alive.

But the squadron commander, who had already lost respect
because of his personal aversion to low flying, was telling the crews
that they must not fly lower than 300 feet during the daytime practice missions when, at the same time, their potential missions into
Iraq called for them to fly at 200 feet at night.

The commander's viewpoint was not without merit. Flying in the

Oman desert was not like flying in the desert around Las Vegas or Phoenix where the crews had trained. In the Sonora and Mojave deserts of the American Southwest the visibility was nearly always unrestricted and judging depth by eyeballs was rarely a problem, at least in daytime, because there was always a definite horizon in view.

That was not the case in Oman. The sand was fine, almost like talcum powder, and because of the persistent winds, it was usually in motion, obscuring the horizon and making it very difficult for crews to rely on visual clues to determine their height above ground. So, it was dangerous to fly low much of the time, at least when using eyeballs to avoid the ground. For that reason, and because the commander was under intense pressure not to lose an airplane, his orders remained firm: No flying below 300 feet.

This restriction, exacerbated undoubtedly both by the anxiety and frustration of the crewmen and the oppressiveness of the desert, soon became a source of contention that caused a schism in the squadron. Many sided with one of the flight commanders, Maj. Pete Hook, a highly respected pilot who had flown a tour with RAF pilots—pilots famous throughout the aviation community for their ability to fly at tree-top levels. Pete Hook was passionate in his belief that the Strike Eagles had to practice flying at 200 feet or lower because, without practice, some of them would get killed trying to do that on a combat mission when they could be distracted by triple-A, SAMs, air-to-air fighters, and the all-consuming task of getting their ordnance on target. "We broke the rules—a lot of us did," admitted one of the pilots. "We flew at 100 and 200 feet because we believed that that was the only way we were going to survive and do our job. You have to remember: War is not Red Flag; it's not a chess game; it's not CNN. You get your job done—you do what it takes and you make sure you survive and your wingman survives. And if you are not prepared to do that, you let yourself down, your wingman down—your squadron, your family, the whole country. It was personally frustrating to go against orders, but it was a case where our consciences said that we had to do that."

Some sided with the squadron commander. "It's no big deal to go from 300 down to 200 feet when you need to," said one of the captains. "What you find—and I've had the Strike Eagle down to 100 feet—is that you are completely task saturated down there; you can't do any scanning; you have to concentrate 100 percent on avoiding the ground. Personally, I didn't think it was that important to practice down there; I felt I could drop down any time I needed to."

But Pete Hook, as a flight commander, pushed the issue. What concerned him was that some of the young pilots were going out and flying low without any step-down training—and that they might get killed in the process. He, along with another highly respected pilot, went to the squadron commander and laid their concerns on the table. "Sir, the guys are out there practicing like each sortie will be their last one before flying in real combat. They are flying at 50 and 100 and 200 feet, busting the altitude you have mandated because they feel they have to train that way if they are going to do that in combat. Please let those of us with experience flying low set up an official, structured, step-down training program for these guys so they can learn to do this safely. We are really concerned. We are afraid somebody is going to get killed if we don't initiate a training program."

The argument fell on deaf ears. "Don't tell me that they are busting altitudes; I don't want to hear about it," said the squadron commander.

"The problem," said one of the pilots, "was that if he officially approved a step-down training program and then lost a jet while practicing, he would be blamed. As it was, those young guys were going out there flying below the level of the sand dunes and if they killed themselves, he could always say that they disobeyed his orders and claim innocence for himself."

The word of that conference got around fast and the morale nose-dived. Flaunting their commander's orders daily was getting to many of them, even while they believed passionately that they must fly their training sorties the way they would fly in combat. Then things got worse. Two aircraft from other bases were lost in training accidents and word came down from Riyadh: No flying below 300 feet, and if you get caught doing that, we take your wings.

That upped the ante, and soon, when the crews were out of earshot of the few who might report them, they held deep philosophical debates among themselves. "It was not unlike the situation on the Caine," said one of the pilots. "Of course, we weren't debating on a mutiny like the Caine's officers were plotting against Captain Queeg. But there was clearly a stiff debate going over whether or not it was a higher duty to our country to train the way we thought we had to in order to be effective. I, myself, especially in retrospect, sort of feel like the lawyer in the story, Barney Greenwald, who, after getting the guys off for the mutiny, turned on them and told them they were wrong in what they did—that they should have obeyed orders. Of course, part of my hindsight is influenced by how we ended up flying in the war. I must admit that at the time all this was going on, I was almost as convinced as the rest of them that we had to bust the 300-foot mandate in order to train realistically."

Pete Hook, an Air Force Academy graduate, was deeply religious and also felt deeply about the leadership responsibility that went with his job as a flight commander in the squadron. He also believed strongly that he should transfer all of the knowledge he had gained to younger crewmen. Said a WSO who knew him intimately, "I had flown with Pete since 1987 when we were in F-4s. We flew at Maple Leaf [a Canadian exercise] for two weeks at Cold Lake; I flew my first ride in the F-15E at Seymour with him. We had flown a lot together and I knew him very, very well. Without question he was the best stick guy I had ever flown with. Period. Dot. But he was also a great teacher—always a teacher. We would be briefing on a four-ship cross-country and he'd say, 'Okay, today we are going to bet. We are going to bet on who can predict their landing fuel the closest.' That was an exercise to make you think—to make you learn something about the airplane. Another day we were briefed to fly and hold near Washington National airport. But Pete wasn't going to waste the time in that holding pattern. He briefed it so that we had five radar offsets that we were to map while in the pattern. One was an entrance to the House of Representatives—another was the White House—and I remember that another was a picnic table in the middle of the Pentagon. And all the while, he planned it so that we were dividing up our radar searching for traffic. It was an exercise in learning—completely unorthodox—but he was that type of person.

"But his passion finally got him in trouble. The squadron commander called an aircrew meeting to talk about tactics—a subject that had been our number one concern since we had arrived. Well, at the end of the meeting, Pete stood up, and with complete respect in his voice, said, 'Sir, I just want to say that I think this is a great idea having this kind of meeting. I'd like to see us hold more of these.' After the meeting, I had to stick around and do some scheduling and I see our commander with Pete Hook over in a corner, the commander's 3,000 PSI finger in Pete's chest. Pete told me later that he had been chewed out—that the squadron commander was extremely disappointed and unhappy with him because Pete had embarrassed him in front of the squadron. I guess, too, that they had a fairly aggressive argument at that time. I'm sure they talked about the step-down training program that Pete wanted—several people raised concerns about that at the meeting. But all anybody got during the meeting was the evil eye if flying lower than 300 feet was mentioned.

"Not long afterwards, at another aircrew meeting, the commander announced that there had been a couple of personnel changes. That Pete Hook was being moved to Assistant Chief of Safety in the squadron and that another pilot, a constant defender of the commander, was to replace him as a flight commander. Everybody dropped their jaw. Nobody could believe it because Pete Hook had been the chief safety officer of a squadron back in 1987. This was a humiliating demotion. After the meeting Pete got his flight together without the new commander and said, 'I found out about this just five minutes before the aircrew meeting. I don't know what to say. I am obviously extremely disappointed.' And we could see that. He was disappointed—extremely so. But he told us that we were professional officers and that he expected us to give the new flight commander 100 percent support. Of course, we all agreed that we would.

"After he got busted, he was very disillusioned about the Air Force, about flying fighters. Very disillusioned overall. His whole dream had been being a flight commander and he took that very, very seriously. He took leadership very seriously. He was not a manager; he was a leader and a very good one. For him it was like his whole world. He didn't understand it; it didn't make sense to him any more.

"But he bounced back. He was a very positive guy—always an upbeat attitude. That was his personality. He tried never to let things get him down. He believed very strongly that the Lord would take care of him. Whatever happened had a greater purpose and that is what kept Pete going."

On the morning of September 30 Pete Hook was in a fantastic mood according to one of the crewmen he was flying with that morning. Said Capt. Rick Henson, "He had talked with his family the night before[2]—his family meant everything to him, and when we went in to brief our two-ship mission he was as upbeat as I'd ever seen him. It was [Capt.] Steve Sanders with me in his pit flying on Pete Hook's wing. Boo Boo [Capt. Jim Poulet] was his pitter. It was a composite mission where we had briefed with some British Jaguar crews who were also based at Thumrait. We were going out to a point and the Jaguars were coming in low level simulating an attack on Thumrait. We were going to tap them twice on that low level, then we were going to do some air-to-air against ourselves and come home.

"The first intercept was briefed as a number two—Steve and I were going to do a high to low conversion. That's where we take the airplane up about 20,000 or so, get in to where we are about ten miles or less from the Jaguars, then roll the airplane upside down and split-S on top of the strike package. Pete and Boo Boo were going to do a level intercept from about 100 to 200 feet. They would stay low and come in on them from the side.

"We took off, we did the systems check, then cruised up beside Pete and Boo Boo, on their right side. Just as we get up on them, Pete does a barrel roll around us. I'd never seen him do that before and I made a comment in the airplane about how unusual that was because it was not as crisp and professional as the way he always

---

[2]By this time the crews had a clandestine phone system at work. It is described in the next chapter.

conducted himself. It seemed odd to me but I quickly dismissed it. He then goes back to do a weapon system check on us and as he is closing on us, I get a radar contact on some very low altitude targets on the nose. I called them out and Pete goes, 'Commit there. Pince!' A pince maneuver is where you have an air-to-air target on your nose and the two airplanes split, one going one way and one the other—where each rolls in on the target in a heart-shaped maneuver.

"As we turned to get some offset in order to come back in, we had a radar problem—the air-to-air radar died. I called that and Pete tells us to go to the holding point that we had briefed, where we were going to start the intercept on the Jaguars that we were supposed to tap—the Jaguars that showed up first and that we started to attack were not a part of the briefed plan. But Pete and Boo Boo continued the attack and I know from listening to the radio and from my situational awareness that they are running intercept on those guys. I hear him call a tally ho, then engaged, but that is the last thing I hear. Shortly thereafter, the real flight of Jaguars checks in—the ones we were supposed to attack—but they are unable to get a Mickey[3] on the radio. They ask why Pete doesn't respond—he doesn't even respond to their check in. I answer up, I pass the Mickey, and I get them set up, but I tell them to stand by because we're orbiting. The air-to-air TACAN [distance measuring instrument] between our jet and Pete's drops off line and Steve makes a comment about that. Without knowing anything is wrong, I have a bad feeling—like when the hair on the back of your neck stands up and you know something is wrong. I didn't know what it was. I tried to call Pete a couple of times and can't get an answer. I then hear over Guard [emergency communications channel], 'Knock it off; knock it off; we have a downed aircraft.'"

---

[3]A time synchronization so they could communicate by secure radio.

4

Turner Takes Command

"Steep Turner turned us into a fighter squadron."
                                        Capt. Chris DiNenna

Rick Henson and Steve Sanders continued to hold and listen to the radio traffic while rescue assets sped to the area. The British Jaguars were the first to report that an airplane had crashed and that no chutes were visible near the scene. It was a gray airplane, they said—at least what was left of it was gray. To the Americans listening, there was still a glimmer of hope. Some of the British airplanes were gray. But then came the definitive word; it was a Strike Eagle. There was no doubt now; Pete Hook and Boo Boo Poulet had ridden it in.

Sanders and Henson continued to hold while rescue assets were mobilized. When they were released they flew at 500 feet over the crash site. They saw a streak in the sand, terminated by part of a wing, a fuel tank, and a dark gray mass that bore no resemblance to an airplane. They did not make another pass or go lower. They had seen all they wanted to see and low flight held no more appeal on this day.

Back in the squadron the commander wavered between shock and disbelief. Some of the crewmen who spoke with him that day and evening believed he was on his way to a nervous breakdown. He had lost the first F-15E. His deepest fear had come to pass.

When there is such a tragedy, the fallen comrades have to be honored. In a memorial service that filled a large hangar, Lt. Col. Dick Hoey gave a moving eulogy for the pilot, Pete Hook, his roommate. For Boo Boo Poulet, the backseater, it was his bachelor friend, Capt.

37

John Pavlock, who rose before the crowd and suppressed his agony long enough to speak of their bright moments in Spain together and tell of the ways his beloved, good-natured, French-speaking comrade had lightened their lives with such homemade phrases as "Taco le Belle" for the fast food restaurant that he enjoyed. The bitterest chore was left for Capt. Jack Ingari, the squadron flight surgeon and sometime WSO who had just flown with Pete Hook and who had been a good friend of both men. It was Ingari's duty to accompany the remains everywhere, first to Dhahran, then to Germany where he had to witness the autopsies, and then on to Seymour Johnson where Pete Hook's wife and children, ages two, four, and six, were grieving.

At Thumrait the alert line was maintained, with airplanes loaded and cocked, but there was no flying for four days. It was time to take stock—time to reevaluate—time to rewire the caution circuitry in the minds of the aircrews. It was also a time when the script for the tragedy had to be deduced.

Within minutes of the reported crash, a team of investigators was on the way to the scene. When they got there, they found a fifty-foot or longer trail in the sand, blackened by the exhaust from the engines, but furrowed by the stabilators[1] of the jet. Clearly, in the milliseconds before the crash, the pilot had the nose high, presumably struggling to alter the course of his sinking airplane. This is an anomaly that is hard for most pilots to comprehend; when you are heading into the ground in most airplanes, you are staring at a windscreen full of the ground that awaits you. However, the nose of the F-15 can be horsed upward, even at slow airspeeds, as the airplane is falling to the earth.

Interviews with the British Jaguar pilots out that morning gave investigators the rest of the picture. Hook and Poulet had continued their half of the pince maneuver after Henson reported the air-to-air radar out in the second jet. Hook and Poulet were successful; they called out a tally ho and that they were engaged. But unknown to Hook and Poulet, the Brits had a "Baron" in trail—a single airplane waiting to pounce on an unsuspecting attacker. Hook, apparently surprised by the attacker,[2] tried to get on his tail with a reversal, a split-S maneuver where the airplane is rolled inverted, then pulled downward like it was on the back side of a loop. It was a split-second judgment call—the kind that fighter pilots must make routinely. However, they were too low for the maneuver—but just barely. The

---

[1]Movable horizontal tail.

[2]These were not the Jaguars with whom they had briefed before the mission—they were still on the ground in Thumrait.

fact that the stabilators were dragging in the sand for a distance
indicates that they almost recovered. The conclusion was that the
pilot had made a mistake in judging altitude. There were also possible mitigating factors. By this time the jets had sand-pitted wind-
screens, which creates a kind of "milk bowl" visual effect when looking outside. Then there was the fact that the jet was loaded with
three external fuel tanks, which was necessary because of their
potential tasking and because it required too much time to take them
off before practice missions. Then there was the desert itself, with
the shifting, blowing, powdery sand creating an indefinite horizon
that made visual altitude judgment difficult.

Morale in the Rockets' squadron was at rock bottom. And it got
worse. Less than a week after the memorial service an RF-4 went in
while practicing a defensive move against a simulated artillery site.
Both crewmen were killed. Less than twenty-four hours later an F-
111F in the theater plowed into the ground recovering from a simulated bomb drop. Again, both crewmen were killed. These accidents
were tragic, but, from the Strike Eagle crewmen's perspective, the
tragedies were on their way to being compounded. Their leadership
all the way up to Riyadh grew paranoiac and, in the aftermath,
raised the minimum practice altitude to 500 feet.

Three hundred feet had been too high for most of them, and during the past weeks, they had grown more convinced than ever that
they had to attack at 200 feet or lower in order to penetrate Saddam
Hussein's defenses. Now they were being told to train at 500 feet.
"That was absurd and idiotic," they groaned. (The expletives the
author heard are deleted.) "The point is," wrote one frustrated pilot
to his diary, "that we must train for the threat, not to prevent accidents. If we focus on training hard but in an organized and logical
way, we will reduce accidents and still train as we need to. One of
the problems now is that people perceive that we are not training
well enough and go out and train on their own. This breaking of the
rules is unsafe, primarily because it is hidden, and not taught and
critiqued as well as it would be in an organized manner."

So the burr under the saddle had created a festering sore. It was
also creating humiliation because the RAF crews, with whom they
were now partying in the Omani Officers' Club, flew at 100 feet or
lower every day—and, of course, reminded their Coalition partners
of their intrepidity regularly. Many of the Strike Eagle crewmen
were also fuming inside because the Brits flew a "missing man" formation during the memorial service for Hook and Poulet but they,
themselves, were not allowed to do the same. "They'll do that at
Seymour," they were told.

Then one of the pilots committed a heinous deed. Someone in the
squadron had designed a new patch to commemorate service in

Desert Shield, the name now being used to describe their defensive operation. In the middle of the patch was a camel covered with cross hairs with the words above and below, "Desert Shield—8,000 miles to smoke a camel." One of the pilots saw the sample patch, fell in love with it, and decided to take some of his own money and order a bunch for all the guys. He did this, of course, contrary to the commander's wishes—my goodness, what if some higher authority took offense at this! Well, somebody snitched after the order was sent, and the pilot, a former F-111 driver who was already in trouble because of the difficulty he was having adapting to the air-to-air role of the Strike Eagle, was severely reprimanded and threatened with an Article 15, which if made to stick, would have abruptly ended his career. Fortunately, the fatherly and well-liked DO, Colonel Eberly, got wind of it all and reassured the distraught pilot that no Article 15 could be levied for such a minor offense.

About this same time another pilot was not so lucky. He got in hot water by trusting the unwritten code of the Doofer Book.

In squadron bars throughout the air force there is some form of composition book (it will have various names) where the aviators can write whatever is on their mind. The comments run the gamut, from wisecracks, advice, jokes, and doggerel to grumbles and fulmi-nations. However, there are unwritten ground rules. First, the book is to be read only by the aviators in the squadron. Second, everyone must sign with their call sign, or their name if they are too new to have a call sign. Third, it cannot be read by O-6s (colonels) or above, and if it is read by an O-5 (lieutenant colonel), that officer must not retaliate to an unfavorable comment in any way. In other words the Doofer Book is a place where high-spirited aviators can vent some of their bottled-up passions without suffering ill consequences.

Or so one pilot thought. This fellow, a U.S. Air Force Academy graduate and a pilot so respected for his leadership that he had been voted 4th Wing Flight Commander of the Year, was called back to Seymour Johnson to help get the Chiefs ready should they be needed in theater. (Actually there were plans being developed that would require the Chiefs, but this was hush-hush stuff—more later.) Just before he left, he noted in the Doofer Book how sad things were in the Rockets (he was a Chief) and that he hoped things would improve. Said the pilot, "I did this out of sincerity, not out of bitter-ness. I was leaving, going back to my family, and I wanted the guys who were stuck there to know that I empathized with them and wished them well."

The recriminations were immediate. By the time the pilot arrived home, his squadron commander, Lt. Col. Pingel, had orders to fire him as a flight commander. However, Pingel hesitated, telling the pilot to report for work and lay low for awhile—often these kinds of reprisals are anger induced and blow over when tempers subside. But that was not to be. There was follow-up and Pingel had to act. Later, when the pilot showed up with the Chiefs when they deployed, he was banished from the base, sent to Riyadh, and would not have flown in the war had not a sympathetic colonel battled to retrieve him. Still, his career was tainted and, after the war, he opted to leave the air force.

A salty military veteran reading the above may be grimacing about now. So, what else is new? he might ask. This kind of petty bullshit is just a routine part of serving in the military. It happens all the time.

The author will admit that stories like the above tend to give a soap opera-like tone to any work. But the reader must understand that such deeds, in the small community of a fighter squadron, breed a contagion of mistrust for a commander. And as the mistrust spreads, the quality of the fighting force diminishes. To be sure, fine professionals do their job anyway; they do what they have to do. But in warfare, that is not always enough. The fighters who win are often those who go beyond their normal capabilities. They mine their bodies and souls for skills and strength and stamina that they never knew they had. And they will do that for a leader they trust. This is hardly the place for history sermons. Yet, the lessons of Washington at Valley Forge and Lee at Gettysburg must not be ignored. The axiom is that for men to give their last full measure in warfare, they must be led by someone they trust. The corollary is that they will never give that full measure for a leader they distrust. So all the petty stuff—the taking of squadron memorabilia from the walls and the overreaction to a squadron patch, and retaliation against comments in a Doofer Book just help explain why the Strike Eagles were not the force they could have been in August, September, and October of 1990. They would have fought, had they been needed. And they would have fought hard. But they would not have fought as effectively as they eventually did for the leader who was about to take over the squadron.

They started getting their hopes up in mid-October when it was learned that their commander was on the colonels list—that he was about to be promoted from lieutenant colonel. "Full colonels do not command squadrons," they reminded each other when they heard the news. "Yes, but are they relieved when combat is imminent?" replied the skeptical ones. No one could be sure, but speculation on the new commander abounded. There was a favorite son waiting in the wings; one who was at the head of nearly everybody's list as a fighter pilot's fighter pilot: Lt. Col. Steep Turner, presently the 4th Wing's weapons officer. But the old-timers who had flown with him for years, first in F-4s and then in Strike Eagles, also knew that he had ticked off the previous wing commander. There was speculation that there was at least one black ball in his file that would keep him from getting the job.

But the 4th Wing commander, Col. Hal Hornburg, who was relatively new in the job and who was everybody's hope for better things, had arrived at Thumrait by now and he liked Turner. Also, Turner had attracted the attention of Ninth Air Force leadership. Those folks liked him, too. So, in late October, when squadron morale was at its lowest, the announcement was made. Steep Turner is going to be the new commander of the Rockets.

The author interviewed more than fifty of the Rockets who were in Thumrait at that time, as well as a dozen Chiefs who had deployed with them. Leafing through the pages of those interviews it is striking to see the same words appearing time after time when the change in command was discussed. "Night and day" was how they described the difference in the squadron after Steep Turner was named commander. A hackneyed phrase, to be sure, but these were fighter pilots, not poets, and, besides, night and day connote both the magnitude and the tenor of the change. Steep Turner changed the squadron into a strong, cohesive fighting force, and he led squadron spirit out of the darkness.

Even before Steep took over, the squadron went to him looking for leadership. The pilot threatened with the Article 15 went to him and asked, "What about the patches, sir?"

"I think they're great. When do they arrive?" was his laughing reply. "And, oh, by the way," he added, "can you make a platform and podium for the change of command ceremony?" (The pilot was a woodworker.)

"Yes, sir, even if I have to stay up nights to do it . . . sir!"

"Good, then I want you to use that platform for the base of a gazebo so the guys can lounge around outside their room when they have a chance."

"Yes, sir! Great idea, sir! Thank you, sir!"

The pilot, along with a fellow carpenter, worked into the wee hours, sawing and hammering and gluing, and in two days had the stage and podium ready for the change-of-command ceremony.

However, the commander first had to have his final flight and a little final flight ceremony afterwards. One of the participants in that ceremony best describes what happened.

"The day before the ceremony I was approached by a senior officer who came up to me and asked, 'Why don't you see about getting a fire truck for the ceremony? You get a fire truck and we'll hose him down when he gets out of the jet.'

"I said, 'I'd love to do that, sir. I would love to do that!'

"I went over to the fire guys and I sat and talked to them—I am pretty good at arranging things under the table. Oh, yeah, we got the biggest fire truck they had and they showed me how to use the nozzle that sits on top of the cab. We tested it out; water came out; it was all primed and ready to go.

"So the commander pulls in with the airplane and parks. I drove the fire truck up and the fire guys reel out one of the little hoses and then another little hose and I'm sitting in the cab with the big nozzle. Everybody is out there and the commander climbs out of the airplane and gets halfway down the ladder, and I turn on the big nozzle. For the first three seconds out comes water—after that, fire retardant foam—theoretically, semi-noncorrosive. However, the canopy is up, he is halfway down the ladder and the foam comes out over the front end of the fire truck and fogs the window and I can't see to aim it. I have it down where I think he is and it is pouring white foam. It is snowing and I am telling the fire guy next to me, turn the windshield wipers on, quick, and how do I turn it off?

"In the meantime, Eberly is yelling and jumping up and down and Hornburg walks over and kicks the fire truck tire, 'Stop it, stop it, stop this, you are ruining the airplane,' he yelled. I looked at the other fire guy there and I said, 'Get out and get the hoses rolled up real fast. Let's back out real quietly and maybe they will never know who we are'—the windows are fogged and they can't see us inside the cab. I backed out and drove the truck back to its parking place. But before we got out, I go, 'Look, here is the story: We tested it, it came out water, and I don't know what happened—we tried to shut it off and it wouldn't shut off.' The three of us agreed to that story. Then I got out of the fire truck, put on my hat, and walked back to the Qs [quarters]. I don't catch a ride; I walk through the desert, away from as many people as possible because I figure I am dead. My only hope was that it was only the senior officer and a few of my friends who knew it was me.

"I stayed out of the way until that night. We had a big celebration that Steep had asked me to set up. I set it up at the club. We had a bunch of booze and everybody is having a good time and I find the senior officer at a quiet moment. I walk up to him and I go, 'Sir, I apologize. I am dejected; I feel terrible, sir. I apologize for ruining the going away ceremony like that. I hope I didn't get you into too much trouble. 'The senior officer starts laughing and patting me on the back.' Best farewell I've ever seen and it couldn't have happened to a better guy.' Then we laughed. I was still nervous but Eberly, who could have investigated, was smart enough not to ask too many questions. He was good about that."

There was the traditional change-of-command ceremony and then the former commander's plane roared off the runway. That night there were loud cheers in the club, everybody gleefully toasting one of their own. They had already heard Steep Turner philosophize about leadership and its burdens. They had already heard him say, "A squadron commander who can't take his best friend out and shoot him can't command worth shit." But they didn't care. They wanted a tough leader. They also wanted one who cared about them more than the airplanes. And when he said, "Guys, I'm your friend, but now I'm your commander. If you make an honest mistake and admit it, I'll fight to the bitter end for you. But if you screw up and do something stupid, I'll run your ass out of here," they cheered again. They were not looking for a patsy. They were not looking for someone to hold their hand and tell them how good they were. They wanted a leader who was, in their terms, a "shit hot aviator," but one who would lead them into battle and then lead them home to their families. That night in early November, when they were toasting their new commander, they were certain that they had their man.

5

A Surprise Move

"Life was beautiful in Oman and we hated it when we heard we were going to Al's garage."

Lt. Col. Mike "Slammer" DeCuir

When the Strike Eagles first arrived in Oman, the crews thought of themselves as merely a speed bump for Saddam Hussein's forces. All they could do at that time was slow an Iraqi offensive against the oil fields of Saudi Arabia. There was no hope that they, along with the thin line of U.S. troopers on the ground, could stop a massive incursion of Saddam Hussein's armor. However, the fact that their planes were not designed and they were not trained for the defensive role they were given, mattered not at all. They were slim, racy, All-American halfbacks, trained for deep penetration into the opponent's territory. But since their coaches, out of necessity, put them into the game as defensive tackles and linebackers, that is what they would try to be.

The offensive coordinators were at work, however, almost from the beginning. In early August, right after Kuwait was overrun by the Iraqis, captains and majors from the different strike aircraft communities received secret orders to report to the Pentagon. But these were not average aviators; these were the pilots and WSOs who, during rigorous training and competitions, had demonstrated extraordinary prowess with their aircraft. President Bush had ordered the military forces to create an offensive plan that could drive Iraqi forces out of Kuwait—if that became necessary. The air power version of that offensive plan was about to be created and the senior commanders responsible for the plan wanted aviators who, when asked what their particular aircraft was capable of doing, would be able to give them an accurate answer—one based on solid experience, not speculation.

One of those aviators, and one of the few who had seen combat, knew from personal experience as a WSO in one of the F-111s on the 1986 Libyan raid the problems and hazards of the deep interdiction missions the Strike Eagles would be tasked to fly. Said Major H.,[1] "There were two of us from the F-15E community, myself and Major W. When we got to the Pentagon, they were going crazy with the logistics of getting everybody over to the desert and they didn't have the staffing to fully develop an offensive air campaign. Then they called in Col. John Warden, who was running Checkmate at the time—Checkmate is the war planning section—and under his leadership we began working on an offensive plan.

"There were about fifty of us—data analysts, some civilians, and some intel folks besides the aviators. Colonel Warden just laid out the president's objectives, which were basically to get the Iraqis out of Kuwait, and then asked us how we were going to do it. We worked 20-hour days and in two and one-half weeks we developed a plan called "Instant Thunder" that was briefed to General Schwarzkopf.

"We all contributed, but Colonel Warden should be given credit for much of the plan. He was awesome. I just enjoyed sitting back and listening to him outline the battle plan so it fit the president's objectives. He was very articulate and his thinking process . . . well, it was just incredible the way he laid out the air campaign in a step-by-step, logical way. And, later, when Desert Storm kicked off, the actual air campaign that was launched basically followed the plan we worked out in those two and one-half weeks."

So in August, while Coalition military forces and world media were totally preoccupied with the defense of Saudi Arabia, President Bush and his advisors had laid the groundwork for a campaign that would drive the Iraqis out of Kuwait.

And it was not long before some of the Strike Eagle crews started looking at the offensive playbook that Colonel Warden and his associates developed. One of the first to do so was Capt. Yogi Alred, a big, easy-going, personable man who was considered by many the best pilot in the Rockets squadron. Typical of the comments heard about him is the following statement a fellow pilot wrote in his diary: "Tomorrow I fly again, another air-to-ground sortie. Captain Alred is leading this one and I greatly respect him. I feel him to be the most knowledgeable man in the squadron on how best to employ and fight with this aircraft."

---

[1]The identification of pilots and WSOs who flew on the Libyan raid are still classified because of potential terrorist reprisals.

Said Alred, "Steep Turner, the wing weapons officer, and I went up to Riyadh August 15—that was my first involvement in the planning that we were calling 'Wolfpack' at the time. Then, about September 15 [Brigadier] General Glosson came over and took charge of the black hole where all the secret planning was done. We went up to Riyadh again and got a look at the plan Glosson brought over from Checkmate. It called for the 15Es to go after the Iraqi Scuds. We didn't care for that; it didn't seem to us like it was the most productive way to use our airplanes, and we told Glosson that when he asked our opinion. We knew it would be worse than looking for a needle in a haystack—trying to find mobile Scud launchers. Even the more permanent sites were a problem. At that time we hadn't done any APG 70 radar work against fences—there was no place to map a fence without a pine tree being in the way on the West Virginia ranges where we had trained. The unique radar signature of the fences around those sites were supposedly what we would be able to see.

"Glosson was checked out in the 15E and knew the capability of the airplane. But he listened patiently while we presented our point of view. Then he launched into a thirty-minute discussion on the predicament that we would be in if the Scuds were not neutralized. It was mainly a political discussion and he made us realize what a problem we would have if Israel got involved because of the Scuds. He took the time with us and was patient. I appreciated that. He also agreed with us. He said, 'I know good and well we can use your airplane better doing other things, but I can tell you right now, we're going to use a lot of your sorties chasing Scuds.'

"I asked, 'But why us?' He looked across the table and said, 'The reason you are going to do it is because nobody else can find them at night. The F-16's radar is not good enough to spot something of this size and there were very few F-16s with targeting pods—which could do the work. There is the same problem with the F-111s—their radar doesn't have the resolution to find something as small as a Scud. During the day I can send out F-16s and A-10s. But only you guys can find them at night.'

"We weren't exactly happy about the idea of flying around western Iraq looking for Scuds. But, at least the Day One mission in the Wolfpack plan was a good one for us. We were to take a big strike package and go after fixed Scud sites deep into western Iraq. That made sense; that was the type of mission that we had been trained for."

In October, after more work on Wolfpack in Riyadh, Alred and Turner went to their wing commander, Colonel Hornburg, and, emphasizing that President Bush might initiate the plan at any time, recommended that the crews be briefed on the top secret operation.

Hornburg agreed, got approval from Riyadh, and Turner took the crews into a secure room, briefed them, and also warned them that they could not discuss the plan anywhere but in the secure area. Soon the crews were studying targets in western Iraq and flying practice missions which, for the most part, resembled the actual mission they flew on the first night of the war—in the operation that was to be renamed "Desert Storm."

Meanwhile, Yogi Alred became involved in another operation—one that would precede Desert Storm—and one far more dangerous.

In the months after Kuwait was overrun by the Iraqis, the United States and its coalition partners had two excruciating problems. First was the problem of the workers from those countries who were in Iraq and Kuwait when Saddam Hussein made his surprise invasion. All of these workers and their dependents were potential hostages whose lives might have to be sacrificed if Kuwait or Iraq were attacked. As it turned out, some were singled out as hostages, but Iraq finally backed away from its barbaric plans to place them where air strikes would kill them. The nationals from the Coalition countries who wanted to leave were eventually given permission to do so.

A greater problem for President Bush was the welfare of the staff and refugees in the American embassy in downtown Kuwait City. They had not been attacked but they were virtual prisoners, surrounded by thousands of Iraqi soldiers equipped with every defensive weapon Saddam had in his inventory. If Operation Desert Storm were launched, what would happen to those folks?

Yogi Alred was about to find out. In November he was picked to join a team that would plan an assault on the Iraqis around the American embassy—an assault that would protect the personnel there while they were being evacuated by helicopters.

Much of that plan, which they named Operation Pacific Wind, needs to remain classified. In our volatile and unstable world a similar plan might need to be implemented at any time. Said Alred, "All I can do is discuss the generalities. We developed the plan with the Special Forces and with an F-117 [Stealth fighter] guy, [Maj.] Bob Eskridge. There were to be twelve F-15Es, four F-117s, and a whole bunch of helicopters—several dozen. It seemed like a good plan at the time, but, in my opinion, based on hindsight, it was unrealistic. We knew of at least seventy-two triple-A pieces within a mile and one-quarter stretch of beach by the embassy—and that didn't include the stuff with the armored divisions in the area.

"After developing the plan, I was sent home to practice it. It was around Thanksgiving and we practiced in Florida, Mississippi, and Alabama. We also brought over [Capt. Mark] Bones Wetzel and put him in another airplane so, if one of us went down, all the information wouldn't be lost. I got back to the desert on Christmas Eve and we flew one more practice mission. Then, on the sixth of January, the president ordered the embassy personnel to get out by going back through Baghdad—and they did, unmolested. If he had not ordered them out, that would have been our signal to go in. Now, I think that would have been disastrous. While planning the operation, I estimated we could lose 2 or 3 out of 12 of our 15Es. After the war was over, when General Schwarzkopf visited, Colonel Hornburg—who had scheduled himself to fly that mission—introduced me to Schwarzkopf who asked me how I thought the operation would have gone. After being shot at all during the war and after seeing the awesome triple-A and missile force they had, I told Schwarzkopf that I estimated we would have lost 9 out of 12 of our airplanes and probably half the helicopters. Also, instead of picking up twenty-seven personnel, we would have left sixty to seventy on the ground. Schwarzkopf just nodded his head without saying anything. I think he knew that it would have been ugly. I know I probably wouldn't have made it—in the plan I had the last run through there. Every triple-A piece in the area would have been waiting for me."

So, from mid-October through November and December, offense more than defense was on the minds of the Strike Eagle crews. And this shift had a significant effect on the morale of everyone who had deployed to the desert. So long as their role was defensive, the trigger that would launch them into action would be a move by the enemy. There would be no waffling around if that happened; President Bush had already made the decision: If Saddam moves into Saudi Arabia, you attack. Period.

As the size of the Coalition force increased dramatically in the area, the possibility of Saddam attacking grew more and more remote. Hence, the need of the Strike Eagles to remain there depended upon their potential role in an offensive operation. But they knew that any decision to attack Iraqi forces and initiate an air campaign was sure to be controversial and loaded with numerous contingencies. So it was now, "Yeah, we'll attack if . . . or when. . . . Their potential for action had gone from a clear-cut, yes, if, to a maybe, depending upon. . . .

They knew that they were drifting in a sea of uncertainty, subject to all the political currents and crosswinds. They all knew what the politicians had done to their uncles and fathers in Vietnam. They grew up hearing horror stories of how fighter pilots had to wait until a missile site fired upon them before they could attack it, and how enemy fighters coming up to kill them could not be fired upon until they were off the ground and their wheels retracted. So they now had a queasy feeling as they attempted to envision their uncertain future—were they or were they not going to war, and if they did, would they be able to fight without being manacled by stupid rules of engagement? This transition from seeing a clear-cut defensive role for themselves to envisioning an offensive role fogged by the inscrutable vagaries of politics greatly increased their anxiety.

But many of them were hopeful. President Bush had been a fighter pilot. He belonged to their fraternity. And he seemed to have more backbone than most of the other politicians they knew, or imagined they knew. Also, they were aware that their senior military leaders were still smarting from all the stupidity they, themselves, had experienced in Vietnam. Several of the crewmen had met Schwarzkopf[2] when he visited Thumrait, and all had heard of his thunderous personality. He, least of all, they presumed, would cave in to stupid rules of engagement, no matter who proposed them.

There were also glimmers of hope from another front—the home front. School kids and senior citizens were writing. Mothers and grandmothers were sending cookies. Members of church groups were signing banners and sending them for display in the squadron and the chow hall. And the message was the opposite of the one their uncles and fathers had received from the American public when they were in Vietnam, or what was received by the F-111 crews who attacked Libya. The messages said, "Go get 'em boys, we're proud of you. Kick ass and take names. We appreciate what you're trying to do over there; we want you to know our hearts are with you. We're saying prayers and lighting candles; may God be with you always."

Those messages helped. They helped a lot, and every person over there was profoundly grateful to know that the home folks were thinking of them. But they were still lonely. And they were frustrated, not knowing what was going to happen, nor when they would ever get home. Their worst fears—that the politicians would debate on and on, or that the international blockade, which had been put in place, would end up being the ultimate strategy to drive Saddam out of Kuwait—meant that they could be over there almost forever, or at least for a long time. The Strike Eagle was an indispensable airplane and would stay over there as long as hostilities were threatened. They knew that fact well, and they also knew that they were almost

---

[2]One of the crews' favorite anecdotes is about Schwarzkopf's visit to Thumrait. Their unpopular squadron commander, not noted for his dynamic speaking ability, gave Schwarzkopf a long, detailed briefing. However, during the briefing, Schwarzkopf kept looking up above the speaker, his mind apparently drifting. When the briefing was over and the commander asked if there was a question, Schwarzkopf was supposed to have replied, "Yes, one question. What kind of a bird is that up there?" Without the commander's knowledge, someone had put Binky, the stuffed puffin—the unofficial squadron mascot—above and behind the commander.

the only ones fully trained to take it into combat. So they were afraid that going home without beating up on Iraq might not be an option they would enjoy anytime soon.

But fighter crewmen are irrepressible and innovative, even under the most adverse circumstances. And those in Thumrait, Oman, were among history's finest and were proving it, even when they were under the iron gaze of their first commander. For example, one innovative captain observed that the Omani Officers' Club was never locked at night and that an international telephone was always accessible. Quickly, by undisclosed means, he got the number for that phone to his wife and soon she, together with other wives who could be trusted not to snitch, had a schedule organized so that on a regular basis, at thirty-minute intervals during the night, the crewmen received calls from home. This was a clandestine activity, probably against the rules, but a morale booster of real magnitude because the mail cycle continued for some time to be three weeks. Of course, the crewmen, just to be safe, did not discuss the system with anybody in the squadron above the rank of major. What the senior officers did not know, they could not terminate or report.

The Brits stationed at Thumrait also helped the Strike Eagle crewmen adapt, and two years after the event many of those interviewed would easily recall names like Andy Kubin, Gus Donald, Ollie Agrebi, and Layton Williams—RAF pilots, hired by the Omanis for the most part, but who went to heroic ends to make life more tolerable for their American cousins. The Brits, of course, were admired for their low-flying skills (Capt. John Norbeck went on two rides with them and saw 50 feet on the altimeter both times), and for their great humor and laid-back cheerfulness. From Day One, when the Americans were greeted with a Heineken beer and, with elfin expressions, the question, "Did you bring any bumpy fronts with you, mates?"—meaning, did you bring any females?—strong and lasting friendships were instantly forged.[3] It was not long afterward that Brits were hosting numerous crewmen to raucous parties in the little bungalows that were their quarters, and some senior officers, not in the clandestine telephone net at the Omani Officers' Club, enjoyed liberal use of the Brits' private telephone lines for calls home to their families. And, since there were no regulations prohibiting the Brits from fraternizing with the American enlisted women, the bumpy fronts were always present in abundance at the parties, which they, themselves, enjoyed immensely.

Life was also becoming easier as the months passed. The desert

---

[3]Two of the Brits have since come to the United States to visit and party with their American friends.

was more kindly now, daytime temperatures were moderate, and the winds were gentle enough so crewmen could keep loose papers in the cockpit without holding them down with one leg. Also, there were occasional R&R breaks from the desolate air base. The sea-coast city of Salalah was about an hour away, and there, in a modern hotel and on pristine beaches largely unused by the locals, the crews enjoyed themselves as best they could without wives and girlfriends and the other attractions of oriental and western cities.

And then there were the monthly Rocket Rampages, elaborately planned parties catered by the Omani Officers' Club, complete with disco sounds and lights, where all the crews, except those on alert, could forget about war and anesthetize their anxieties.

They were flying, too, which was the best tonic of all; and under Steep Turner's leadership, their enthusiasm for their airplane and their mission was growing dramatically. Also, they were becoming more competent, especially at night as their training became more realistic. Many missions were flown all the way up near the borders of Iraq and Kuwait, and night tanking was practiced in full view of Iraqi radars. They were almost certain that their first mission, should war break out, would be a large package sent to destroy fixed Scud sites in western Iraq—a mission that would require tanking before they crossed the border. So, before the war, they wanted the Iraqis to see lots of activity near the borders and be lulled into thinking that the actual combat mission they would fly was just a routine night training mission.

So life was good now for the Strike Eagle crews in Oman—at least as good as life could be in a desolate, Muslim country, away from home and family. But ugly rumors were circulating—rumors that, if true, would eliminate the pleasant little niche they had carved out of the desert. What disturbed them was the disappearance of Col. Ray Davies, their hard-driving Deputy Commander for Maintenance. It was rumored that he and some of his key personnel had departed to some other location in Saudi Arabia. A few days later, base engineering types began disappearing. Was a new base being prepared closer to Iraq? That was what was in the rumor mill. And they feared it was true.

Their worst fears could not compare to those of Colonel Davies. Said he, "About the tenth of November, General Horner sent down his head of logistics and told Colonel Hornburg that we were going to be moving up to Saudi Arabia. The next day or so, Eberly and myself flew up to Riyadh and drove seventy-five miles south to see a 10,000-foot runway and ten million square feet of ramp—and nothing else. The town of Al Kharj was fifteen miles away and there was nothing for miles around but desert. I was then told that I was in charge of creating an air base out there that would serve five fighter squadrons, two C-130 squadrons, and with housing and facilities for five thousand personnel—and the base had to be ready for the first units by December 18.

"We went back to Oman and I got with the engineers and started a crash design program for building a new base. In a couple of days we had blueprints for what we wanted. Meanwhile I got the Red Horse Engineers—an Air Force unit somewhat like the U.S. Navy Seabees—working on the plans. Of course, we profited by all our experiences erecting facilities at Thumrait, but we had some incredible problems that we didn't experience there.

"At the beginning we had a problem just getting on the base—the Saudis wouldn't give us clearance for a while and it was November 25 before we even set foot on the place. Then we encountered another hurdle. All of our assets—everything we needed for construction—had to be brought in by air. But the Saudi in charge of the place decided to play God, and he would not let our aircraft land. We even had airplanes inbound and he put jeeps on the runway so they couldn't land. Finally, Col. Bill Ryder, the head air force logistician, who was to work a hundred miracles for us in Riyadh, got that problem through the Saudi bureaucracy. But then we ran into a massive new problem.

"The land surface there was pure sand; it was impossible to drive on [with ordinary vehicles] or to put down tent stakes that would hold. There were a few paved roads and a large area covered with packed clay suitable for erecting tents on that we planned to use. But the Saudis didn't think there was going to be a war and they decided that it would be better if we did not use those roads or the packed area—they might need it in three or four months and we would be in the way. So they moved our location. They drove us around and finally showed us the area we could use—which was pure sand and about a mile and a half from the flight line. There wasn't even a good road to the area.

"Well, we started digging with the limited equipment that we had, hoping to get down to a hardpan that would be solid enough to use as a base for roads and for construction. We dug and scraped sand with our bulldozers the first two days while waiting for our airlift to be approved, but we never hit anything hard. Even with our tinkertoy equipment, we had an area approximately 40 by 1,200 feet dug 4 feet deep, but we hit nothing but sand. And we had to have an area 1,500 by 3,000 feet ready before we could do anything!

"Some civilian contractors had been working there and one of them, a Greek company, had just finished a project and had a small mountain of clay left over. The head of that company, who spoke excellent English, came over to see us one day—he was real friendly—and told us that we were just pissing in the wind, that all we would ever hit was sand and the only way we were ever going to build anything was to lay a clay base on top of the sand—a base eight inches to a foot thick—then spread it, wet it down, and roll it into a hard surface. Of course, we didn't have clay or dump trucks so I asked him what were the chances that he could move that clay mountain over for us to use—they were going to move it but to a location the Saudis had specified. He saw that we were overwhelmed, and, strictly out of the goodness of his heart, agreed to do what he could in the three or four days remaining before his crew had to leave. We worked all night to build a dirt road over a culvert and then, without paying him a dime and with no authority on my part to ask for his help, he worked his trucks and men on twelve-hour shifts, and in three days we had the mountain moved. As it turned out, that was only a quarter of what we needed.

"Then I went to one of the Saudi contractors and they had an American engineer, Malcolm Lloyd, working for them. I explained my problem and Lloyd managed to arrange a big luncheon with the sheik who owned the company. The sheik came out in his big Mercedes, we explained what we needed and that we had no money, and he generously agreed to work his crews from 4:00 P.M. until midnight in support of our operation.

"Then I had to fight Riyadh. The problem was that our clay surface was not suitable for roads. Torrential rains were in the forecast for the upcoming winter season and clay, when soggy wet, is impossible to drive on. On the other hand, if it is not kept slightly wet, traffic disintegrates it into sand and powder. So the only option I could see was to pave over the clay with asphalt. I recommended that, but got a lot of static from Riyadh—I was accused of trying to gold plate the place. That problem got solved, thanks to Bill Ryder, and soon we had a steady stream of asphalt trucks coming from Riyadh. We paved all roads, including a 160-foot-wide, 1.5-mile-long road around the whole camp.

"With the logistics people sending supplies and the Red Horse Engineers working with my crews, we managed not only to have housing and operations facilities set up by December 18, the deadline, but also built a 700-seat theater, two large chow halls, two all-rank clubs, and even a weight lifting/exercise facility complete with mirrors and thousands of dollars of equipment donated by Arnold Schwarzenegger. By Christmas Eve, at 11:45 P.M., we finished the base chapel just in time to seat three hundred personnel for midnight services."

In December, while Ray Davies was engaged in probably the most frenetic base-building enterprise in U.S. Air Force history, the troops in Oman were being told, "Yes, you are going to be here for Christmas." There were the skeptical ones, of course, and some who had been tipped off about the impending move. But things went along normally. They trained hard, and several of them described the atmosphere at the time as being like it is before a big game. In their spare time, they readied themselves for the holidays, decorating artificial Christmas trees with anything they could find, including, in the case of Capt. David Castillo, the jalapeños that his wife had sent him.

Then the blow fell. "No, you are not spending Christmas in Oman after all. You are going to Saudi Arabia,[4] to a place called Al Kharj.

"Where?"

"Al Kharj."

"Al's garage. That's what I thought you said."

"Not Al's garage, dummy. Al Kharj."

"I hear you loud and clear, buddy. It's Al's garage, and I damn sure don't want to go."

---

[4]Capt. Kevin Thompson said, after reading this, "One day Mark Stevens and I were about to climb the ladder when the crew chief says, 'Hey, sir, I heard we're going to move to Saudi Arabia.' At the time I thought that was the dumbest thing I'd ever heard. I said, 'No way, chief, we're not going anywhere.' Two days later we were packing. Now I know to talk to the crew chiefs or the guys running the hot pit if I want to keep up with what is going on."

6

War Clouds Rising

"I knew war was terrible but I was drawn to it like a moth to a flame."

Capt. Richard Crandall

Some crewmen flew up to Al Kharj on December 14. They were the advance party, charged with buying lumber and tools so they could build a floor and partitions in the squadron operations building. The rest of the crewmen followed on Monday, December 17, and immediately went to work erecting the four-man tents that would be their living quarters. A few hours later, after the tents were up and after they had assembled Saudi-purchased closets and night-stands from China, beds from East Germany, and covered their foam mattresses from Yugoslavia with sheets from the USSR, they were ready to take a break and have an MRE (meal ready to eat—combat ration) on one of the picnic tables that the advance party had constructed for them. The weather was beautiful now. The desert was calm, and the sun's heat actually felt good as it soaked into their Nomex flight suits.

And they were in a talkative mood despite the depressing environment they had moved into. Two weeks prior they learned of the United Nations resolution to use force if necessary to drive Iraq out of Kuwait. Now that they had been moved closer to their potential enemy, they talked incessantly of tactics and the ways they were going to avoid the thousands of Iraqi air defense weapons that were plotted on the intel maps they studied. And, while many of them had kept in shape by running and weight lifting when they were in Oman, these conditioning activities took on a more serious aspect in

Al Kharj. Keeping in shape was not their priority now. If shot down, survival in the desert, where they might have to walk a hundred miles to freedom, was their new priority.

They also talked about the desolation of their area—desolation of the kind they had never seen before. Said Capt. Garrett Lacey, who would arrive soon, "We had seen desert of all kinds, but even in Death Valley there were some plants and bushes. But not in that desert. There was absolutely nothing—except one hundred miles from nowhere you would see herds of camels—dark brown or black camels—and sometimes a tent with Bedouins. How they lived out there I'll never understand. When we were on training flights, it was a problem finding a target to practice on out there. Occasionally, we'd go over an oasis, but they weren't like we had them pictured in our minds. Typically, there was just a tank with water and nothing else—no waving palm trees, for sure. I think some of those camels that lived out there must have had to walk one hundred miles to get to one of those tanks. But they were interesting to watch. When we flew low over them they would turn their heads and follow us with their eyes. Animals at home, like cows and horses, never do that."

Everybody soon learned that there were more than camels in that desert. Poisonous sand vipers could be found anywhere. So could scorpions and camel spiders, both of which could inflict painful stings or bites.[1] It soon became a standard precaution for everyone to empty their boots before putting them on. Empty boots were a favorite haven for those arachnid pests.

But were they going to war? Although skeptical of the politicians who were debating and negotiating their fate, they were seeing stronger and stronger signs that war, indeed, was likely. For example, they discovered that they were not going to occupy the base alone. A squadron of F-15Cs—air-to-air Albinos—soon arrived from Bitberg, Germany, along with two squadrons of F-16 Vipers, one a U.S. National Guard squadron from South Carolina and the other a National Guard squadron from Syracuse, New York. In addition, they were to receive two squadrons of C-130s, one from Dyess Air Force Base, Abilene, Texas, the other a New Jersey National Guard squadron. More significant, their sister squadron, the Chiefs from Seymour Johnson—the only other F-15E squadron that had airplanes and crews mission ready (or soon to be mission ready)—were

---

[1]When things got boring on the flight line, maintenance crews would catch a scorpion and a camel spider and put them in a box together to see what they would do. Mortal enemies, they always fought, but neither had a clear-cut advantage; sometimes the scorpion killed the spider, sometimes the spider killed the scorpion.

slated to arrive in about a week. Although they had received no official word that they were going to war, the massing of aircraft assets
at their base and the bringing in of another Strike Eagle squadron
had ominous implications. At this time most would have bet that
they would soon be at war.

And they weren't unhappy about that. They felt sure they were not
going home until the Iraqis were out of Kuwait. And few believed
that Saddam would cave in to political pressure and withdraw without a fight. From their intelligence briefings they knew that he had
built huge mine fields and networks of oil-fed fire trenches—trenches designed to funnel attacking forces into a waiting maw of deadly
artillery fire. They also knew that he had positioned three of his elite
Republican Guard divisions deeper into Kuwait, ready to counterat-
tack should any part of his defensive lines be breached. These troops
were armed with the latest and best high-tech weapons money could
buy, including thousands of triple-A pieces and SAMs. Saddam
owned Kuwait and its oil fields now—a highly valuable prize—and it
did not require rocket-scientist intelligence to see that he intended to
keep it.

While the crewmen at Al Kharj were getting settled, the Chiefs
back in Seymour Johnson were in an intense training phase. They
had learned in November that they were going to join the Rockets in
Saudi sometime after Christmas. But they were a young squadron,
with several "nuggets"—young lieutenants right out of flight or navi-
gator training and the "Basic" school at Luke Air Force Base, where
they were introduced to the Strike Eagle. Also, there were several in
the squadron who had just recently transitioned from the F-4—crewmen with good overall experience but not much time in the new airplane. Lt. Col. Steve Pingel, the Chiefs' squadron commander, had
visited Saudi and knew the general plan for the air campaign that
was planned. He knew there were some tough missions ahead if they
went to war and he wanted to give his crewmen as much realistic
training as possible. So he had them flying with full loads of bombs,[2]
at night, and in as large a package as possible just to make their
training more realistic. He also tried to get them experience with
air-to-air refueling in a variety of conditions, but that training
proved difficult to arrange because so many tankers had already
deployed to the desert.

On December 26 the Chiefs attended a mass brief for their twenty-
ship deployment, which was to begin with six-ship cells departing at
thirty-minute intervals the next afternoon. (The two remaining
Strike Eagles were to be joined by two F-15C Albinos from Langley

---

[2]They were not live bombs; they were called Mark-82 inerts.

Air Force Base.) But the weather turned sour, as it had for the Rockets' deployment in August, with visibility down to one mile or less. Then, as the first cell was ready to depart, other traffic caused a delay of forty minutes—a delay insignificant to the Strike Eagles, but miserable for the families gathered on one of the taxiways waiting to wave their last goodbyes. The waiting did not deter them, however. Grimly they stood their ground, waving and cheering as cold sheets of torrential rain lashed them. And, as it had with the Rockets earlier that year, the retained visions of those loved ones huddled together in the rain, waving and cheering, would remain exceptionally vivid in the memories of the Chiefs who departed that day.

Earlier, while the Chiefs were preparing for their deployment, Betty Jane Turner, the wife of Rockets commander Steve "Steep" Turner, had been hard at work. This dynamo of a lady, the mother of two children and a full-time professor of history at the local college, was determined to make Christmas a little brighter for those in her husband's squadron. Said she, "It was the end of the quarter and I had one hundred term papers and one hundred exams to grade and I had my own Christmas to get ready for when I got this wild idea that we should do something for those guys over there. I went out and bought about a two-dollar stocking and a one-gallon Ziploc bag that would hold everything that could be stuffed into the stocking.

Char Gruver [Lt. Col. Bob Gruver, the Rockets' operations officer's wife] and I then talked it over and decided that we should get all the wives together and have them decorate a stocking and fill a zip-lock bag with personal stuff. Fortunately, my mother lived close enough to come down and help make chili for the event and, together, we decorated and packed seventy or eighty bags for the guys' stockings.

"Of course, I had promised the wives that I would get them shipped over. But just after we got them ready, they canceled all the morale type of flights and it was going to cost me a small fortune to ship them privately. Steve happened to call right at that time and I explained my problem to him. I was really desperate to find a way to get that stuff over there and he jumped on the problem. I don't know for sure what he did, but he asked for some help from somebody over there. He knew if there was ever anything that would help morale, this was it. Thankfully, the leadership over there agreed and they opened up a flight for us.

"The stockings and plastic bags arrived in Thumrait just before the crews were scheduled to leave. Steve passed out the stockings, but kept the bags hidden. Later, on Christmas Eve up in Al Kharj, he dressed up as Santa Claus—with a red hat and white beard but in G.I. "chocolate chip" desert fatigues—and led his guys through the tent area, caroling. When the guys came back to the squadron, they found the bags—he had arranged to have them laid out—and those grown men had tears in their eyes when they saw the things their wives had sent. It wasn't just candy; it was very personal things that meant a lot to them."[3]

Most of the Rocket crewmen chuckled when they described Steep Turner in his chocolate-chip Santa uniform, leading his ever-growing body of carolers, many of whom were humming the melodies of the carols because they had forgotten the words. But their chuckles were not in any way derisive. Almost two months had passed since he had taken over the squadron and, despite some tough acts—he had fired and sent home one of his flight commanders and had stood up before the squadron and told them why—he was more popular than ever. Several said that even before the war started, before they saw him perform truly heroic acts of leadership, they were ready to follow him to hell and back.

And hell was not far away. President Bush, using a mandate from the United Nations Security Council, had issued an ultimatum to Iraq: Get out of Kuwait by January 15 or Coalition forces will drive you out. And on January 13 the crewmen learned that the U.S. Senate had voted to support Bush and that the U.S. House of Representatives would probably vote the same way. That news brought immense relief to them all. The last thing they wanted was a political brouhaha that would drag on at home. They were ready for action. They wanted to do what they had been trained to do, then go home and forget about Saudi Arabia, Kuwait, Iraq, and this damned miserable desert.

The weather had changed, and was now increasing their misery. It was cold, especially at night, which was when all of them were flying now. Thermal underwear, which they never dreamed they would have worn last August, was hauled out and worn under their flight suits. And there was rain, too, steady twenty-four-hour downpours that flooded their tent floors and made the unpaved, clay-covered areas seem like slimy, sticky tar pits.

In January the training intensity increased. It was night flying only now, and the Chiefs, who had flown mostly in the daytime back in North Carolina, were on a steep learning curve that made them uneasy, particularly their leaders. Said one of the Rockets who was involved in the planning of the first missions to be flown, "There was a big difference in the two squadrons' relative experience. We aver-

---

[3]Besides the stuffing material for the stockings, the Rockets also enjoyed an enormous treat thanks to Yogi Alred and Bones Wetzel, who returned on Christmas Eve from practicing Operation Pacific Wind in the United States and Germany. While in Germany these two bought $200 worth of pizza and stored it in the travel pod of their jet.

aged about 400 hours in the airplane; they averaged about 150. It was my philosophy that we should fly the most difficult and dangerous missions the first two nights of the war, not implying that we were better than them, but that we were better adapted to night flying than they were and we would be better able to survive—which was our main goal—to do the job we had to do and get everybody home. They didn't like that at all; they thought I was trying to degrade their capabilities. They argued and managed to get some of their guys on the big twenty-four-ship package we were to fly the first night. But when I stood up to plead with them to let us take the most dangerous mission on the second night, I was told to sit down and shut up, which I promptly did because I was a captain at the time. And they got what they wanted, which turned out to be pure hell. Later, after that meeting, Steep Turner just kind of wiped his brow in relief and said, 'Well, we tried; at least my guys are more survivable.'"

As the days of January passed and the deadline approached, everybody in the squadron became more tense. Said Capt. Rick Henson, "I figured we would lose 25 percent that first night. The threats were tremendous—they had a lot of guns and we assumed that they had all been well trained by the Russians. I think a lot of guys felt that way. I know I owed Chainsaw [Jim McCullough] thirty dollars because he had sent some flowers to my wife when he went back to Oman. I made it a point to pay him just before the deadline because I figured there was a 1 in 4 chance I might not be coming back.

"I also had quite an argument with my frontseater, Skippy [Brian] Shipman. He had a back problem and had had recent surgery. Somehow he got them to put him back on flight status even though they told him if he had to eject, he could become paralyzed and disabled. He agreed to take that chance and he argued with me and tried to get me to promise that if we had to punch out, I would leave him and look after my own survival. I finally promised him I would do that just to get him off the subject, but I knew I could never have done it."

Safety was also on the minds of the leaders and they called a big safety meeting of all the crewmen and invited all the Vietnam veterans they could find to give the crews survival advice. The younger airmen listened intently to their elders during that meeting and heard how many airmen had been killed in Vietnam because of stupid mistakes—like making multiple passes where gunners could predict an airplane's flight path and lay up barrage fire—straight-up fire—that would blow an airplane apart. And they were told tales of how some were killed simply because they carelessly flew their airplanes into the ground. These latter tales were particularly chilling for the Strike Eagle crewmen because their first mission required them to ingress to their target at 300 feet and at night.

On January 13 another meeting was called. Brigadier General Glosson was making the rounds of all the bases, explaining the total air campaign to crewmen. This was unprecedented, but Glosson and his boss, Lt. Gen. Charles Horner, had resented how they had been kept in the dark in Vietnam (they said they had been "mushrooms") and never knew how their mission efforts dovetailed with others that were being flown. The crewmen listened intently, and while many of them already knew quite a lot about the air campaign, they were still in awe at the magnitude and precision of the plan.

They were exceptionally buoyed by one of Glosson's promises. At the end of his speech he said, roughly—the author heard at least twenty versions—"Boys, you go out there and do a good job and after this is all over we'll sit down together, have a beer, and toast your good work." Nobody was having any beer now—they were in Saudi Arabia where General Order No. 1 prohibited the consumption of alcoholic beverages—and many were tense and uncomfortable because of their forced withdrawal. So Glosson's words rang bells and cemented themselves permanently in their minds. "Ha, we do our job and old Glosson's gonna bring us down a truckload of beer and we're gonna celebrate." That was what they thought, more or less, and his promise is what they would constantly use to cheer each other up in the depressing days of abstinence that were ahead.

Except for occasional short flights for maintenance checks, all the Strike Eagles were grounded as the January 15 deadline approached. There were forty-eight of them on the ramp and forty-four of them were loaded and ready for the first night's missions—missions that, for the most part, had been planned and rehearsed since October. Steep Turner could see that his crews were tense—some said the atmosphere was like that in a locker room before a big game—and he decided to hold a barbecue and try to relax his guys. But it was no Rocket Rampage—it couldn't be without proper spirits—and while it was a pleasant event, there was little relaxing.

Most were eager to go, but for reasons that defied logic. It was the moth-candle attraction, deadly but irresistible. It was a toss-up, of course, trying to assess the most lethal of the threats they faced. For many it was the SAMs, the computer-brained killers that could slither through the air undetected, hunting them relentlessly like evil cyborgs. For others it was the triple-A, especially the red hose streams of the radar-guided, four-barrel, ZSU ("Zeus") 23mm machine gun. "Guys, listen to me; every seventh bullet is an incendiary and yet it makes a red hose stream—does that tell you how dangerous that sucker is?" That was the warning that was ringing and reverberating in their ears now.

For some the most serious threat, perhaps because avoiding or defeating it depended so much upon their alertness and skills, was the air-to-air threat. Capt. David Castillo's attitude about the Iraqi fighters was typical. Said Castillo, "We were always getting briefings on their capabilities and my reaction was that we were underestimating the threat. They kept saying that they [the Iraqis] had a lot of old airplanes. Well, I used to fly in an F4D model. We used to do pretty good. If someone were coming to bomb my country, I wouldn't care how old the airplane was—I would be wanting to kill someone. While we were waiting for that first mission, I just felt that it was going to be a lot uglier than anybody was predicting."

Capt. Jeff Latas was probably the first of the crewmen to learn when the war was going to start. Said Latas, "It was after the barbecue and I was working as the scheduler in the squadron—it was after eleven o'clock on January 15. We had only flown two sorties that night—just maintenance checks—so it was quiet and I was reading the frag [first night's mission breakdown], refreshing my mind on the sequence. Then the phone rang back in the mission planning room. I picked it up and it was an EF-111 [electronic jammer] guy. I had been an F-111 pilot before getting into the Strike Eagle and I knew some people who flew the EF—they were from Mountain Home [AFB, Idaho]. I asked if he knew this one friend of mine and he said, 'Yeah, but he's flying.' Then he asked to talk to the mission commander for the next day's mission. I thought that was strange; we didn't have a mission commander for tomorrow—we just had a two-ship flight scheduled for local things. I said, 'Well, he's not here. Are you talking about mission so and so,' and he goes, 'No, this is the mission number,' and he reads off the mission number of the frag that I happened to have in my hand. I said, 'Say that number again, and are we talking about the same mission? Is it something that I don't know about?' He says, 'You don't know?' Then I handed the phone to the Ops officer and said, 'I think you'd better talk to this guy.'"

The next morning they made the rounds of the crew quarters. David Castillo was making a tape recording for his parents when he was informed. Said Castillo, "I didn't listen to the tape before I sent it, nor have I listened to it since then. But everyone who heard it said that they could see a huge change in me in the middle of it. They said I was real cheerful and jovial and then, suddenly, I got pretty serious. I must have been feeling pretty emotional. I was ready to go and it was no surprise when the word came. But at the same time I was thinking, not everybody is coming back.

The word that Castillo and the others got that morning was that they were definitely going to war. The air campaign would begin after midnight that night. It would be January 17, two days after the United Nations deadline.

7

The First Night

"The colors were so vivid it was surrealistic . . . a pitch black velvet night, with triple-A going off, bombs going off, and then a MiG hit the ground and sprayed red flames across the horizon. After that, a ruby red column of flames shot up and it looked like hell had opened up."

Capt. David Castillo

The main mission the first night was a "gorilla package"—twenty-two Strike Eagles teamed with two radar-jamming EF-111s. The Strike Eagles would depart just after midnight, fly out to western Saudi Arabia, rendezvous with seven KC-135 tankers flying in from the west, then run deep into northwest Iraq to attack five different Scud launching sites. Timing was critical. They were to drop their first bombs at 0305 hours—exactly the same time that other packages of F-117s, F-111s, and British Tornados would begin unloading theirs on other targets in Iraq. The planners of the missions hoped to achieve total surprise. They wanted to minimize threats from the Iraqi air defense system, especially the air-to-air fighters, which they hoped would be caught on the ground and unable to attack until the strikers were on their way out of the country.

It was an ambitious plan, but it had been briefed numerous times (with slight variations) and, except for an odd-ball method of tanking, which would turn out to be a small nightmare for them, it had been rehearsed several times, at least by the Rockets. Four Chief airplanes were added to the package and those crews were not as experienced.

The crews for the gorilla mission had their mass brief at 2130 hours. It was a short brief, conducted by Capt. Yogi Alred, the mission leader. Said Alred, "I just hit the highlights of the plan—everybody knew it by heart—and most of the time was spent on E&E [escape and evasion] and IFF [identification, friend or foe] procedures. There was definitely none of the rah rah rah, go-win-the-game type stuff. It was a serious atmosphere; there was none of the levity that usually crops up from somewhere during peacetime briefs."

Most of the others remembered two things from that mass briefing. As they filed in to take their seats, there was a slide on the screen saying, "Please Lord, forgive us for we are not going to show any mercy." That, as much as anything, set the tone for all of those in the fighter community who were preparing for war that night. Fed up with the desert, feeling ostracized in a Muslim culture that hated them, and homesick for loved ones that war might keep them from ever seeing again, they were not in any mood for mercy. They wanted a quick and violent war. There was little thought about Kuwait; it was Saddam and his military power they were after. Kuwait's freedom was an afterthought; Kuwait would automatically be free once Saddam and his military forces were destroyed. And after that, the absolutely most important thing of all: a flight home with all their buds tucked in on their wing.

And home was at the heart of the second thing they remembered most about the mass briefing. At the end, just before they rose to file out, Steep Turner, the Rockets commander, stood up. Then, said lst Lt. Brad Freels, a young WSO "with the butterflies not quite kicking yet," who vividly remembers the event: "I will never forget Colonel Turner standing up there saying, 'I don't question anybody's abilities in this room. I know all you guys will go out there and do what you are supposed to do tonight and do it well. But I'm going to tell you right now, my job is to make sure that I take every one of you home with me when this thing is over.'" That message struck deep; he was saying that there was nothing out there tonight worth dying for—that yes, you will be a first-class professional and do your job, but going back home together has a higher priority.

For the mission itself, they would take off and fly in trail formation, one behind the other, slightly offset in what they called a twenty-two-ship "train." (The EF-111s from another base would fly a separate route.) However, at specific points inside Iraq, the train would split into smaller groups—most into three-ship "packages"—and head for their respective targets. So, after the mass brief, the crewmen flying in the separate packages got together, briefed their specific mission one more time, then were left with forty minutes to an hour before they "stepped"—before they left their squadron to go to their airplanes.

For those who shared their private thoughts with the author, those minutes before stepping were the hardest. Their guts were telling them that they were heading into a caldron. Although they hoped for surprise, few realistically expected that to happen. Iraq had an excellent French-designed early-warning radar network, and even though their briefing emphasized that they would cross the border undetected,[1] that was a nebulous promise, a Murphy's Law proposition. "Yeah, they say that, but I've seen fancy plans like that go to hell in Red Flag and Maple Leaf." That was typical of their thinking. Also, it had been briefed that AWACS planes would be airborne at high altitudes calling out air-to-air threats and there would be Albinos flying high-altitude protective cover, ready to be vectored against enemy aircraft. But the crews were skeptical of those services, too. Said one crewman, "You could always depend upon some screw-up in our exercises at home—a frequency screw-up, or something. Basically, our attitude was, if AWACS can call out the threats, fine, but we're not going to count on it. And the CAP [Combat Air Patrol—the F-15 Albinos], well, we figured that some of the bandits would get through and we would have to look after ourselves."

The ultimate test was getting closer now and doubts were lurking in the shadows. "Will I be able to control my fear? Can I keep from screwing up? That was what they were asking themselves, and they were probably the same questions that have worried nascent warriors for centuries. And, like the warriors of old, when a split-second movement of shield or sword, or a reflexive thrust or parry, meant the difference between life or death, they in their high-tech machines, streaking through the moonless night at 300 feet and 600 miles per hour, were equally dependent upon motor skills, finely tuned and reflexly conditioned. In the moments before they were to thrust themselves into the black night there was contemplative time—time to weigh potential actions and reactions. But ahead of them, when the war would erupt, they knew that fear, if not controlled, could invade their synapses like viscous tentacles, causing all their finely tuned motor skills to be off by a half beat. For that they could ruin their mission. And for that they could die.

Most, if not all, had experienced fear and knew its consequences. They knew how their voice rises to a higher pitch and then gets husky, and how a radio frequency commonly used can suddenly become unretrievable, and how one foot will spontaneously start shaking on a rudder pedal, and how one can struggle just to remember the call sign of an airplane. Those were lessons learned when they first started to fly—lessons their instructors wanted them to learn. They wanted them to learn what fear can do and how to man-

---

[1]Some knew that the Iraqi radar site located where they were going to penetrate was scheduled to be destroyed.

age it. In addition, fear builds respect. And fear builds caution. Flying any kind of airplane is inherently dangerous and an incautious aviator without respect for the inherent dangers of flying is not likely to survive. Some fear, then, was healthy; they knew that and they knew how to handle it. But mega-fear was something else, something new, but something inevitable considering where they were going. So, in the last moments, while they waited, many were priming themselves in their own ways, programming their synapses to dissolve away the viscid tentacles, and resolving to themselves that, no matter what, they would remain keenly focused on the tasks that had to be done.

And the first task was to get to the airplanes and get organized— and, for some, that was a problem. Said one of the WSOs, Dave Castillo, "Here I am, trying to get to the jet, and I'm loaded down. I've got my combat vest, my chem gear, maps, evasion kits, mission package—it was almost comical trying to walk out to the airplane carrying so much junk. Then when I got into the jet, I was wondering, where am I going to stick all this stuff? It must have taken me thirty minutes to get completely organized."

Capt. Bill "Moon" Mullins, the pilot of the third airplane in the train, remembers the apprehension he felt when he climbed into the cockpit. "We had been practicing for this mission a long time, but there was one difference. That first night we went out with airplanes completely loaded. We had two bags [auxiliary tanks] of fuel and twelve Mark-20s [500-pound rockeye bombs]. And the scary part was that they had to download two of our four AIM-9s [infrared seeking, air-to-air missiles] in order to get us down to a max gross weight of 81,000 pounds. I had never flown an 81,000-pound jet before and we were surprised when we started taxiing. We felt a thump, thump, thump underneath us and we were concerned until we realized that all that weight standing on the tires for forty-eight hours had molded a temporary flat spot on them."

After launching, they flew more than an hour to western Saudi Arabia where they were to rendezvous with their KC-135 tankers, take on 25,000 pounds of fuel, then proceed north into Iraq. The tankers, separated by five hundred feet vertically, would be flying a pre-planned profile called a "step-down" pattern—they would fly at one altitude for a period, then descend to a lower altitude, and so on—the idea being that, as they flew closer to the Iraqi border in their profile, they would be harder to see on enemy radar, and the Strike Eagles would be at a lower altitude in preparation for ingress to the border.

Practically every crewman who flew that night felt that the tanking was almost as dangerous as the mission. Said Capt. Nick Sandwick, who was number two in the train behind Yogi Alred and

Maj. Bill Polowitzer, "It was a real goat rope—we were radio silent [no radio communication allowed] from the time we left and we get up to the tankers and all their lights are off. There was no moon and we were IMC [instrument meteorological conditions—flying totally on instruments in clouds] in lousy weather, and then I get a mild case of vertigo as we're jumping off and on the boom, descending through the weather. Capt. Jay "K-9" Kreighbaum, his WSO, added, "It took all of our concentration—it was totally black, no lights of any kind on the damned tanker. Zip. Nothing. We rendezvoused on radar, then tried to see them on the FLIR [forward-looking infrared device—which provides, in the heads-up display (HUD) on their windscreen, a visual image that looks somewhat like a black-and-white photographic negative]. It was totally idiotic. They were surrounded by all these jets armed to the teeth and they were worried about being attacked by enemy fighters."

The biggest problem was that the pilots had to get on the boom without the help of the two guidance lights on the bottom of the tanker. One of the lights guides the pilot to the proper fore and aft position, the other to the proper up-down position. As it was, with no guidance lights, no communication between the airplanes, in turbulent clouds, fighting the throttles of their lethargic, 81,000-pound airplanes while tobogganing downhill and trying to stay on the boom—all in abject darkness, it was an aviator's nightmare.

And then there was the problem of finding a tanker that did not have a flight of fighters queuing up for fuel. Said Maj. Lee Lewis, who was leading the flight of Chiefs at the tail end of the train, "We [with Capt. Dave "Two Pigs" Breeden] were scanning our radar and FLIR, trying to sort out the tankers and the receivers scattered out ahead, staggered at all different altitudes. I led the group into the mass of airplanes, looking for a lone tanker. But it was 'ump, he's full, ump, he's full,' and that's the way it went as we went through the package. I was worried then, because if we got through them without finding a tanker, or, if we did find one without receivers and it was out of fuel, we are not going to make it. But we kept going and the front tanker was empty [it had no receivers]. I put my four-ship on him and by the time my last guy got gas, the tanker was at the bottom of its profile, had turned around, and was heading south away from the border."

Nineteen of them crossed the border—two in one flight of three had to abort because of systems malfunctions, while the third was prohibited from proceeding alone. Said Bill Polowitzer, the WSO in Dodge One-One, the lead airplane of the strike package and of the three-ship Dodge flight that was going to the northernmost target, "After refueling, everybody went down to 500 feet, then we had to worry about making our TOT [time over target] of 0305. My job, as the lead WSO, was to make sure the navigation was correct, and to do that I had update points—radar significant places I could pick out and use to tighten up the INS [places with known geographic coordinates that they could program into their inertial navigation systems]. So we're motoring along at low level, trying to get our SA [situational awareness] up—it was a tense moment—and when we were about fifty miles from the border, Yogi said, 'Holy shit, somebody's shooting something.' It was the Apaches taking out the EW GCI site [the early-warning radar site that would have picked up the strike package as they crossed the border]. It was exactly on time and it was a perfect job. As a matter of fact, it was one of my geographic update points, but after they blew it up, I couldn't use it. I tried to map it on radar and couldn't even get a fix on it."

The explosions, created by Apache gunships of the U.S. Army (escorted by U.S. Air Force Special Forces Pave Low helos), heartened all of the Strike Eagles in the train. The tankers, despite their lights out problem, had been exactly where they were supposed to be, and the profiles they flew were exactly as briefed. There was no screw-up there. Now, exactly on time, the Army had taken out the radar site that would have reported their crossing into Iraq. Even among the skeptics there was now some hope building that they might, in fact, get to their targets undetected.

Bill Polowitzer in Dodge One-One describes those next few moments. "It was total darkness when we crossed the border—I've never seen it so dark—it was like sitting in a closet in a chair, or like being in a simulator. Then we started crossing highways and there was traffic with their lights on. Everybody was breathing heavy then, thinking, Christ, I hope nobody pulls over and makes a call telling somebody that we're flying over."

It was assumed that most, if not all the vehicles they flew over were Iraqi military vehicles, and a train of Strike Eagles flying at 500 feet or lower makes one hell of a noise. The crews knew now that any soldier who had a two-way radio could report that they were in country.

High in the sky, AWACS—the huge Boeing airplanes with ungainly looking, flat mushroom-type antennas on top of their fuselages—were also doing their job. In their high orbits they were scanning their sectors for enemy aircraft, and were broadcasting what they saw to all the strikers. "Picture clear," meaning that their radars were painting no threats, was the message the Strike Eagles heard while they were tanking. But shortly after the radar early-warning sites were blown away, the Eagles received this call from AWACS, "Threat north, bulls-eye Manny, 330 for 60, medium altitude, heading south."

As all WSOs do when they are going into action, Bill Polowitzer was gripping the hand controllers on each side of his cockpit.[2] Instantly he fingered the concave knob on his right controller, slewing the air-to-air radar in the direction of the threat. Within seconds he was painting a contact on his middle-right MPD—one of four in an array in front of him. "Got a contact, 30 right for 50," he said to his front seater, Yogi Alred.

"Do you have an ID on it?" Alred asked quickly.

Polowitzer, using all of their secret IFF procedures, was never able to confirm that the bogey (unidentified aircraft) was actually an enemy aircraft, or "bandit." However, he watched the little blip on his screen intently, until, at thirty miles it changed direction and flew away from them. Breathing a sigh of relief, he assumed that he had been watching an Iraqi jet on routine patrol, flying a triangular pattern that had been observed for several nights and described in their preflight briefing.

But they were still wary. Said Polowitzer, "It seemed like it was taking us forever to get up to the target—which was only twenty-three minutes away from the border. But I kept busy all the time—constantly scrolling[3] through the displays, checking the progress of the flight and fuel consumption, scanning the air-to-air radar, and just keeping my SA up. Yogi and I had flown together for a long time—first in F-4s in Germany. We were good friends and a good team. We worked well together. But I was concerned. We wanted to hit our TOT exactly and the navigation was my responsibility. If we were on time everybody else would be on time.

"But our time was good, the radar was clean, and at the flight plan check point for minimum fuel we were three thousand pounds fat—so we were good to go. Next we had to cross over some troop concentrations, then we skirted to the side of some SA-2 sites. Nothing was on the RWR [radar warning receiver, pronounced "raw"], the radar was clean, and we're getting to the final update point thirty-five miles from the target. We could map this without

---

[2]Shaped like the pilot's control stick, each hand controller is festooned with buttons and knobs with unique shapes recognizable by feel.

[3]Using a "coolie" switch on each hand controller—the switch so named because it is shaped like a coolie hat—he was constantly changing the displays that were "layered" on his four MPDs. On one MPD, for example, he could scroll from a HUD display (seeing what the pilot was observing in the head's-up display on his windscreen), an HSI display to check flight plan route and TACAN distance from other aircraft, and a terrain-following (TF) display showing the relationship of the airplane to the ground. Each WSO has a favorite way to layer the displays in each MPD.

going off course[4]—it was already offset—and if, for some reason, we couldn't map the actual target, the coordinates were good on the update point, which was a metal fence corner around a pumping station at H-1 airfield, and we could bomb off that. At that point I told Yogi that I was coming off air-to-air [not monitoring the air-to-air radar] and now I'm mapping, getting a 1.3 [large-scale image] then zooming to a .67 [an image covering .67 nautical miles—about four thousand square feet], and thirty seconds later I tell him it's designated [mapped and fed into the computer for potential use during the bombing run]. After that I checked steering [heading] and then checked the PACS [programmable armament control system], confirming that we had twelve bombs, and the intervalometer, which controls the timed interval spacing between each bomb coming off—so all twelve don't come off together. I can't remember now whether I set it for six pairs or a ripple [coming off one at a time].

"Now we're twenty miles from the target, which is just south of the town of Al Qaim, right where the Euphrates River enters Iraq from Syria. At that point, Yogi steers left so I can map the target, which is now on the right. I'm mapping now but the quality isn't good. I don't see shit and I tell him. 'Okay, I'll pop it up to 1,000 feet,' he said. I had my RWR up [on the MPD] and the volume up [so he would not miss the sounds of radar lockup by a SAM] and as we climbed up, the quality got better—it was a fixed Scud site with a metal fence around it that showed up clearly on the radar. I extended the map now to .67, designated it, then gave the steering to Yogi. He put the pipper [aiming designator] on the target and then transmits—for the first time that night, 'Dodge [flight], showtime, green 'em up.' It wasn't likely, but he did not want anybody approaching the target with the master arm switch off.

"From that point on I'm mostly outside—my contract is to check 3 to 9 [the back half of an imaginary sphere around the airplane] for missiles, but I'm also cross referencing the HUD and the TFR [terrain-following radar] to make sure there's nothing in front of us. We're good; our airspeed is good, we're between 300 and 500 feet, and now I'm outside looking but it's so dark you can't see shit.

---

[4]The Strike Eagle has a synthetic aperture radar that returns signals and processes them into a "God's-eye" image. A WSO who "maps" a target thirty-five miles away can obtain an image that appears as though it was taken from directly overhead. The only problems are that it is sometimes difficult to get a good map at very low altitudes, and the mapping procedure cannot be performed at the airplane's twelve o'clock position. Mapping can be done anywhere between 8 and 60 degrees off the nose; it is usually done between 30 and 50 degrees.

"Then the bombs come off; you can feel the canisters release. I come inside and look on the PACS page to make sure nothing is hung. It's clean. Then our Rockeye starts going off. It looks like huge sparklers—showers of sparkles. Very impressive. Then holy shit! It's triple-A, and it's unbelievable! It looks like a waterfall, or like a wave or surf over us. We're like inside a black tunnel with the stuff arcing over our head. I can't believe the amount of fireworks. There are missiles coming up—unguided, because the RWR's clean. But I'm dispensing chaff[5] just in case. Then I take one hand off the controller and grip the sissy bar [bracing bar] on the panel so I can twist in my seat. Yogi's turning and pulling Gs and that's the only way I can turn and see over my shoulder. And it's awesome. It looks like everything coming up is coming at you, and it's so lit up by the triple-A I'm visual on Nick [Dodge One-Two] at seven o'clock, coming off the target. But I can't see Mullins [Dodge One-Three].

K-9, the WSO in Dodge One-Two picks up the story, "We're coming into the target—I've got a good map of the pumping station at H-1, which was sixty miles or so from the target and we could bomb from that. But I'm hoping to get a good map of the target itself. We are heading to the target now, keeping Yogi [Dodge One-One] in sight—we could do that four ways: We could see him on the air-to-air radar, we could see him on the air-to-air TACAN [distance measuring device] on the HSI, we could hold down the air interrogator and see his squawk [from a transponder that emits a coded IFF signal], and we could see him on the HUD display, which is an image from our FLIR. We wanted to keep from four to eight miles back, and at six miles during the attack. We're afraid, of course, but it was just the right amount of fear to give extra alertness without degrading our concentration. At times it seemed like a training flight—we had trained hard for five months and we were as sharp as we would ever be. The mission tasks were automatic and I had to keep reminding myself that we're in Iraq, in Saddam's backyard, and they want us dead—that they will try to kill us.

"We're coming into the target now. Nick checks left and I see the whole complex—all six [fixed Scud] sites. I zoom in, from a four-mile scale to a three-mile, and then I get it down to a .67. I squeeze the trigger and get a frame on display. In the meantime I'm processing another and then I got a good map and I tell Nick we're designated. About then I heard Yogi transmit, 'Dodge, showtime, green 'em up.' Nick had already hit the toggle switch for the master arm control. Also, I was feeling pretty good; I had a good map of the tar-

---

[5]Shredded, aluminized Mylar cut in different lengths to jam different radar wavelengths. Used to confuse any radar-guided missile or triple-A weapon.

get and now everything was in the hands of the pilot and the air-plane's systems.

"Just then I see Yogi and Polo's bombs go off, and seconds later the triple-A starts coming up. We're still about eight miles from the target—at nine miles a minute, we were fifty to fifty-five seconds out. From this time on I'm in temporal distortion. The triple-A, when it opened up, scared the shit out of both of us. I was watching it, mes-merized, an orange and red cascade of triple-A going over and under us. From then on there was no question that we were going to get hit. I was basically waiting to die—there was just so much of it. It was arcing over the top of us and going underneath us, too. And some was coming right toward us, the tracers burning out just prior to getting to us. I just knew at any second there would be a big whap and we'd be hit. Also, it was growing in intensity by the second. I couldn't wait to get to the target so we could leave our straight and level flight path. Nick jinked once—it was harder on him because he had a lot more glass to look through—he could see it go across his nose. But after that one jink, he kept it rock steady, pickled the bombs, then did a hard left and a hard dive toward the ground—I was punching chaff and Nick rolled it 120 degrees and pulled, slic-ing toward the ground. I'm holding the hand controllers, thighs flexed, grunting. And I'm totally mesmerized by the triple-A—like a fascination with a cobra. I'm padlocked on it—I can't believe there is so much of it. It was orange and red and I'm watching it, trying to see how close it is. Then I see it moving away and I grab the sissy bar and twist in my seat, looking for Dodge One-Three, but I was really expecting to see a fireball back there. I figured we were lucky, but another airplane was not going to make it through that gauntlet. The fire is more intense now. There was just no way Moon [Mullins] and Rich [Horan] were going to make it."

Mullins and Horan in Dodge One-Three pick up the action now:

Mullins: "We're coming into the target now and it's still seeming like a peacetime mission. There is low humidity so there is very good visibility in the FLIR. I'm seeing two white spots—the two hot engines of Nick and K-9's airplane—and my concern is to keep my spacing so we don't run into their bombs."

Horan: "I was more concerned going in because the Iraqis had fourth-generation Soviet fighters and the latest, high-tech missiles. I wasn't thinking much about the triple-A threat.

Mullins: "Rich had the target designated and I turned in and I'm checking off the bearing and range to the target, which are in my HUD.

Horan: "About this time I'm saying to Moon that it isn't too bad—we may get in and out without being detected. Then he says, 'Yogi's bombs should be going off about now.' I say, 'I'm looking,' and then we see the flashes and Yogi in the HUD crossing left to right. Then Moon says, 'Uh, guns, give me 300 [feet].' I don't see the guns immediately, but we're at 500 and I punch in 300 [so the pilot doesn't have to take his hands from the stick and throttle] and say, 'Do you want to do a loft?' That is a maneuver that would allow us to drop our bombs and stay farther from the target. He goes, 'No,' and then I look out to the right and my comment on the tape is that it is the Fourth of July. Suddenly it's the most impressive fireworks display I've seen in my whole life—those I've seen in some of the big cities were nothing in comparison."

Mullins: "It was no surprise that they opened up the instant Yogi's bombs went off—they were warned after the EW GCI [radar warning site] sites were blown; they were on alert sitting at their guns. But what was surprising was the volume of triple-A, and nothing in our training prepared us for that."

Horan: "I think intel was more concerned about the high-tech stuff—the air-to-air and the missiles—and they tended to discount the triple-A. Also, intel didn't tell us that Al Qaim was where the Iraqis had their secret chemical and biological warfare research and production. Had we known that we would have expected it to be more heavily defended."

Mullins: "We're on the target run now and to this day I do not know how we got through the triple-A. However, when we dropped down to 300, we were flying under a lot of it—I don't know if they couldn't depress their guns lower, or if we just lucked out. I made a couple of jinks, first left, then right, then lined up with three miles and twenty seconds to fly straight and level to the target."

Horan: "For a fraction of a second the triple-A looked beautiful, then reality says, these are bullets and only every seventh is a tracer. So we are flying through what must have been almost a solid wall of the stuff and how we were not hit, I do not know. Actually, it was mesmerizing, and it is impossible in words to describe how much there was. If you've seen tapes of the triple-A over Baghdad that first night, that is just a small fraction of what we were seeing. Greg Hasty was forty miles away in another package and he said it was the most awesome fireworks display he had ever seen in his life."

Mullins: "We're almost to the target now and it was like flying under a bridge—the stuff forming an arch over the top of us. I'm going down the steer line and when it hits the pipper, that's the release point, and I pickle—which is really a consent to release because the computer actually releases the bombs."

Horan: "I've designated a target with a bright spot that looked like a missile erect in firing position. Then, just before he pickled, Moon says, 'I think I see one.' Later, in our debrief, the tape of the HUD shows the missile in the firing position. Then our bombs release and we get a very large secondary explosion—we assume it was the fully fueled Scud.

Mullins: "Now I can't think of a good way to get away. Then I'm thinking a hard left turn, put it on my tail and try to outrun it. I do a hard left, pull six and one-half Gs—I over-G severely and Bitching Betty [the synthesized female voice that automatically comes on with various warnings] is yelling 'Over G, Over-G,' and then I look over my shoulder to see if the tracers are heading toward us."

Horan: About the time we pickle, more guns are opening up. We were supposed to come off in a right-hand turn behind Yogi and Nick, but Moon makes a very aggressive turn to the left—at what he thinks is a safe altitude. As he is doing that we get a RWR spike [an indication that a SAM radar is targeting them] and I look off to the right expecting a SAM launch. More guns are opening up now and Moon has made a 95- or 100-degree banked turn rather than a 90. He doesn't realize it but we are heading toward the ground.

Mullins: It seemed like only seconds after I turned when the radar altimeter goes off and Bitching Betty is saying, 'Low altitude, low altitude.' I look through the HUD and see the ground coming up."

Horan: I'm looking out at right 4 to 5 [o'clock] for a SAM, then turn back and see the ground just in time to yell, 'Watch it!' Moon has probably already realized what's happened. He rolls wings level and does a six or seven-G pullup—we over-G again and we're breathing hard. We were within a second of hitting the ground. [The videotape of the HUD later showed that they had descended to 90 feet.] We scared the hell out of each other but we didn't have time to think about it. We're still in the triple-A and Moon asks, 'Where's Nick?' I look at the radar while Moon makes one or two weaves. I tell him to weave right, then Yogi comes up on the radio, 'Dodge One-Three, are you still with me?' Moon comes back, 'Rog,' and I say over the intercom [just to the pilot], 'Yeah, crap in the pants and all, Yogi.'"

Moon Mullins and Rich Horan were not the only ones experiencing stark terror at 0308 hours that morning. About seventy-five miles south of where Dodge flight was attacking, Col. Steep Turner, the Rockets' commander, was leading the five-ship[6] Chevy flight in an attack on fixed Scud sites located on H-2, an Iraqi air base. But they were using a different tactic. There were five Roland missile sites on H-2, and these French-built SAMs were deadly against aircraft flying

---

[6]Chevy flight started as a six-ship, but Chevy One-Six, crewed by Captains Brian Shipman and Rick Henson, kept losing systems—the loss of any one of which would have been sufficient justification for turning back—and finally, while heading into Iraq, they aborted after losing their terrain-following radar, which was absolutely essential for low-level night flight.

as low as 300 to 500 feet. To avoid the Roland missiles they had to pickle bombs above 10,000 feet. However, this precluded using the Mark-20 Rockeyes that all the others in the gorilla package were using that night because the fuzing for releasing the 247 bomblets in the Rockeye canister was not reliable from high altitude—the canister could open prematurely, scattering bomblets over a huge area and negating their destructive effect. So Turner's airplanes were carrying twelve Mark-82s—500-pound general purpose bombs—and they would drop them at a 20-degree diving angle after zooming up to 20,000 feet just before they reached the target.

Turner and his WSO, Bones Wetzel (who, with Yogi Alred, had helped plan Operation Pacific Wind), approached the target and as they started their climb they were amazed that they were not detected on enemy radar. That they were not detected was evident by the appearance of the H-2 airfield. "It was lit up like Raleigh International," said Turner. "We could easily have dropped our gear and landed."

In the climb, Wetzel found and mapped the Scud site that was their target, and at 21,000 Turner rolled inverted, pulled the nose down, rolled upright, leveled his wings and, while diving, followed the steering line in his HUD until it was time to pickle. In the meantime he was ignoring calls from AWACS reporting bandits west of bulls-eye Manny—which just happened to be H-2 airfield, which they were attacking.

Then it happened, just like at Al Qaim. Seconds after their bombs went off—but after Chevy One-One had pulled off and away from the airfield—triple-A from more than one hundred guns began ripping through the skies. Visible were the burning, red-hot tracers, orange and red in color, and deadly ominous as the others in Chevy flight stared in horror and with the realization that the tracers they were seeing were only a fraction of the hot, deadly metal that was filling the airspace over their target.

Grimly, Captains Matt Riehl and Mike Cloutier dove into the erupting caldron where, at their dive angle, every tracer seemed to be coming right at the pilot's fragile windscreen. Said Cloutier, "Intel later told us there were 136 guns at H-2. I believe all of them were firing; everything was lit up around us, and at the same time we were getting RWR indications. This is where training paid off. You do what you have always done, but it is an absolute eternity with all that stuff zipping by the jet and waiting for the bombs to come off."

Next it was Col. Dave Eberly and Capt. Tom Two Dogs McIntyre's turn, and they were followed by Capt. Steve Killer Kwast and Maj. Steve Chilton. They, too, made it through. And then, with the hornet's nest completely roiled, it was time for "tailend Charlie," Chevy

One-Five: Capt. Chris DiNenna the pilot and Capt. Reno Pelletier, the WSO. Said the two:

DiNenna: "Steep [Turner] was about ten miles ahead of us, probably about to start diving on the target when I started popping up. And it was incredible looking down at that time. There was a major highway below us and all the traffic was motoring along with lights on. Then, the flashes of light from the bombs going off at Al Qaim became visible at one or two o'clock. But looking straight down at H-2, it was lit up like a Christmas tree. The blue taxiway lights were on; the runway lights were on; the running rabbit [rippling strobe lights illuminating the final approach path] was on; and even the revolving beacon was visible on top of the tower. I'm going, 'Jesus, I can't believe this, but tally ho, there is the target.'"

Pelletier: "We checked [turned to an offset heading for radar mapping purposes] at twenty miles and as we climbed I was busy finding the target and mapping. That turned out to be easy because I had the runway and some shelters at the west end to guide me to the Scud launch pad that we were after. I got a good .67 patch map and about that time, as I looked outside, Steep's bombs went off. All the airfield lights went off immediately—I mean in a second or two, and then the triple-A started."

DiNenna: "By this time the place is lit up like you can't believe. I have never seen anything like this in my lifetime and I was totally scared. The airplane is climbing and I'm stroking the burners a little bit to keep the knots on it. I'm looking out and I forgot to pull down—we are just climbing and we are slowing down. We are at about 31,000 feet and down to 200 knots with a heavy airplane. I come back inside and I go, 'Oh, shit!' We are hanging over the top of the airfield and about as slow as we can get."

Pelletier: "After I designated, my inside job was over so during the climb I was outside, grabbing the sissy bar first with one hand, then the other, turning in the seat, checking six because I didn't want to get assholed by a SAM. And I'm thinking there can't be that many gun barrels in all of Iraq. I mean the triple-A was so thick you could get out and walk across the top of the airfield at 20,000 feet. Then I hear Chris say, 'Oh, shit! Airspeed down to 200,' and I go, 'Unload, unload, but don't use the burner.' We were terrified because at that low speed we had no energy to outmaneuver a missile if one came on us—and it was the missiles that we had thought would be the greatest threat—not the Rolands at this altitude, but the SA-2 that was on the field."

DiNenna: "Sometime about then, as I'm bunting over, unloading, AWACS calls out a bandit 20 west of Manny, which was where we were. Reno says that's going to be a factor on egress, but we ignored the call—we were both too occupied. We are moving down now and

I'm staring at a windscreen full of all this crap out there—and those guys on the ground are as mad as they're going to get. I just kept steering through streams of red golf balls and I pickle. The bombs came off a bit later and I do a big right 130-degree turn toward the east and as I start downhill we get stroked by the SA-2. I've got the jet up to 600 knots cal [calibrated airspeed] in about 20 degrees of dive and then a light flashes—INS [inertial navigation system] limit, then it says TF [terrain following] fail. I said, 'Oh, great.' I was looking in the FLIR at the ground and I start rounding out to level off. And now AWACS says we have a bandit chasing us."

Pelletier: "AWACS said, 'Hey, Chevy Five, you've got a MiG-23 and he's on you.' We're doing 560 cal now and we're at 500 [feet]. I say, 'Let's get down to 300,' and Chris rogered. I punched in 300 and then I get a spike on the RWR. I have the audio up—it's a high-pitched tone. I eyeball the RWR and this MiG—it's a Flogger—is at our six. My pinky is on the chaff switch on the left controller and I mash it aft and the spike goes away. I'm looking back now and we get another spike. I check the RWR and he's at our five, maybe ten to fifteen miles back. [The F-15E air-to-air radar only covers a 120-degree angle in front, so the exact distance was unknown.] I release more chaff and it goes away again. I knew what was happening. The chaff was causing his radar to break lock. Then we got a couple more spikes, I chaffed, and finally he either gave up or ran low on gas. With his wings swept back and with his big engine in full blower [afterburner], he could have caught us—but it would have cost him a lot of gas. However, the Flogger does not have look-down, shoot-down capability, so we were probably safe at 300. Now the Fulcrums [MiG-29]—they are another story; they do have the look-down, shoot-down capability. And right about then we had two of them coming down the line, in the opposite direction, looking for us as we motored south."

Firebird flight was leading the train out of Iraq and they were the first to encounter the MiG-29 Fulcrums. Captains Mark Stevens and Kevin Thompson ran the IFF codes and confirmed that they, indeed, had a bandit at their one o'clock position and twenty to twenty-five miles. Said Thompson, "I don't remember ever getting a call from AWACS, but we ID'd the airplane as a bandit. It was a Fulcrum on a reciprocal heading at 4,500 feet and 400 knots. Mark had a hard time getting a good tone on the AIM-9 but he finally did and he fired one—it came off the rail on the right wing. We had pitched up just a little, but after the missile opened its eyes to track, it couldn't pick up the heat signal and went stupid. It pitched up and over us and smacked the dirt at our left eight or nine o'clock. Just about then, number three called out that his ID was friendly. That confused us for a moment and by then the bandit had slid by our right side."

(Mark Stevens, in a later interview, said the Fulcrum passed within three thousand feet of them and that he could see its double tail in the FLIR.)

Capt. Rich Crandall and Maj. Al Gale were in trail behind them and they were busy trying to authenticate their target when the missile was fired by Stevens and Thompson. Said Crandall, "Actually, Firebird Three-One had picked up a MiG-29 over Mudaysis [Iraqi air base] but it slowed down to 70 knots, then broke [radar] lock as it landed. Then we picked up one of them coming north and as we followed him, Turner's Chevy flight passed right through us—at least three or four of their airplanes slid through us. That scared us. Then AWACS makes a bandit call on this Fulcrum. They said it appeared to be running on us. Kevin [Thompson] locked him up and Mark [Stevens] called saying he was engaging the bandit. Then I hear 'Fox two,'—the call that the AIM-9 is off. I see a flash of light but didn't realize it was Mark's AIM-9. It looked like the MiG shot at them.

"Meanwhile, Al [Gale] locked up the same guy and says, 'He's a bandit.' But I go, 'Did you check the modes?' He says, 'Yes I did,' and I say, 'Check them again.' I didn't want to take a chance in killing a friendly. I wanted to be sure. That's when I saw the flash and then I see the airplane is coming from slightly to my left to my right, and as he pulled within four to five miles, I climbed into him. He was at 4,200 feet and at 350 knots. I pulled hard and over-G'd the airplane—I didn't know it at the time but I had a hung bomb— and selected the heat seeker [AIM-9] and uncaged the missile. In the meantime I didn't tell Al what I was doing—things were happening fast—and he is yelling at me, 'What are you doing?' Here I was trading the low-altitude sanctuary and climbing up where he could detect us. But I don't answer; I'm trying to get a shot at this guy. But I made a switch error. When we lock up a bandit with radar, the missile is slaved to it and starts tracking the target. But to be sure, we cut off the radar and if the missile is still tracking we get an audio tone. Well, I forgot to turn up the volume, so I didn't get a tone. So I hesitated firing and just then the bandit goes by and I'm too close to shoot it. It was a real breakdown in crew coordination because Al was sitting back there hearing the tone and if he knew what I wanted, he would have yelled, 'Shoot! Shoot!' Anyhow, I passed slightly below him and could see him out the right side in my FLIR. I was well within 500 feet of him and could actually see his double tail."

Capt. Jeff Latas and lst Lt. Russ "Smack" Mack were just behind Crandall and Gale. They pick up the story.

Latas: "We saw Mark's AIM-9 go off and can see that it goes to the left while the target is to the right. But just then we were getting a friendly ID on the guy coming this way. I say, 'Understand friendly,' and Kevin Thompson comes back, 'Interrogation bad,' but I'm only 98 percent positive I was getting a bad interrogation and it was actually a hostile airplane."

Mack: "The problem was that Firebird One was too close to the MiG and the radar could not determine what was good and what was bad. Our other system said, 'bandit,' but by our ROE [rules of engagement] we did not have all the criteria. We had a good tone on our heat-seeker and could have shot him."

Latas: "So we can't shoot at this guy and he is now about two and a half miles from me. Then I saw a launch—from his airplane. I am looking up into this black sky and I see a definite missile plume—a definite elongated flame that turned into a ball and it looked like it might have turned down. My first reaction was that it was coming toward me. I pushed down, very aggressive—negative-G situation. We were 300 feet and now I thought, 'I'm going to hit the ground!' All this happened within a split second."

Mack: "When he saw the flash, I was head down in the radar, then, suddenly, I was pinned against the canopy. It was negative Gs and I think I said, 'Climb, you idiot.'"

Latas: "I had pushed the nose down then realized I can't do this at 300 feet. Then, as Bitching Betty was yelling at me for low altitude, I put the stick in my lap and pulled. Now Smack is back there yelling at me to pull up, pull up—I must have buried his head in his lap and he didn't know that I was actually climbing, and Bitching Betty is yelling, 'Over-G, over-G.' And I was wondering if I was disoriented and actually pulling down. I was pretty sure I wasn't, but at night it is easy to get confused. Then, by that time the missile had passed over the canopy and the MiG had passed to my right. My heart rate must have been 500 from the adrenaline overdose. I leveled off at 1,000 feet, eased back down to 300 and took a look at the overload system displayed on one of our MPDs. I brought up the page and saw that I had over-G'd the airplane—negative when I pushed over, and positive when I pulled up."

Mack: "You are trained to think of any negative-G maneuver at 300 feet as deadly; it is automatic: You are going to die if you feel negative Gs at 300 feet. I was absolutely sure I was dead because we were traveling in excess of 550 knots. That's when I realized that the fun was no longer there—that we were doing a deadly job."

Captains DiNenna and Pelletier, who had just managed to escape the MiG-23 Flogger bearing down on their tail, were the next in line to see the Fulcrum passing along their column. Said DiNenna, "Just after this guy takes a shot at Jeff [Latas] and Russ [Mack], we come inside and Reno starts painting it with the air-to-air interrogator and he sees somebody coming down the right side of the scope. He's not squawking [a friendly code], so we lock this guy up. He is two miles at our right two o'clock and he's pulling lead on us like he's going to intercept us. Both of us go outside [looking through the canopy] at right two o'clock, getting ready to break for a missile because this guy is going to be right there real fast. Then a huge fireball erupts at two o'clock and about a mile. This guy runs into the ground! I know he did it; I saw it. He smacked the ground and he just went ksssh.

"What happened? I think he was trying to get below us to get a look-up shot, which was pretty sporty—and he was below any altitude he had ever flown at—we were at 200 feet. It was pitch black and he probably just got overloaded and didn't know what he was doing. They're not trained to do that kind of stuff at night."

Captains Matt Riehl and Mike Cloutier were in Chevy Four-Two, ahead of DiNenna and Pelletier, with another MiG-29 running toward them. Said Riehl, "We've got this guy running down the string and we lock him up. But the ROE to shoot BVR [beyond visual range] were real particular—we had to check all his IFF codes and make sure he was out of the block [the block of airspace above 4,000 feet where none of the strikers were supposed to be]. He's at close range now and I'm still not sure—the system was fairly new and untested and sometimes you misidentify. I just wasn't real sure so I told Klute [Cloutier] to run through the criteria again—that I don't want to shoot some stupid lieutenant in an F-15 [Albino] who is out cruising around and lost. We started running through the criteria again and before we could satisfy the second time, we see that he is passing by us. We said, 'Screw it,' we didn't think he saw us because we hadn't gotten any RWR indications from him. I'm thinking he doesn't know where we are and as low as we are we can push it up and run away from him. We would have a good headstart and I didn't think he would have the gas to run us down. I had Klute punch up a lower setting on the terrain-following radar, and about that time, at our right three o'clock, he blew up in mid-air.[7] He was about three miles—real close—it was a beautiful, symmetrical fireball, well above us. Then it descended until it hit the ground and it blew up a second time, spreading out over the ground."

Those behind Riehl and Cloutier also saw the explosion. Bill Polowitzer (with Yogi Alred) was perhaps next closest and watched the enemy airplane descend in a flat spin after the initial explosion. Capt. David Castillo in another airplane watched the second explosion when it hit the ground and thought it looked like hell had opened up.

---

[7]No Coalition fighter claimed a Fulcrum kill in that region. It has been speculated that the bandit was shot by his own wingman because Iraqi fighters follow Soviet doctrine and fly with the "hammer down"—meaning that their missiles fire when they lock on a target.

At the very back of the train, Captains Mullins and Horan, who had somehow made it through the solid mass of triple-A over their target near Al Qaim, were now sweating out a Fulcrum that was coming down the line toward them. Said Horan, "Dodge One-One had been following him, then Polo [WSO in Dodge One-One] called out that he's off their scope. Then Nick [pilot in Dodge One-Two] says he's off their scope, then he [the bandit] puts his nose on us. We make a call that we're reacting to him. Then we lock him up and he does a defensive maneuver—a beam maneuver—then turns back on course. We can't shoot him at eight or ten miles. We didn't have a radar missile [AIM-7] so we would have had to chase him. Soon he was fifteen miles away and not a threat and we decided to let somebody else take care of it. There was a package of sixteen F-15Cs supposed to be coming in to take on these guys and I make a comment, 'Where the hell are those Albinos; send in the cavalry.' We were both feeling like we had dodged the [silver] bullet from the ground and now we're sweating the Iraqi MiGs. Then fifteen potatoes [seconds] after I said that, we see missiles streaking across the sky. That's when the Albinos started shooting."

Maj. Robert Graeter, who was leading a four-ship flight of F-15Cs, was one of the Albinos that showed up fifteen potatoes after Horan's comment. Said Graeter, "We had been holding south of the border so they would not see us on their radars. Our push time [time for crossing the border] was 0308—then we were going to come across and sweep the area that included Mudaysis, an Iraqi air base. While we waited, we had a real eye-watering experience—I mean I was the most scared I have ever been in an airplane. We were IMC, bouncing around in clouds, and we had to refuel with tankers that had no lights. Looking back, I wonder how we did it.

"Well, we get our gas and we're holding at 400 to 500 AGL [above ground level] to avoid radar detection, and the mission director sees all this fighter activity around the F-15Es and we end up pushing a couple of minutes after three—just about the time of the strikers' TOT. We're popping up to the 30s now, heading north for this early commit and we see some [MiG] 29 activity up around Al Assad [an Iraqi air base] and also 29s north of Mudaysis, which is in the sector for my four-ship. What I saw initially was 29s trailing the 15Es out— I had all of them on Mode-4 [IFF system]—there was a forty- or fifty-mile train of 15Es egressing and the head of the train was about fifty miles north of us. Then I see some bandits trailing them out—they're ten miles or so away from the 15Es. I'm fifty miles away and can't do anything—all I have is radar information. But then [Capt.] Rick Tollini, who is in another element east of us peels off and starts running on that element of bandits. He had those guys at about thirty miles.

"Now, prior to me getting in close enough to help those guys, I pick up bandits scrambling out of Mudaysis. They were about ten miles south of the egress track of the E-models. First there was a single, then a total of three. They were F-1s—French-built Mirages. [He found that out later.] They had taken off from a southeast to northwest runway, and as one of them was making a left-hand turnout, he was about twenty-five miles on my nose. [1st Lt.] Scott Maw, my wingman, and I started descending, taking a look at these guys, sorting them out. My first contact was at 4,000 on the clock [altimeter] and at that same time AWACS calls out that he is a bandit. He continues in an easy left-hand turn and ends up at a 160 [degree] heading. He should have seen a spike on his RWR from my radar, but I break lock because the range is twenty-two miles, and I pick up the second guy, three to four miles in trail. He's heading northwest, then makes a gentle left-hand turn. I'm getting excited now and I break lock on the second guy and lock the lead guy again. He's now at sixteen miles range and climbing through 6,000. I'm at 29 to 30 [thousand] ramping downhill and I'm on the radio to AWACS to confirm a bandit. I know the E-models are around and I'm concerned about fratricide. But the target climbed out of the safe passage zone [below 4,000 feet—a briefed zone where the Strike Eagles would be safe and all potential bandits would have to be confirmed by AWACS]. I do the AAI [air-to-air interrogator]—I'm checking his squawk and it's not friendly.

"I've been running the castle switch on the throttle and the TDC [target designator controller]. I've got the shoot cue on the HUD and the missile is ready to go. I am convinced the guy is definitely a bandit now, and AWACS had already called it a bandit. The whole ID process took about twenty to thirty seconds and I'm going downhill rapidly. I made up my mind to shoot and I bunted over [pushed the stick forward] to get steering and I mash the red pickle button on the top of the stick and fire the missile.

"It takes about a second and a half to come off, then I get the clunk and hear the motor. I'm not supposed to watch it at night because the flash will cause temporary blindness. But sure enough, I watched it go away from the right side of the airplane and saw that it was guiding. I came back inside—I'm still going downhill rapidly—and I went into an F-pole maneuver—a hard turn to the left which would force his [the bandit's] missile, if he shot one, to fly farther to reach me. It was a defensive maneuver. Then I'm looking for my missile and lose it, so I concentrate on the radar to make sure I didn't gimbal [lose radar coverage] the guy, and then the missile goes off at my right two o'clock. It detonates and I see a V-shaped charge go off in the missile. Then, simultaneously, there is a very large fireball that spews across the sky. It was a bit like a World War

II flamethrower—a long drooping flame with chunks of metal flying through the air. It was eerie because there was no noise.

"He was seven miles south of Mudaysis, heading 160 degrees and had passed through 7,000 feet when the missile hit. I watch the fireball and I'm down to 16,000 when I go to auto guns, which is an automatic search mode on the radar. It's like a scanner and it locks up the first thing it sees. I'm looking for the other guy now—Scott Maw is on the tail of the third one in a chase—and then the biggest parts of the airplane I shot hit the ground causing another secondary explosion. I see that over my shoulder, then I come back to the front and three or four seconds later the second guy hits the ground at my right one o'clock and two to three miles.

"It's just speculation on my part, but when I locked him up the first time, he should have seen the spike on his RWR. So he was probably running at low altitude. Then he saw his leader blow up and, in a defensive maneuver, could have overbanked and pulled into the ground. I mean, put yourself in his shoes. He had probably just gotten out of bed and was launched off alert—he doesn't have a FLIR, so he's seeing nothing until his leader is a fireball. It would be easy for him to get disoriented and pull into the ground.

"In the meantime Scott Maw has the third guy locked up in a tail chase and I call him off. The E-models are coming south—they're still north of Mudaysis—and we need to stay where we can help them if they get jumped."

The E-models do not get jumped again. The three jets taking off from Mudaysis were the last threats they encountered. But there was still a minor shock to be experienced. After they crossed the border, they began turning on their navigation lights—red on the left wing, green on the right, and white on the tail. "It was like being in the middle of a Christmas tree," exclaimed Capt. David Castillo. "I went, 'Oh, wow, where were you guys fifteen minutes ago?' Coming out we couldn't see the guys who were above us and to the side. Now, I was amazed that we were all running so close together."

Firebird Three-Two, crewed by Crandall and Gale, had a hung bomb and, with Three-One as an escort, they detoured into the Saudi desert and released it. So Firebird Three-Three, with Captains Jeff Latas and Russ Mack, was the first to land at Al Kharj. Said Latas, "Because I had over-G'd the airplane in that stupid maneuver trying to evade the missile, we didn't hot pit [take fuel with engines running] but taxied directly to the ramp. It is now five or six in the morning and the F-16s are gearing up and getting ready to go. We taxied right in front of their Ops and in front of our Ops and they were all lined up there. They are all standing out with big thumbs up and smiles and cheering—all the maintenance people from the F-16s and F-15s. It was very gratifying to know that they were out there and we had big smiles even though we were still somewhat shaken."

Capt. Jim "Boomer" Henry and his pilot Capt. Randy "R-2" Roberts had spent the night on Scud alert—their INS programmed with eight different Scud zones should they get scrambled. It was a boring night for them, but then, as Latas came taxiing in, everything changed. Said Boomer Henry, "We saw those guys come in that morning and I don't know if I will every have that surge of emotion again in my life. The way I felt when I saw those jets come back in the morning and all the troops on the line cheering and waving flags—it was one of the highlights of my life."

The crews were pumped up and the adrenaline had not quit flowing as they climbed down from their airplanes and waddled through the cheering crowd that greeted them. And they were buoyed by the good news that every airplane that had gone out with them had either come home or was known to be safe. There was no formal debrief, but crews from the different elements gathered informally and reviewed some of their videos—and talked excitedly about their individual experiences.

Then, after a leisurely breakfast, they ambled off to their tents and slowly succumbed to some not-so-pleasant thoughts. Some probably felt like Jay Kreighbaum, who said, "You get to where it is quiet and you start thinking. You realize that you were incredibly lucky just to have survived the mission. And you know that you have to go back, and back again, and back again, and you know then that it is just a matter of time. You know you are vulnerable now and a dread sets in. You haven't learned to live with that fear yet—that comes—so after that first mission I was down. I was real unhappy."

The Strike Eagles had, indeed, been very lucky that first night. But, in their tents, alone now, they were tormented with thoughts that have aggrieved combat aviators of every generation. Yes, I survived the first battle. But I am in an air campaign and there are more missions to fly—many more, probably. And luck is an ephemeral commodity; today I had it, tomorrow I may not. One only hits so many flushes with a one-card draw. Keep playing and betting those odds and you're going to go bust. Sobering thoughts, those. Not good thoughts to go to sleep on.

But like all the combat aviators who went before them, they would finally sleep. And when they awoke, they would grimly go about the duty to which they were committed. In the night they would again streak into the black and dangerous skies of Iraq. And they would all know that the Strike Eagles could never be so lucky again.

8

The Basrah Raid

*"King Kong with a noose around my nuts could not drag me
down to low altitude again."*

Capt. Chris Hill

Capt. Merrick Krause was dragging when he came in from his
first mission. Unlike the others who flew the first night, he had not
had the opportunity to sleep the day before. He had spent the day
planning an entirely new mission. Initially, he and his backseater,
Maj. Joe Seidl, had been scheduled to spend the first night sitting on
the ramp on Scud alert. But U.S. intelligence discovered that
Saddam Hussein had installed a new telecommunications link
between Kuwait and Baghdad, built with the latest fiber optics technology and with relay stations powered by arrays of solar panels.
One day before the air campaign was to start, word came down from
Riyadh to send a four-ship flight against two of the relay stations.
Krause and his wingman, who were Chiefs, were tasked along with
two airplanes from the Rockets to go against those relay stations the
first night. And, technically, before the mission, Krause was supposed to be in crew rest. But he could not sleep. He spent the day
poring over his maps, memorizing ingress and egress routes, and
every landmark in the corridor that would take them to As
Samawah, where their target was an array of solar panels.

Krause was a highly respected instructor pilot (IP) in his
squadron and a meticulous planner. But that, alone, does not fully
explain why he was unable to sleep. Said Krause, "I'm Jewish, and I
thought I might have a little more to consider than the other guys
when it came to attacking Iraq. I didn't want to take any chances. If

I got shot down I did not want to be captured. So I really prepared. I mean I went overboard in comparison to some of the guys. I memorized everything. I carried extra clothing, an extra survival kit with extra parachute cord, extra water bottles along with plastic tubing to siphon water out of rock crevices in the wadis [dry creekbeds], and three or four extra flashlights. I also carried a Glock [automatic pistol] with an extra ammo clip; my dog tags had no indicator of religion on them, and I had even stayed out of the sun so my skin would not darken."

The first night the two-ship Rocket flight that was to attack a relay station near the Tallil airfield had to abort because one of the airplanes had a vital system malfunction. But Krause and Seidl, along with wingmen Captains Chris Hill and Ray Smith, went to their target. "Even though we had no photo imagery," said Seidl, "the coordinates were accurate. We were going after the solar panels and with our radar it was like taking candy from a baby. The target was so distinctive anybody could have found it. The panel array was a little bigger than a soccer field. And except for a few muzzle flashes, which didn't appear to be any threat, the attack was a piece of cake. We did have an eye-watering experience coming out. A four-ship flight of British Tornados flew right in front of us and we almost had a mid-air. But we lucked out compared to most of the other guys [who went out that first night]."

The next day, those who flew during the night were sleeping, or trying to sleep. Except for Merrick Krause. Said he, "I just couldn't sleep. The mission coming up was going to be a rough one. The six-ship flight I was in was going to attack a POL [petroleum, oil, and lubricants] site near Basrah and it was heavily defended. There were SA-3s, SA-6s, and SA-8s—all deadly, and all kinds of triple-A. In addition, the site was going to be hit first by a U.S. Navy package, which meant that the defenses would be alert and all stirred up when we came in. We were coming in line, on one axis, so we would be easy targets. I knew it would be ugly, and there is no way I could have slept."

Ugly indeed. Joe Seidl, a frustrated historian—he had to take "hard courses" in college in order to get his ROTC commission—was comparing it to the Ploesti raid of World War II, when B-24s went in at tree-top level to destroy a Romanian oil refinery that supplied a major portion of Germany's war needs—a mission that was tragic because of all the losses. The main difference in the Basrah raid, other than magnitude, was that the Strike Eagles were not attempting to permanently destroy the refinery itself. The goal was not to cripple Iraq's future refining ability; in fact, the crews were briefed to avoid all refinery processing equipment such as cracking towers. Their targets were strictly the fuel storage tanks because planners wanted to deny gasoline and diesel fuel to the armored forces in the Kuwait theater and throw sand in the Iraqi logistics machinery.

The leader of the six-ship package was Capt. Mark "Chairman" Mouw. He and his WSO, Capt. Tom "Radar" O'Reilly, had not flown the first night. They had spent the previous day and evening fine-tuning all the little details involved in getting their six-ship flight to the target and back. The night of the mission, they briefed with two other packages—one a four-ship flight of Rockets attacking bridges north of Basrah, and the other a six-ship flight of Chiefs attacking an electric power plant in the same area.

After the mass brief for the sixteen-ship package, of which Mouw's six-ship T-bird flight was a part, each flight broke up and briefed separately. Then they launched, on time, and flew northward where they had the same unpleasant experience some had had the night before. Their tankers were in their briefed position, but they had their lights off. All sixteen airplanes got their fuel but not without a lot of anguish, cursing, and sweaty palms. Said Krause, "It was an unbelievable joke the way those tankers flew in the weather with their lights off. Tanking was the most dangerous part of many missions."

Trying to get on the tanker boom while bouncing around in clouds and with no lights for guidance can also create other problems. Without visual clues, and with the fluid in the semicircular canals of the inner ear sloshing around and creating novel stimuli, the processors in the brain that sort out those stimuli sometimes get confused. In short, the conditions the pilots experienced trying to tank in the turbulent conditions can easily bring on vertigo—a dangerous condition because the pilot gets mixed signals about the attitude of his airplane. The night before, when the Rockets were tanking, one pilot had vertigo and fought it successfully while coping with all the other problems he was experiencing with his heavy airplane. This night, it was another pilot's turn to suffer. Capt. Chris Hill, who was piloting T-bird Four, suffered nausea and was so disoriented for a few moments he was afraid he might have to return to base. However, like most WSOs, Capt. Ray Smith, who was in the backseat, was fully capable of flying the airplane.[1]

Said Smith, "We had just come off the tanker and suddenly we popped up above it and one wing started dropping. I said, 'What's

---

[1]Capt. Ray Smith had 200 hours of civilian flying time, but like most WSOs he had also been given plenty of "stick time" by the pilots he flew with. Because WSOs have limited forward visibility, they become competent instrument pilots because they must rely on their instruments rather than on visual references whenever they are in control of the airplane.

going on? Where are we going?' Chris had his head down and didn't answer me. I said again, 'Hey, what's going on?'—by that time we had really started to roll. I knew then he was having a problem. I took the stick and rolled us level, then said, 'Hey, Chris, are you having a problem?' He said, 'Things are starting to tumble,' and then I started talking to him while flying the airplane. It was the standard litany, 'You're not climbing. You're not diving. Look at the ADI; see what it is telling you'—then Merrick called, 'T-bird Four, are you having a problem?' I said, 'Standby,' and kept on working with Chris. 'Look at the ADI. Your wings are level. You're not rolling. You're not climbing. You're not diving. Look at the ADI. Believe the ADI. We're straight and level.' That's all it took—just a few minutes of that and he was okay. It was just a momentary thing. By the time everybody was off the tanker he was fine and we started heading toward the Iraqi border."

They were letting down now, on a northerly heading just west of the tri-border area[2] when, out of the night, tracers streaked by the canopy of T-bird Three. Said Seidl, the WSO, "My RWR had gone off indicating that a MiG-29 was at our six [o'clock] but that could have been an ambiguity. About that time the tracers flew by and for a second I thought a MiG had rolled into the middle of the flight. Then I realized that the fire hose of tracers was coming from below and I looked outside and saw the gun firing at our left seven-thirty to eight o'clock. Merrick reacted with a climbing right-hand turn and the fire hose followed us. That meant that the gunner must have had some kind of night vision device and was optical on us."

"It was close," said Krause. "It was maybe forty feet—less than a wingspan from us, leading us and getting closer. I rolled left and continued with a barrel roll right over the gun. It was a tight barrel roll, but sluggish in this pig of an airplane. We had two bags of gas, twelve Mark-82s, two LANTIRN pods, and four Sidewinders—and we had just come off the tanker. But I remembered what an old German IP at Shepard [AFB—where he learned to fly] said. He said that the key to staying alive at low altitude is to 'pull before you roll' and I did that—a 4-G pull. The gunner lost us and after we rolled upright. I was pretty tense and had to force myself not to hyperventilate and to concentrate on keeping in formation."

Keeping in formation was a problem for all of them now because the leader, Chairman Mouw, was ahead of schedule. He throttled back, creating an accordion effect as he slowed and the others closed the gap. Because they were in offset trail, as the gap closed, they were flying more side-by-side than in trail. Then number three in the formation, Krause and Seidl, had their second scare of the

---

[2]The acute angle of western Kuwait that borders Iraq and Saudi Arabia.

night. Said Krause, "As Chairman slowed, we lost sight of number two in the radar [because of its limited 60-degree coverage] and then he looms up in my HUD and I have to over-G the airplane pulling away from him. Then, out the side I just caught a bit of canopy glint as number four passed by us."

Lt. Col. Robin "Scottie" Scott, respected for his flying skills and well liked for his good humor, was having the latter severely strained while piloting T-bird Five that night. Said Scott, "The night before, we had spent three long hours flying around a tanker, holding for contingency tasking into Iraq. We were IMC half the time, and with the tanker's lights out we were in constant danger of a mid-air. Finally, after bugging AWACS to cut us loose, they finally sent us to a target and we dropped our bombs. But it was a long night, and here we are on the second night and it's the same thing—number four cuts in front of my nose and I'm thinking we're in more danger of a mid-air than we are from anything the enemy can throw at us. [Scott was to change his mind in a few minutes.] I am seriously debating whether or not it is worth going to the target area anymore. In my mind I'm saying I'm not comfortable with the way this train is headed down the track. We're weaving around, with everybody doing S-turns and flying at 280 knots, and I'm going, 'What in the hell are we doing?'"

After a few more minutes of flying the "goat rope," they were back on schedule, flying at high speed, with a safe three or four miles separating them, and approaching the initial point (IP) where they would turn and fly directly to the target. Their route to the IP had taken them to a swampy area near the confluence of the Tigris and Euphrates rivers—the idea being that they could turn southeast toward Basrah at the IP and be relatively safe from Iraqi triple-A and SAMs while flying over the swamp. It was a good plan, but there were a lot of bad things working against them.

First, the weather was not as predicted. The predicted high overcast was down to three or four thousand feet.

Second, the Navy had already hit the targets and fires from the burning gasoline tanks were casting light against the overcast and the reflection was creating almost daylight conditions in the area. This meant that the six Strike Eagles in their near-black jets were clearly visible against the cloud backdrop as they flew over what they thought would be a sanctuary. They knew the Iraqis could not position triple-A pieces and SAM launchers in a swamp.

What they did not know was that the Iraqis had one, perhaps two, divisions of Republican Guards bivouacked along a road that paralleled the swamp. After the navy raid, these elite Iraqi troops were alert and manning every air-to-air weapon they owned just as the Strike Eagles roared in from the IP. So, as they headed for their target, strung out in trail formation and highlighted against the cloud deck above them, they were a gunner's dream. All the compressed trail flying the Strike Eagles did that night had been for the purpose of getting all six aircraft over the target in a short time—before the defenses could get into action. But now, with the Republican Guards as an unexpected factor along their ingress route, all their agonies of formation flying were negated. Highlighted perhaps better than in daylight, they would now have to fly through a long, angry gauntlet of fire, and then fly through the triple-A and missiles fired by the now alert defensive forces guarding the Basrah refinery.

Chairman Mouw and Radar O'Reilly were in the lead and when they saw the fires raging, Mouw called his flight and told them to make a small change in their tactics. They were all planning to loft their bombs; they were going to fly to a predetermined distance from the target, zoom up, and release their bombs so they would be thrown forward upon the target. But now, with the fires' intense heat washing out the infrared symbology in his HUD, Mouw told everybody to loft at maximum range. At the altitude and speed they were traveling this would allow them to loft their bombs about four miles from the target. That would keep them farther from the exploding gasoline tanks and give them a few seconds less exposure to the deadly triple-A fire near the refinery.

Capt. Ned "Neckless" Rudd, the powerfully built ex-academy football player who was flying T-bird Two, doesn't even remember hearing that call. Said Rudd, "As we were coming down the swamp, our plan was at twenty or twenty-five miles from the target to check south and get a map out the left side. But as we turn from the IP, all hell breaks loose—triple-A coming up from everywhere. I was initially flying in at 500 feet, but I stepped down to 300 feet, then 200 feet, then 100 feet. I was down there. And, at that time, I've got like 60 hours in the airplane and I'm at 100 feet with bullets coming from both sides over the top of me. I have my hands full of airplane and I'm flying the little TF [terrain following] box and I have this FLIR imagery helping me keep from hitting the ground. I check for the map, then I'm jinking like crazy and, of course, after every jink that I made, I didn't have the confidence to go level so I would go up a little bit and then down a little bit and then I would go back up. I am trying to move the airplane and be unpredictable going in there. As I'm trying to move the airplane the next thing I hear out of T-Bull [Lt. Col. Keith Trumbull,[3] the WSO] is, 'Take your steering.'

"I said, 'What?' The last thing in my mind was taking a target attack run. I was trying to save our butt. He said again, 'Take your

_____

[3]Considered by many with whom the author spoke one of the finest WSOs in the fighter community.

steering.' I mean this guy, T-Bull is a warrior; he has ice water running through his veins. I mean, I am sucking this seat cushion up
into my sphincter and jinking and trying to avoid the ground and the
bullets and trying to keep some semblance of where the guy is out in
front of me and T-Bull is back there commanding a map. How he
did it I don't know. For certain, I could not have done the countdown, make the map, and designate with all the crap flying through
the air while knowing that a 60-hour pilot is maybe going to run me
into the ground. But he is telling me to take my steering. He has
mapped and designated and I have a carrot in the HUD telling me
exactly where I have to fly to get to the target. I turn till the carrot is
on the nose and lo and behold, right in front of the nose is this big
flame coming out of the target. I start looking down. I'm supposed to
pull at two and one-half miles for my loft and I start watching the
distance countdown. It is going in slow motion even though I'm
probably going 600 knots and the stuff is going over the top of me. I
had no place to go; I had to keep the steering. I'm like shooting a
curl in surfing; there is nowhere to go but straight ahead, and I don't
want to go straight ahead.

"We get in to about six miles and I know I have to go straight
now; it would be silly to go through all this and miss the target
because I jinked. I start easing the altitude down and I'm bending
the throttles forward without going into afterburner, flying my steering and watching the countdown. 'Oh, God, two and one-half will
never get here,' I'm thinking. But it eventually did and I pulled into
my loft. Now I have bullets going over me and underneath me. I
come off hard to the left and I'm trying to avoid all this stuff—and
I've lost track of Chairman. I knew he was in front of me and I knew
I wasn't going to hit him, but I didn't have him on the radar. Now
I'm pulling down from my loft recovery and I'm watching out for the
ground and I kind of level off, and I'm jinking trying to avoid bullets.
Then I hear T-Bull in his calm voice saying, 'You are at 2,000 feet
and 280 knots.' What a mouthful that is. He is saying, 'Get down and
speed up. Now!' But in his ice-cold voice, he just says 2,000 feet and
280 knots—which told me everything I needed to know. I plunk the
nose over, we take the steering, then make a couple of sweeps for
Chairman [on the radar], can't find him, and I said to myself, 'The
hell with it; we're going home.'

The gunners had taken all the practice shots they needed by the
time T-bird Three with Krause and Seidl started down the gauntlet.
Said Seidl, "The triple-A really got intense by the time we left the IP
and headed inbound. I mean, it was everywhere—lots of 14.5 [mm]
and quite a bit of 23 [mm]—like red fire hoses—that's how it had
been described and that is how it looked. I had taken an offset map
before we reached the IP, but now I'm starting to worry about the

designation. I'm looking through the targeting pod[4] and I see what I perceive to be our DMPI [desired mean point of impact—pronounced "dimpy"]—I recognize the cracking plant from the photo we saw before the mission and from it, I picked up the cluster of storage tanks that we were to hit. Then all hell really starts breaking loose as even more triple-A starts coming up. It's been said a million times but I'll say it again; it was the greatest Fourth of July display I have ever seen. For awhile it was barrage fire—they were firing straight up hoping that we would fly through it. The manuals say to fly around barrage fire, but I'm thinking this stuff is twenty to thirty miles wide and there was no way to go around it. We just had to suck it up and go through it, hoping it would be like the World War II B-17 movies where the planes get through even though they are shot full of holes."

Krause, the pilot, continues, "We did a mapping leg and then a jink, and we were smack in the middle of the triple-A again. Then a red stream that looked like it was aimed started coming toward the nose. I pulled hard to the left, then decided to do a maneuver that Chairman and I had practiced at Seymour and which he briefed for the mission. If any of us had to deviate for triple-A, we could take a reciprocal heading, pick up those behind us on the radar, then swing back in line behind the sixth airplane. I said to Joe, 'Shit, that guy's got a bead on us. We're out of here; we can't make it.' Then I pulled hard to the left and got out of the flow."

T-bird Four, with Captains Chris Hill and Ray Smith, was next in line.

Said Hill, "The triple-A was incredible. It was nothing like I could ever have imagined. Picture a football field with firemen along the sidelines. Each one has a high-pressure hose and out of those hoses comes red and orange Kool Aid. That's just what the tracers looked like. They only put tracers every seventh bullet, so for every one thousand tracers there are six times as many bullets. We were told in training to simply move the airplane to where they're not shooting. But for us that night, there was no place they were not shooting. It was like trying to make it from one end zone to the other and back while every Iraqi with a gun was trying to hose us. And sometimes they would draw a bead on you. When they did that, you would see the red whip start moving toward your airplane. The only thing to do is to move a little away from it and hope a gunner on the other side doesn't see you—or flow to the back of the train like Merrick and Joe did in T-bird Three."

Said Smith, "About the time we were turning in, Chairman radios

---

[4]The function of the targeting pod will be explained in chapter 11.

for everybody to max loft instead of using a mini loft because the target is so hot. We disagreed in our jet. We could have pulled sooner, but we also would have had to pull higher and that we didn't want to do. We're getting closer to the target and now we can see features on the ground, and the gun emplacements, and even make out the individual guns. There were a lot of single 23s. I'm watching the radar now and see Two do his loft, then we're in and Chris pulls and we toss the bombs on our DMPI, which is a cluster of tanks. Just then a Zeus [ZSU 23-4, a radar-guided, four-barrel weapon] starts its fire hose on us. Chris maneuvers left, then another Zeus opens up on the left side. In addition, there are tracers coming from everywhere and lots of small arms fire coming up. While maneuvering, a third Zeus opened up and as Chris reacted to it, I looked outside and see the ground coming up. I'm yelling, 'Recover the jet, recover the jet!' and as he pulls, I look inside and see that we have descended below 75 feet."

Scotty Scott and Larry Bowers are in T-bird Five behind Hill and Smith. They continue the story.

Scott: "As soon as we turned in [at the IP] it looked like a tunnel of guns ahead of us. They had gun pits on both sides of the river—one pit every mile and each pit had six or eight guns. They were pointed like a giant water fountain and we had them firing on both sides of us. So we are just going down this tunnel, looking at all these guns, and now the adrenaline is really pumping and I am going, 'Holy shit, you have to be kidding me.' That is when I learned what war is all about."

Bowers: "After we turned at the IP, I had to concentrate on getting a map of the target. Before we left, I picked the southwestern portion of a cloverleaf, right where the northwest highway out of Basrah intersects an overpass. I had those coordinates programmed and now, as we flew toward them, Scottie did not have to check right and fly into the triple-A. I did a map and designated on this offset, then the computer did the math and gave us steering directly to the target. When I finished, Scottie had the carrot—a diamond on the HUD pointing to the heading in degrees that he was to fly. Also, on the lower right side of the HUD he has the distance in tenths of a nautical mile. When I finished I went outside and was amazed at what I was seeing. None of our training even came close to preparing us for this."

Scott: "Time has slowed down now and I just want the airplane to give me the pull-up cue for the loft. It seemed like it was forever; it wasn't passing fast enough. Finally I get the pull cue, I start the pull and the hammer is down [pickle button is down giving computer consent to release bombs] and Larry goes, 'Scotty, when you get a chance break left'—which isn't the normal call you make. Normally a break call means you are about to die, you had better move the airplane."

Bowers: "While he is in the loft, I'm looking outside at my right one-thirtyish and I've got a steady stream of bullets coming toward us. It was obvious they could see us and that it was aimed fire. This is a steady stream that is catching up with us but I know Scotty is paying attention to his job, just sitting there waiting."

Scott: "I am glued to the release key."

Bowers: "To get accurate weapons he has to track right up the line: I know that is what he is doing. And I'm like, oh, my God, they are coming on us."

Scott: "I've got the airplane in a climb at 3 Gs and at about 35 or 40 degrees and the weapons finally come off. I pull hard and am in over-G, Bitching Betty is yelling at me, and Larry is saying, 'Watch the jet!' and I'm saying, 'Watch the guns, watch the guns!' and I'm pulling down and jinking—kind of S-turning our way down and then I get too far south and have to come back around. The jet was 6,000 pounds lighter now and it was easier to maneuver it."

Bowers: "As we checked to the south there was a big explosion that I thought was a secondary until I realized it was away from the target. I make a comment to Scotty, 'Whoa, somebody's bombs hit way short.' At the time that is what I assumed had happened."

About this same time Merrick Krause and Joe Seidl were taking their place at the back of the train behind T-bird Six. They pick up the story.

Krause: "When we got back in line I checked right to get Joe an angle for mapping and we were right in the thickest of the triple-A. It was everything: Small arms, a couple of Zeuses—lots of 37 and 57mm. Also, the heat of the fires at the refinery had my HUD almost completely washed out—I had trouble reading the symbology. But I could see a black spot ahead of me. It was Six—Teek [Maj. Tom Koritz] and Donnie [Maj. Donnie Holland]—and I could see Five pulling off the target. I radioed Six and told them to call off target because I couldn't do everything I had to do and watch them. They acknowledged that they would."

Seidl: "After Merrick's call I looked through the targeting pod and found a group of oil tanks that were not burning yet so I said, 'Hey, this is a good place to put the bombs.' I designated that point. Merrick and I had not flown together all that much so he makes a comment, 'Say when,' and I thought he meant when I was designated. So I said, 'Okay, I'm designated, you are clear to pickle.' He interpreted it to mean that he was cleared to pull. He started pulling and actually pulled about two seconds too early, which now put us outside the loft basket [the bombs could not be released]. So here we are, in all this triple-A, pulling up into it and the bombs aren't going to come off."

Krause: "I'm going up and I can see the fires and the clouds above us and all that triple-A right smack in the middle of the HUD and over the top of the canopy. I'm still flying the steering but it's real obvious that we're going to be at 2,500 feet and right in the middle of the triple-A—and the gunners down there had just seen five guys with similar spacing doing the same thing. Right then I decided to do a direct pop—a maneuver we weren't allowed to practice at Seymour but one I'd learned at Luke—it's to be used on rare occasions when you can't complete a loft maneuver. I was climbing 30 degrees nose high and I unloaded the airplane—pushed forward lightly on the stick—added a little left rudder and a lot of left stick— and rolled it upside down. While doing that I pressed down on the castle switch and moved it forward, which gave me command of the HUD and now, without pressing any buttons on scopes, I can change my delivery method from automatic to manual. Then I'm pulling the nose back down, five degrees nose low, then I unloaded and rolled to the left—half an aileron roll. The nose scoops out but is on the same heading. I could see the target—the whole refinery is on fire. I picked a tank that we were supposed to be hitting, put my pipper on it, pickled, and started pulling up again to stay above secondary explosions and the frag. I turned hard left—I knew Teek and Donnie were off—they had called off target—so there was no deconfliction problem. The last I saw of the target, the flames were several hundred to a thousand feet high, there were explosions, and big fireballs were coming off the refinery. While doing the hard left turn, I reached down and jettisoned the gas tanks. And just then I looked out to the left and said something to the effect that somebody's bombs fell short."

Seidl: "Merrick's pulling left, and the FLIR and the TF are going crazy because they are saying, 'obstacle ahead, warning, caution,' and all this other stuff. I'm thinking, well, shit, I don't care; we've got to get back down to low altitude. Merrick could see the ground— it was that bright—so he makes a visual recovery and as he is crossing, probably about three to four miles away from the target now, going outbound, he says, 'Oh, somebody missed,' meaning that somebody's bombs missed the target. We fly over a bunch of flames and debris and smoke coming up—we flew right through the smoke. Then, as we continue egressing, Chairman calls for a flight check. He goes, 'T-bird flight, check.' We hear Two. Merrick checks us in— we're Three. We hear Chris and Ray—they're Four, then Scottie and Larry—they're Five. But Six does not check in. There is just silence and Merrick goes, 'Oh, shit!' Merrick realizes that that big flame and all that debris short of the target was not somebody's bombs that had missed, but that it was the other airplane.

"Then Chairman calls again for a flight check. But we get the same. Six doesn't answer. Then Chairman asks Scotty to try and check him in—thinking that he, himself, might be out of radio range but that Scotty might raise him. Scotty tries but has no luck. He goes, 'T-bird Five checked. No answer.' Then Merrick comes up and says, 'This is T-bird Three. We're behind the package. We are the last ones out and the last we heard is Six calling off target. Then Chairman says, 'If you are the last guys in the flight, look on the radar to see how many people you have out in front.' I get into the radar and I count four airplanes out in front of us. Four in front plus us is five, and that's all we have. By now, Merrick and I are pretty sure that the wreckage we flew over was Six."

Krause: "About that time Joe is on the radio alerting RESCAP [rescue forces] and I'm flying and checking radar when the RWR starts beeping. I quickly look out at the left where the Republican Guards were firing. It's a lot of triple-A but a mile away, but then Joe goes, 'Break left!' I look left—it's only three or four guns at a distance and, thinking he was confused, I broke right."

Seidl: "I was on the radar and all of a sudden my RWR gear goes off—I'm in the radar trying to find the other airplane. The RWR goes off but I didn't have the receiver up on one of my scopes because I had taken it down to figure out where everybody was. My first impression was that it is my wingman behind me that is tripping off my RWR gear. Your mind works at 20,000 times normal speed and I am thinking, 'Wait a minute; my wingman is not behind me anymore because I'm the last guy out here.' So I thumb over to the scope to get my RWR gear up and there is a flashing R in the middle of the scopes, which means there has been a Roland launch. I tell Merrick to break left. He breaks right but I was happy because there were Gs on the airplane. Even if it is the wrong direction it was better than nothing at all. We break and sure enough there is a Roland; we see it launch off the ground. It looks kind of like a white candle with a rocket motor. I pump out chaff, but I am also bumping the switch to get flares out, too, because the Roland has both a radar and an IR version."

Krause: "When I realized what was happening I did a hard left, then a hard right turn, the over-G warning going off all the time. After about the third turn, a missile came over the top of the right wing—it lit it up enough that I could see detail on the wing as it flew by—then exploded in front of us."

Seidl: "Distance is hard to judge at night, but that explosion was extremely close. Merrick continues jinking and finally the RWR goes away and we ease back down to low altitude and start pressing out.

While all this is going on, Merrick also comes on the radio and goes, 'T-bird Three is engaged with a Roland,' to let the other people know. Once this is over, Chairman goes, 'Okay, T-bird check. We get Two, Three, Four, but Five doesn't answer. That is Scotty and Larry. We had seen a flash and I'm going, 'Oh, God!' Right then I knew they had bought it—that the Roland had tripped our RWR but that they had launched on Scotty.

"Now we're trying to raise Scotty and no reply so I get on the radio to AWACS to start a SAR [search and rescue effort] on T-bird Five. I had the mark point on my INS where the launch was and I gave those coordinates to the AWACS guys. But there was nothing else we could do—if we're in an area where there's a Roland, we couldn't really orbit around and try to mark positions or any of that stuff. After that, we headed home and it was an extremely depressing ride."

Scott and Bowers were not lost, however. They had been tied up on other frequencies, talking with AWACS and monitoring the Guard frequency, which all downed aviators use for ground-to-air communications. It was their wingmen who were lost and their diligence in trying to locate them that caused the confusion. Eventually the matter was resolved when AWACS called Mouw and explained that they had been in radio contact with T-bird Five and that he was not missing.

But that word did not get back to their home base. When they landed, they taxied directly to the chocks rather than hot pitting because every one of them had over-G'd[5] their airplanes and maintenance did not want full tanks when they checked them over. Scott and Bowers then walked into the squadron and to an eerie greeting. Said Scott, "It looked like a tree full of owls when we walked in that door. Tech. Sgt. D. K. Austin looked at me, his eyes all white, and he says, 'Well, I never thought I would see you again.' That hit me as kind of a funny thing to say—I mean for a guy who has just come back from a relatively hard mission. Then number Four [Capt. Chris Hill] comes up to me and says, 'Man, when you guys checked in on the radio I was so happy.' I was thinking, 'What the hell are you talking about?' We were oblivious to the whole thing. We didn't know we had been reported missing."

Senior officers were waiting in the squadron and Mouw was asked about the missing plane. Then, when Krause and Seidl arrived

---

[5]The reader who is an aviator may wonder how a pilot can over-G an airplane such as the F-15E, which is built to handle nine positive Gs. The answer is that the G-limit varies inversely to the load the airplane is carrying; that is, the G-limit decreases as the load is increased. Most of the over-Gs occurred while the airplanes were heavily loaded.

and reported that they had T-bird Six's airplane on their tape, every-one gathered around a video machine and watched it. The tape clearly showed Koritz and Holland in their loft maneuver, and the audio confirmed that Donnie Holland had called bombs off. Then the airplane disappeared from the tape—Three's HUD was almost completely washed out from the heat of the fires—and there was nothing further until Three was about four miles from the target and the tape picked up burning debris on the ground.

The senior officers took the tape and retired to make their report to Riyadh. The crews mingled briefly with others who had returned from other missions, then caught one of the shuttle vans to their tents that were two miles away. Meanwhile, Capt. Jack Ingari, the Chiefs' flight surgeon and sometime WSO, was agonizing in his own private little hell. Said Ingari, "Tom Koritz and I were close friends. He was smart enough to be both a doctor and a fighter pilot—but he was born to fly—that is what he loved, and he waived his Geneva rights to fly combat. He said he wanted to fly so he could understand circadian rhythms—so he died doing what he wanted to do. I didn't know Donnie Holland as well, but he was a wonderful guy, he loved golf—he was Chief Dimpled Balls[6]—and he was highly respected by all the guys. The night they were killed I went to my tent and tried to decide what I should do in regard to the crews that were flying with them that night. I knew that some of them had gathered in Scotty's tent, which was just across from mine. Personally, I wanted to join them, to find out what happened, and, professionally, I needed to assess how the trauma of the night had affected them. But flyers are a close group and trauma brings them closer. I didn't want to intrude and I felt like I might be doing that if I barged in on them.

"As I was trying to make a decision, which none of our manuals or textbooks cover, I kept remembering recurring scenes from a novel I had read. It was Mark Berent's *Rolling Thunder*, a novel about Vietnam flyers. In the novel there was this roly-poly flight sur-geon who, when the guys returned from tough missions, took a bot-tle of scotch and joined them, assuming that his proper role was that of a counselor. Finally, with that in mind, I decided that tonight I

---

[6]The Chiefs squadron is said by many to have the most heritage of any squadron in the U.S. Air Force. One of their traditions is to call all new members of the squadron "boy." Then, at a time determined by the Big Chief—the oldest in the squadron, but not the squadron commander—they meet in the woods, take everyone's car keys away, build a big fire, and sit around for the entire night dreaming up appropriate names for the inductees. Some, like Chris Hill's name, "Chief Inverted Gully," are plays on the person's name. Others, like Chief Bald Eagle for squadron commander Steve Pingel, allude to a physical characteristic. In the case of Donnie Holland, "Chief Dimpled Balls" referred to his passion for golf.

should be a counselor, too. So, I took the scotch my wife had sent in a Listerine bottle and went to their tent."

There was a bare light bulb hanging from the front part of the tent, its filaments casting a garish yellow light, which, after being reflected from the amber-green walls of the tent, created a bilious pall over the six crewmen who were gathered there. They were in the front half of the tent, partitioned by the wardrobes that separated the four bunks from the living area. In the shadows around the periphery of the living area there was a water cooler—Narjan water from Saudi Arabia—Donnie Holland's teapot, Scotty's boombox, pages of Larry Bowers's "Far Side" calendar glued to the walls of a wardrobe, and a dart board—a legacy of Donnie Holland's tour with the British air force. "It was a somber group," said Ingari. "I've played a lot of rugby and football and it reminded me a little of the locker room after a losing game, except that these guys were in worse shape. Their hair was matted to their heads, their faces were gaunt and covered with dried sweat, and every one of them had dark circles under their eyes. They were fatigued and they were down, Scotty most of all because Teek and Donnie, his tentmates, had also been his wingmen and he had lost them. I got paper cups and poured each of them a drink. Besides Scotty and Larry, who lived in the tent, there was Chris Hill and Ray Smith, and Merrick Krause and Joe Seidl. We drank a toast to Teek and Donnie, and then I asked them to tell me what happened. Nobody said anything for awhile. They weren't hostile; they didn't appear to resent my question. They were just numb, I think. They just stared; it was the classic thousand-mile stare that I had read about. Finally, Scottie started talking: 'Doc, it was like this,' and he began describing the triple-A— he said it was like flying through the Holland tunnel, he couldn't go right or left, and sometimes the radar altimeter showed minus fifty feet—that they were skimming the ground as their only hope of surviving. Then Larry Bowers took up the story. His slender face was gaunt and his eyes were sunk in the back of his head. He said, 'It was unbelievable, Doc, going in there through all that.' And he said, when he told about Chairman breaking radio silence calling for a flight check—he said when Koritz didn't check in, it was the longest silence he ever heard."

Ingari left the tent and was still not sure that he had done the right thing by joining them. But, professionally, he went away convinced that he would not have to ground them and take them out of the war for a day. Soon, Krause and Seidl, then Hill and Smith, also left, leaving Scott and Bowers alone to do the dismal chore that had to be done. There were four bunks in the back of their tent. They would have to occupy two of them and try to sleep while trying to forget that the other two might forever be empty.

Chris Hill still had a duty to perform when he reached his tent. He had vowed that he would keep a diary of the war, so he wrote and described the mission, then his concluding thoughts. The quotation at the beginning of this chapter was taken from those comments. So was the following:

I met Tom Koritz at Luke during RTU. When Michele and I started going to church downtown, we met Tom's wife, Julie, and three great looking boys. I know God is with them now.

Donnie Holland was like a father to me. As my flight commander in F-4's he probably was one of the biggest reasons I got to transition to the Strike Eagle. He loved to play golf. Made his own clubs. He was a good friend and the kind of person I often looked to as a role model. Not just as an officer, but as a parent and a person. I was sitting at the duty desk in the squadron with him on the 15th when he called home to talk with his wife and son. He told them he loved them. I think it was the last time. I will miss him. Farewell to "Chief Dimpled Balls."

The mission last night was intense by any standard. Losing a very dear friend has taken whatever romance there was out of the war. It is now a matter of killing and surviving. I wondered how I would feel about killing people. Well, no qualms about it now. The more of them I get, the sooner this ends and we all go home.

9

Political Pawns

"If these missions are all going to be like this, it's going to be a long war."

Lt. Col. Robin "Scotty" Scott

About the time Flight Surgeon Ingari was dispensing medicine to the distraught fliers in Scott and Bowers' tent at Al Kharj, seven Scud missiles were launched from western Iraq. Their primitive computer brains were programmed with coordinates in Israel, and moments later when one of them exploded in an apartment complex in Tel Aviv, Saddam Hussein had announced to the world, via wailing sirens and garish night-scope footage on CNN, that his war of revenge was underway. If attacked, he would burn half of Israel with chemical weapons, he had vowed earlier. Now, it appeared that he was keeping his promise.

But the Scuds were not carrying chemical warheads. And the minuscule 160-pound explosive warhead with which the Scud was armed, was, according to General Norman Schwarzkopf, "terrible for anyone it happened to land on, but in the grand scheme of warfare, a mosquito."

For decades the Israelis have had their own grand scheme of warfare as they have struggled to exist as a nation while surrounded by Arab nations determined to destroy them. Their grand scheme is called instant, massive retaliation, and they have unleashed countless attacks in retribution for minor assaults with one-pound hand grenades. So it was really no surprise that 160-pound high-explosive warheads, descending in the dark of the night to explode on a terrorized civilian population, would unleash a quick and vicious retaliatory response. Their grand scheme, when boiled down, was essentially, "kill one of us and we will kill one hundred of you." Undoubtedly, ratios of that magnitude were on the minds of the Israeli commanders when they launched "dozens" of their attack jets two hours after the first Scud landed in Tel Aviv.

In Riyadh, Schwarzkopf received word of the Israeli jets being launched and in his memoirs he confessed, "We waited grimly for them to strike Iraq in retaliation." Except to chase our own jets out of western Iraq to eliminate the danger of inadvertent conflict, there was nothing else Schwarzkopf or anyone else in the theater could do. If the Israelis pursued the "grand scheme" that had guided them since their existence, Iraqi targets would be attacked and the precarious coalition of Muslims and infidels that Schwarzkopf had forged was probably doomed.

That did not happen, of course, and in the way of explanation, all Schwarzkopf says in his memoirs is that a tired-sounding Colin Powell called that morning saying that "Washington" had persuaded Israel to recall its jets, at least for the present.

But the next night three more Scuds exploded in Tel Aviv and Jerusalem. Israeli tempers boiled over now and any attempt to restrain them would be like trying to restrain Americans after Pearl Harbor was bombed. "Get the yellow bastards!" was the revenge cry the author heard as a boy when hundreds of thousands volunteered to do just that. And Pearl Harbor at that time was not even in the United States. Hawaii was a territory and like a foreign country then.

So the fires of revenge were lit in Israel. Soon after the Scuds exploded the second night, Schwarzkopf received a message outlining the Israeli plan for massive retaliation the next day. They would launch one hundred airplanes in the morning, one hundred more in the afternoon, and follow with commando and Apache gunship raids during the night. And all the raids were to traverse Saudi air space enroute to Iraq.

At the highest levels the phone links between Washington and Tel Aviv were humming, and ultimately it became President Bush's difficult chore to plead with Israel's prime minister Yitzak Shamir to call off their attack. According to Schwarzkopf, Bush argued that Coalition bombs had already destroyed all the known launching sites, that Scud hunting would continue on a more massive scale than Israel could ever match, and that just a single retaliatory raid by Israel would fracture the Coalition.

The high-level diplomacy worked—at what ultimate cost, no one has said. Israel did call off its attack. But that forced General Horner and the Coalition air forces to greatly modify their plans for the air campaign. The promise of Scud-hunting on a more massive scale

than Israel could match had to be fulfilled. And, of course, what airplanes had the endurance to fly out into western Iraq, then loiter
and search where, because of their limited range, Scuds had to be
launched in order to reach Israel? Answer: The A-10 Warthogs and
the F-15E Strike Eagles.

Suddenly, A-10 pilots who launched to attack artillery and armor
in Kuwait received orders to fly out to an unheard-of airfield in western Saudi Arabia. Once they got there, they found orders sending
them north into Iraq looking for Scud mobile launchers they had
only seen on badly photocopied pages from *Jane's* that were handed
to them in their cockpits as they refueled. Correction: Some saw the
pictures; others went off with only a verbal description. "Look for
something about as big as a fuel transport truck," some were told.
"And don't be surprised if the missiles themselves are hidden under
Bedouin-type tents."

The Strike Eagle community got a little more professional intro-
duction to their new tasking. It was about 1100 hours at the Tactical
Air Command Center (TACC) in the basement of the Royal Saudi Air
Force building in Riyadh when Capt. Joel Strabala finished his
duties in the frag shop where all the missions were planned. As he
stood waiting for the printer to spit out the next day's frag document
for the Strike Eagles, Brig. Gen. Buster Glosson rushed up to him,
anxiety obvious in his expression. Said Strabala, "He came up and
said to cancel twenty-four of the F-15E lines [sorties] for tonight—
that we had to send a whole squadron back up to northwest Iraq to
hit H-2 and the fixed Scud launching sites northwest of H-2, and
that the first TOT up there would be at 2300 hours. That didn't put
us in a panic—we had a reasonably decent time to refrag the guys—
but it took a lot of work. That afternoon, working with [Capt.]
Charlie Bowman, the F-15E FIDO [fighter duty officer], we did a lot
of ad-lib coordinating with tankers, and with [Maj.] Charlie Heald,
whose job was to break out the frag and do the mission assignments
at Al Kharj. I know they went through hell on the flight line up
there, changing the ordnance three times on the jets.

"We knew, of course, that these missions were probably unneces-
sary. Those fixed Scud sites had all been hit. But the BDA [bomb
damage assessment] in that war really sucked. It was okay for the F-
111s and F-117s because they were using laser-guided munitions
and could bring back videotape from their infrared sensors to show
their results. That was the video footage people first saw on CNN—
the bomb going down the airshaft kind of shot. That was very pretty.
But the Strike Eagles only had videotapes of their HUDs, so when
the pilot pulled off target after bomb release, there was no way the
tapes could show results. Also, many people wondered why spy
satellites couldn't photograph the sites and send back pictures. Well,

they could do that if they happened to pass over them when there was no cloud cover. But there weren't that many satellites passing over Iraq and to change the orbit even by five degrees would cut the station time of the satellite in half. In addition, during the first days of the air war, there was an unusually large amount of cloud cover over western Iraq."

The Strike Eagle crews at Al Kharj were unaware of the knuckleball that had been thrown at them. Most had taken "no-go" pills sometime before dawn and were sleeping soundly despite the noise of F-16s and C-130s taking off only a half mile from their tents. What woke them up the following afternoon were the extraneous noises— the shrill whine of circular saws at work, or the raucous honking of horns by third-country nationals who worked on the base.

For Captains John "Norbs" Norbeck and Keith "Spitter" Johnson, who on the previous night had been on a raid against a power plant north of Basrah, it was business as usual when they got to the Chiefs' squadron ops tent in the late afternoon. The frag that had come down called for a four-ship raid against an ammunition dump in Iraq. Norbeck and Johnson were on the schedule to lead that mission, and ordnance crews on the flight line were loading each of their four airplanes with two Mark-84 2,000-pound bombs—they could have carried four each but Mark-84s were in short supply— plus three bags of gas and four AIM-9s. Then came the surprise.

Said Spitter Johnson, "We spent all the late afternoon and evening planning and then the other guys came in and Norbs and I briefed the mission. Then, just as we were about to step, Slammer [Lt. Col. Mike Decuir] picks up the phone and guess what, we're refragged to go out to Al Qaim where Yogi Alred and the Rockets went the first night. I said, 'I don't believe this; we're going out there into some of the worst triple-A and in all those SAM rings, and we're not going to have Weasels and no idea if the EF-111s would be there for support and we've got thirty minutes to plan, brief and get off the ground—and they're saying to us, are you guys going to get there or not?'"

It was "Yes, sir! We'll get there, sir!" because good crews salute smartly, suck up their misgivings, and do the best they can whatever the circumstances. So, without changing ordnance, Norbeck and Johnson's four-ship Sting Ray flight launched and flew out to the westernmost tanker track in Saudi Arabia. The tankers were in their "Chuck Berry" track as expected, and even though they were still flying with their lights off, the fighters were flying visually and there was none of the wild, downhill tobogganing the crews had experienced the first night.

Norbeck and Johnson tell what happened next:

Norbeck: "After coming off the tanker we crossed the border immediately and headed up to the target in the low 20s—we had decided after the guys' experience the first night over Al Qaim and the second night going into Basrah, that we'd rather take our chances with the SAMs and the air-to-air threat than have to fly through the wall of triple-A that we knew was up there. However, as we passed H-2, we skirted the SA-2 and SA-3 SAM rings before heading northeast to Al Qaim."

Johnson: "I'm thinking, 'My God, it's quiet up here tonight.' There was nothing on the radar—no triple-A—nothing on the RWR. I mean it was too quiet; the hair on the back of my neck was standing up. Also, I remember thinking to myself when we were walking out to the airplane, 'You don't actually think we're going to hit our target tonight.' I mean, with intel briefing us on all those SA-2 and SA-3 rings up there—and we're going to be all alone, without support.

"Anyhow, we're driving in, we get to the IP, and Norbs checks right 40 degrees for me to map. I pick up a Scud site on a 3.3 [nautical mile scale] and nothing there, which is what I expected. Then I squeeze off a .67 map and the Scud site looms up just like it was described. It was a square fenced-in area—real easy to designate. I tell Norbs he is designated. He checks back, puts the target on the nose and is going to do an auto-toss delivery—that's a diving delivery where he has the carrot on the heading and when he gets the pipper on it and hits the pickle button, he will make a smooth pull off and the bombs will come off. It's kind of a combination between a dive-bomb delivery and a loft."

Norbeck: "I'm designated and then I roll inverted, pull 30 degrees nose down, then roll out and, suddenly, the whole place is lit up. I mean, I can see the ground it is so light."

Johnson: "No kidding, it was like someone had turned on a light switch; the whole world just erupted. It was like a flowing river of light. The whole earth was a different color, with white, orange, and red fireballs coming up."

Norbeck: "I yelled, 'Whoa, I'm not putting my nose in that.'"

Johnson: "And I mumbled, 'Yeah, good idea.' He switched to the manual mode, pickled and bottomed off at 15,000. I'm completely outside now, left hand on the chaff and flare button and my right hand on the sissy bar because I'm checking to the left, looking for the bombs. The triple-A is all around us but there's nothing on the RWR—no symbology indicating SAM launches."

Norbeck: "I'm coming left on the egress, thinking maybe we're going to get out of the stuff when Spitter yells, 'SAM, break left!'"

Johnson: "I was watching for the bomb splash but never did see them because it was so bright down there—and, normally, you can see the flash of Mark-84s a hundred miles away on a clear night. Then, as I was looking back, I caught a bright flash out of the corner of my eye. It took me a microsecond to process the information, then I realized that was the booster phase of a missile. It was a SAM launch and there was a second one right behind it. They rose real fast. I yelled for Norbs to break left and he goes into a 10.5-G break turn [they discovered later]. Bitching Betty is yelling at us and I'm going, 'No kidding, lady; I don't care right now.'"

Norbeck: "The first one is tracking on us—I break into it and it can't make the hard break and it blew up at ten o'clock."

Johnson: "It detonated about 1,500 feet in front of us—I think; it's hard to judge distance at night. I had a momentary feeling of relief, but no time to rejoice because the second one was right on our tail."

Norbeck: "I'm breaking into it, trying to force an overshoot, but it repositions and is on us again. I do out of plane maneuvering and break into it again, trying to get it to square the corner and lose energy. But it was still following us. I unloaded and went down, and as the SAM followed us, I broke up into it again. It was still on us after three maneuvers so I had to do the last-ditch maneuver, which is to wait until the last five seconds and do an orthogonal roll, keeping my lift vector perpendicular to the missile—it was almost like a barrel roll."

Johnson: "He does a great maneuver. The missile couldn't hack the corner. It sailed over the top of the canopy and blows up at three o'clock. It was close. There was a huge flash that lights up the inside of the cockpit and we didn't discover it until later, but part of a frag-mentation rod blew through one of the conformal tanks and through the side of the airplane just behind my seat. We didn't feel it, though for an instant I saw chunks of the warhead flying off just after it exploded. Then I saw a third SAM and yelled, 'SAM, break left!'"

Norbeck: "Spitter yells, and for whatever reason, I could tell that it wasn't on us. But I'm slow and I stroke the burner to get some ener-gy in case I do have to maneuver."

Johnson: "I mean we are slow—down to 250 knots so we can't maneuver if another SAM is on us. But the burner lights us up like a big blow torch. It's a huge glare and the gunners can see it and they're saying, 'Thank you very much.' But we're pretty well out of the triple-A by now."

Norbeck: "And ten seconds later I tell Spitter to turn off the tape and then I just screamed."

Johnson: "He doesn't remember but I had already turned the tape off and we both went 'Aaaaaah!'"

Captains James "Chainsaw" McCullough and Ansel "Elvis" Mangrum were in the second ship of Sting Ray flight. They pick up the story:

McCullough: "We were ingressing to the target at medium altitude and there was nothing on the radar, no SAMS, no triple-A, no nothing. We drove one hundred miles through Iraq and nothing."

Mangrum: "When we left the tanker, I was worried about bandits. The first night we were on the tail end of the big package out here and had one run on us from behind. We could see his big burner plume, but then it went out and nothing happened. After that a Flogger goes through the HUD five hundred feet across our nose. So as we're motoring in and I'm really in the air-to-air radar—I don't want to miss anything. We're at medium altitude and it was going to be a lot easier for them to find us."

McCullough: "So here we are, it's quiet—I mean nothing. Then, when we turn in and we're fifteen miles from the target, the sky just lights up."

Mangrum: "It's heavy triple-A and we're above most of it. But then we start getting SAM activity on the RWR."

McCullough: "I see the SAMs coming now—there were nine altogether we found out later—but I saw three. It was whoosh, whoosh, whoosh. I'm watching them and I pull off to the left to put them on the beam, I roll out, and they are coming from my right side. I jettison my wing tanks and now pull back and Elvis goes, 'We are five miles from the target.' I had forgotten the target. Now I had to get our bombs off."

Mangrum: "I was throwing chaff wholesale and was looking left while Chainsaw was following the one on the right. That was my contract, but it was very hard to keep from looking right. But that saved our ass because I picked up one coming from the left."

McCullough: "I had hit combat jet [jettison] one, which got rid of the tanks, then came back right, put the steering on the nose, and I'm watching the SAMs and they are basically going up—they're not coming down on me at all. I drop the bombs on the target and get the hell out of there. At the time I am getting out of there, I am looking inside the turn coming off to the south and I see some more SAMs coming at us. Elvis is putting out chaff the whole time and I get the big minimum light up in my cockpit that says, 'Oh shit, we're almost out of chaff.' I said, 'Elvis save some of that chaff; we might need it to get the rest of the way out of here.' He comes off the button; he had already put out ninety bundles."

Mangrum: "About that time, Chainsaw stroked the burners and it looked like we lit up the sky. I was looking back and it looked like two of the SAMs were tracking us on a tail shot."

McCullough: "Then we heard lots of calls from behind us. The SAMs were on Three and Four and we heard them jettisoning tanks and bombs."

The last two planes in the flight had no chance at all. Their flight pattern was now predictable and the SAM operators were waiting. Soon their sky was full of SA-2s and SA-3s—estimates of numbers range from seven to fourteen—and as they turned into the target they were totally engaged. Captains Mark "Chairman" Mouw and Tom "Radar" O'Reilly were number Three in the flight. They had led the Basrah raid the night before and had seen "all the triple-A in the world." Now, in a new fight for their lives, they jettisoned their tanks and their bombs and concentrated solely on saving their lives and their airplane. It was a fight, with hard breaks left and right, an orthogonal roll and a diving, high-speed race out of the area.

Behind them, two young first lieutenants, Jeff Mase and Brian Killough, saw three SAMs fired at them. Said Mase, "You see three big balls of fire coming up at you. You get your radar warning saying, 'SA-2.' You see them flying at you. We chaffed and I did a couple of maneuvers. But they are tracking on us. You know they are tracking on you when they don't move in the canopy. They just freeze. They have a pure pursuit curve and you know one of them is going to hit you. I do a maneuver and jettison tanks. Everybody else is going to the target with their bombs [he thinks] and I'm trying. But, I can't maneuver very well with the extra weight of my bombs.

"After the last break they slid on the canopy, which means my maneuver worked. Then they restabilized, which means they figured out the guidance and they are tracking again. I do another vertical maneuver and they are about twenty seconds away. The books say three to five seconds prior to impact do an orthogonal break. I got rid of the bombs for this last-ditch maneuver. We pulled 8.7 Gs in the break—and never felt it. The missiles just slid off after that. There was no way they could make the turn. They exploded at our six [o'clock]."

Brian Killough, who was in the backseat, saw what happened. Said Killough, "I saw the whole thing. After Jeff's maneuver, they locked on to one of the chaff bundles that I had released. All three may have locked on the same bundle because they appeared to have exploded at the same point in space. Since we had turned right in the last break, we kept going in that direction just to get away from the area. By then the rest of the flight had egressed in the other direction and we had no idea where they were."

About that time Norbeck called for a flight check and was relieved to hear "Two," "Three," and "Four." They had all come up on the radio and all were safely out of the target area. From then on it was a quiet flight home, each crewman reflecting heavily on the night's experiences. And by the time they got there, some were in a fighting mood.

"I was pissed," said Norbeck. "It was suicide to send airplanes up into all those SAM rings without Weasel support. We had been told to call the TACC in Riyadh if we experienced anything significant up there. Well, as soon as I could get to a telephone, I called and told them about all the SAMs and that our RWR gear did not give us a single indication of all those SA-2 launches. It was not a malfunctioning instrument, either. We had done the self-check on it on the line. It was fine. It just didn't have the programming to pick up the band they were using up there."

Norbeck talked with Capt. Mike Smyth, the F-15E FIDO on the night shift. Said Smyth, "I remember the call from Norbs—he said he had never seen so many SAMs in his life. That impressed me at the time and I passed it on to the O-6 [colonel] in charge, who I assumed passed it on to [Major] General [John] Corder, who was under Horner, and in charge of the TACC at night. I assumed that this information would also come through intel and affect the next night's frag."

That did not happen. Day four turned out to be a real goat rope.

It started in panic when Israel announced that it was sending two hundred airplanes, Apache helicopters, and an unknown number of commando raiders into Iraq. Sometime during the day, that effort was quashed, but in the fervor of the moment, all systematic fragging of the air campaign came to a halt. And ideas for solving the Scud problem were sprouting like weeds. Said Capt. Charlie Bowman, the daytime FIDO in the TACC, "There were all kinds of options discussed that day. One of them was to send a mass of planes over western Iraq and map it all, and in the process, find the Scuds. That was off the wall because we didn't have near enough assets to do that. Another was for intel to send up weather balloons that we use to check the winds, but equip the balloons with sensors that could pick up the electronic emissions before the Scuds launched. That would have been a real needle-in-the-haystack approach. Finally, they decided to send some of the airplanes out to hang on a tanker for nine or ten hours until they were told where to go."

Then, at about 3:30 in the afternoon, General Glosson ordered Capt. Strabala to frag another half-squadron of F-15Es on the Scud sites in western Iraq. "We were jumping through our assholes after that," said Strabala. "We had four hours to plan and coordinate tankers and Weasels—Mike Smyth, who had taken Norbs's call the night before, had insisted that Weasels were necessary because of the SAMs. It was a real goat rope because we couldn't get enough tankers; we had the gas but not enough booms to get them refueled and across the border at the same time. Finally, we did some creative, ad hoc tanker scheduling and worked it out. The other problem was that the Weasels had to come all the way up from Bahrain and they needed to refuel midway up through Saudi, then again before they crossed the border into Iraq."

Lt. Col. Robin "Scotty" Scott and Capt. Larry Bowers had spent the whole previous night planning a twelve-ship raid on an ammunition dump east of Tallil airfield in Iraq. It was a meticulous plan, with Weasel and EF-111 support confirmed, and it was based on high-quality target photography—a rarity during the whole war. They went to bed the following morning confident that they had done everything possible to avoid the nighmarish mission they had flown the night before into Basrah.

"Then when we walked in late in the afternoon to get ready for the briefing," said Scott, "we were told that the mission to the ammunition dump was off—that we were going out west against Scud sites. Suddenly, we were faced with the problem of developing a whole new plan. And there was a critical void in our information—we did not know that Norbs and the guys who went up there the night before had run into a whole bunch of SAMs—that it was so bad that some of them didn't get to the target with their bombs.

"We did our best in the time that we had. Larry did a lot of the route planning while I got on the telephone and tried to coordinate Weasels and EF-111s so we would have their support. But then they kept calling from Riyadh and changing the TOTs—moving them up. We got three changes which I phoned to the Weasels and EF-111s, but because the Weasels were so far away, they didn't get the last one. They had to take off early because they had to tank hop to get out west. And as it turned out, they also had trouble with the weather and their tankers—their tankers didn't have all the gas they were supposed to have because they had been diverted from other tracks at the last minute for this new mission.

"We launch and get out west and the weather is terrible. Somehow we managed to get on the tankers and get our fuel, but the Weasels are late. They show up when we're ready to push across the border. They say, 'We're on time,' but, of course they weren't. So I had a critical decision to make at this time. Do I wait for the Weasels to tanker [they take on fuel at half the rate of the Strike Eagles], knowing that to do that I'm going to have to let everybody else get low on gas—and there is no more gas in the tankers? Or do I go without them? Not knowing about all the SAMs that were shot the night before, I elected to go."

In the meantime, the news about all the SAMs being shot at the Strike Eagles the night before finally filtered down to the TACC in Riyadh. Said Joel Strabala, "That news really bothered me. Intel said that there was now confirmation that there were a lot—with capital letters, L-O-T—of SAMs up by Al Qaim where one of the flights was going. Right then Charlie Bowman [the FIDO] and I were convinced that the mission going up to Al Qaim should be canceled. We didn't know that the Weasels would be late, but we knew there were only two of them to cover flights that would be striking targets eighty to a hundred miles apart. We talked about it, then went to General Corder and convinced him that the one mission should be called back. But there was a problem. We didn't know the call sign of the flight going to Al Qaim—that was left for the wing to work out. So all General Corder could do was request that AWACS transmit a message to cancel the flight going to the northernmost target. I heard the message being transmitted to AWACS and I heard them say that their message was never acknowledged."

Scott and Bowers, who were leading Corvette flight to the Al Qaim area, never heard the AWACS transmission.[1] Said they:

Scott: "As we ingressed I was still livid because of the half-assed way we were tasked for this mission. Moving the TOTs up on us caused us to go with maybe a five-minute brief and we didn't even get our target information until about ten minutes before we stepped.

Bowers: "We had no photography, nothing. It was just coordinates and I remember Scotty standing over the map with the guys in the flight and he turned to Colonel Eberly who was number Three and said to him, 'Sir, this is the kind of mission that people get killed on.' Colonel Eberly just looked at him. He didn't say a word."

Scott: "Well, we're approaching the target area now and the guns opened up."

Bowers: "They were big guns—bigger than we saw at Basrah, and they started when we were twenty miles from the target. You would see a red streak go boof and it would pop way high."

Scott: "We see it on our mapping leg and the adrenaline is going up. But we are at medium altitude and much of it is not getting up to us. And we're thinking, this is good, this is good, we were right being at medium altitude. That is the answer. Now we get the mapping leg done and I come in and roll down the chute. Then, just as the bombs are coming off, Larry says, 'Punch the tanks, break right!' Okay, religiously, because I believe in my pitter, I slam all the tanks off the airplane, make a hard-breaking right-hand turn, and no shit, here comes an SA-2 right at us."

Bowers: "That night the RWR worked. I had indications of a launch, but looking out, there was a problem because they had shot up a bunch of ground-launch flares—parachute flares. These things topped out at around 13,000 feet.

Scott: "They looked like huge bottle rockets. They lit up the whole sky."

---

[1]In fact they did not know about the transmission until after the war, when the subject was brought up by the author.

Bowers: "They would go whoosh, pop, and they would then hang and slowly fall in the air. They were everywhere just to light us up."

Scott: "It was an old World War II technique and it worked like a champ."

Bowers: "Scotty breaks right and down into the missile and it pops behind us. It popped higher than us and probably went after some of the chaff I was punching out. Then we got another launch and I'm watching it and Scotty is breaking right, then left. Then we got indications of an SA-3 launch."

Scott: "We estimated that there were ten to fourteen SAMs launched against our package that night and all the guys were breaking for them. It was chaos and as we egressed we were waddling back up to altitude to get away from the triple-A and my mouth is like cotton. Then, remembering the Basrah mission, I checked my flight as soon as I could. Two checked in and Four checked in. But no Three. I called, 'Four, have you seen Three?' 'Negative,' was the reply. Three was Colonel Eberly and Tom Griffith. Nobody saw them get hit. Nobody saw them go down. They were just not there anymore. Now, we are climbing out, trying to get on SAR freqs, reporting to AWACS, and coming back out."

Bowers: "When I heard all that, I said, 'Oh, shit!' This is my third mission and twice we have had people from the package go down.' I knew then that I might as well get used to this. But it was not a good feeling."

After the initial calls to AWACS the radios fell silent. For most of the crews the black night enclosing them was peaceful and benign, and after they had crossed the border and were back into Saudi, the sudden appearance of the blinking lights of their comrades gave them a warm and secure feeling. With the peace of the gentle night around them, their tapes would record a slower rhythm of breathing in their masks, and their muscles, grown rigid in the terror, would slowly begin to relax. Some would use these tranquil moments to mutter prayers of thanks. Others would allow their disciplined minds freedom to wander as they gazed out their canopies in awe of the myriads of shooting stars streaking across the black sky.

But Scottie Scott was doing none of this. His emotions were raw and painful, and he was as tense as he had been in the maelstrom. Two nights before he had lost his wingmen and tentmates. Tonight, he had lost his friend, Tom Griffith, and Dave Eberly, the 4th Wing's Deputy Commander for Operations. Now his earlier decision was haunting him. He had elected to go without the Weasels. With them, their HARM missiles could have put the radars guiding the SA-2s and SA-3s out of business and kept the missiles from guiding. But how was he to know that there would be so many missiles? In the hellhole of Basrah it had been all triple-A. And that is mostly what

Fourth Wing Commander, Col. Hal Hornburg. He became commander of all the squadrons that ended up at Al Kharj in Saudi Arabia. Courtesy USAF

Col. Dave Eberly, the 4th Wing director of operations (DO), before he was shot down and imprisoned by the Iraqis. Courtesy USAF

Col. Dave "Bull" Baker, who replaced Colonel Eberly as DO after Eberly was shot down. Baker's twin brother on a Navy carrier gave the Strike Eagles intelligence that resulted in one of their most successful raids. Courtesy D. Baker

The highly respected Lt. Col. Steve "Steep" Turner took over the Rocketeers Squadron in Oman. Author

Maj. John "Taco" Martinez, assistant operations officer of the Chiefs, was the driving force who pushed to get laser-guided bombs on the F-15E. Author

Lt. Col. Mike "Slammer" Decuir was the operations officer of the Chiefs and the F-15E pilot who dropped the first laser-guided bombs in combat. Author

Maj. Pete Hook being awarded "Flight Commander of the Year" honors. He was killed in Oman on a training mission. Courtesy J. D. Pohle

Maj. Tom Griffith was the WSO in Col. Eberly's aircraft when it was shot down. He was captured and imprisoned. Courtesy T. Griffith

Capt. Mark "Chairman" Mouw (left) and Capt. Tom "Radar" O'Reilly planned and led the Basrah raid. Author

Col. Ray Davies (right) showing CBS anchorman Dan Rather the base at Al Kharj. Davies was considered a miracle worker for his leadership in quickly building a complete air base along a bare runway in the desert. Courtesy R. Davies

Maj. Donnie Holland, known as "Chief Dimpled Balls" because of his passion for golf, was killed during the Basrah raid. Courtesy C. Holland

Close friends Capt. John "Holmes" Pavlock and Jim "Boo Boo" Poulet in happier days. Poulet, a weapons systems officer (WSO), was killed on a training mission. Courtesy J. Pavlock

Capt. Tim Bennett (top) and Maj. Dan Bakke made history with the first air-to-air kill by a laser-guided bomb. Author

Capt. Mark "Yogi" Alred, who led the first night's "gorilla package" and helped plan Operation Pacific Wind, was one of the most respected F-15E pilots in Desert Storm. Author

Capt. Laura Warn (née Berry) (left) and S/Sgt. Lori Helms were honored after the war for their diligence in finding worthwhile alternative targets for the F-15Es that flew the Scud patrol. Courtesy USAF

Maj. Joe Seidl (left) and Capt. Merrick Krause led the first element of Strike Eagles to penetrate severe thunderstorms and drop ordnance on Iraqis trying to escape Kuwait City. Courtesy M. Krause

Maj. Tom Koritz, flight surgeon and fighter pilot, was killed during the Basrah raid. Courtesy J. Koritz

Maj. Paul "PB" Burns and Capt. Mark "Bones" Wetzel were selected as the WSOs who could best be trusted to steer laser-guided bombs onto Iraqi aircraft placed near the historical ziggurat at Ur. Author

The Planes

Business end of a loaded-up F-15E Strike Eagle. Courtesy McDonnell Douglas

F-15E of the 4th Tactical Fighter Wing staff. Courtesy McDonnell Douglas

Typical conditions in the Southwest Asian theater of operations. Courtesy F. Serna, *Airman* magazine

One of the test models of the F-15E. Courtesy F. Serna, *Airman* magazine

Mock-up of F-15E cockpit with simulated background. Pilot's seat has been removed to show instruments. The two display terminals in the WSO's station are the FLIR targeting video (left) and synthetic aperture radar display (right). Courtesy McDonnell Douglas

Aircraft from the 4th Tactical Fighter Wing. From top right, 334th Tactical Fighter Squadron, wing staff, 335th Tactical Fighter Squadron, and 336th Tactical Fighter Squadron. Courtesy F. Serna, *Airman* magazine

Strike Eagles of the 336th Tactical Fighter Squadron. Courtesy F. Serna, *Airman* magazine

F-15Es of the 336th during mid-air refueling. Courtesy D. Wise

Another mission: Strike Eagles of the 336th shortly before takeoff. Courtesy F. Serna, *Airman* magazine

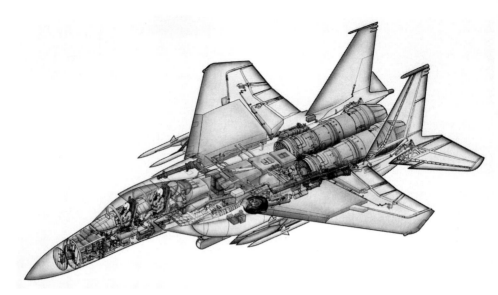

Schematic view of the Strike Eagle showing major systems and components. Courtesy McDonnell Douglas

F-15Es of the (from top) 336th and 335th Tactical Fighter squadrons with an albino F-15 of the 36th Tactical Fighter Wing fly over Iraqi aircraft shelters hit by precision-guided munitions. Note dark gray camouflage of Strike Eagles. Courtesy McDonnell Douglas

had been reported in the Al Qaim region by those who had gone in there the first night.

"We didn't say a word coming home," said Scott. "I had used up about all the adrenaline I had and I was physically drained. But you can't help going over everything that had happened. It was like a checklist; if I had done this, what if? I went over everything in my mind, questioning myself. We were supposedly on a high-priority mission—I mean they had canceled our regular mission and had us jumping through our skirts for this new one. So, believing that it was high priority, I didn't expect that they would want me to say, 'Okay, boys, let's go home,' when the two Wild Weasels didn't show up on time. I decided that we should go, and today, considering what I knew then, I would make the same decision again."

10

Search and Rescue Becomes a Myth

"After we saw the videotape of Eberly in Baghdad, our confidence in JRCC went to zero."

Lt. Col. Steve Turner

Every war is a tragedy for those who have to fight it. However, despite all the bad things that happen in war, some of the combatants win the good-luck lottery and fate allows them to survive when they could have been killed. As it turned out, on the night of January 19, 1991, when flight leader Scotty Scott was agonizing over the decision he had made to continue his mission without Weasel support, Dave Eberly and Tom Griffith, whom he feared he had lost, managed, with the help of luck and the marvelous engineering of the Aces-II ejection seat, to escape from their stricken airplane. Here is their story:[1]

Eberly: "We were ten miles out, with the final targeting maps made, when I turned to put the target on the nose. Just then we got a SAM alert and at about seven miles, I looked off to the right side and saw what looked like an oil well fire. Instinctively, my training told me it was the fire plume of the SAM. I did a hard turn to the right to force it to overshoot, then turned back to put the target on the nose."

---

[1]The reader will note that Griffith relates their experience in more detail. Most of Eberly's story has been published in *Crusade: The Untold Story of the Persian Gulf War*.

Griffith: "Coming in from the IP I was concerned with getting a good map and finding the target. It was a Scud site in one of the tributaries of a wadi out there—easy to recognize with the radar after I found it. I got a good .67 map and the two guys in front were just getting to the target when we turned in. It looked like solid lights underneath us. It was triple-A and I was impressed with how much there was—it looked like we could get out and walk on it. Then, about eight miles from the target, we got a missile launch indication at right two o'clock. It was a flashing, SA-2 indication with a high-pitched steady tone in the headset. I'm outside now since the designation and I see two fireballs that look like they are coming up at the airplane. I watch them but don't want to jink against missiles not guiding. But these looked like they were not moving. I put out chaff and asked Eberly to come left and kick them to four o'clock on our beam. He turned left and I put out more chaff, and as we are coming back to the right, there is an explosion on the left side of the airplane. There was a bright light, and almost an immediate impact on the airplane— it felt like it almost stopped in midair. I had never hit anything in an airplane but it was instantly recognizable that we had hit something."

Eberly: "Just as I rolled back to put the target on the nose there was a blinding white light and a stunning sensation of impact. My eyes were pulled to the left side of the cockpit where the fire lights are located. I struggled to focus. Something was different. The lighting was foggy.[2] Instinctively, almost subconsciously, I knew we'd been hit [by a SAM], that we were still alive, but must get out immediately. My hands had already grasped the handles and I could feel the slight friction as I rotated them to initiate ejection."

Griffith: "I know we've hit something and that Eberly had his hands full fighting the jet. The first thing I wanted to do was make a radio call because Teek and Donnie had gone down without saying anything. I reached for the foot mike [a microphone switch on the floor much like the old-fashioned automobile dimmer switch] but before I could reach it, I was up the rails. The first sensation I had was that I'm falling in my seat. It was black and I couldn't see anything, but I was worried: I didn't want to hit the ground in the seat. I needed to get a parachute—now I'm getting some temporal distortion—and I tried to manually deploy the parachute. It deployed automatically and with the opening shock I was thanking God that I had a parachute and was still alive. I'm looking down now and I see that I'm coming down into all the triple-A—we were probably at 21,000 when we were hit and the chute was supposed to open at 14,000.

---

[2]It was determined later that this was from the rapid decompression caused by shrapnel from the exploding SAM penetrating the left forward section of the canopy.

Now I'm thinking they are shooting at me—that was my first reaction—then I realized that no, they're not, I just happened to be in the wrong place. I didn't see the airplane hit but I'm aware of a big fire underneath me. I don't know if it is the airplane but I tried to steer away from it. Also, I realized that I hadn't made a call when in the airplane so now I took my survival radio and tried to make a call on guard [emergency frequency monitored by other aircraft]. But I don't think I was successful; my fingers were cold and I couldn't get them to work on the radio. I fooled around a couple of minutes it seemed, and as I became aware of the ground coming up, I started putting the radio away. I was not ready when I hit and I twisted my left knee—it was pretty hard and gravelly where I landed."

Eberly: "The next thing I can remember after reaching for the handles was that I was kneeling on the ground, staring at a fire in the distance. It was deathly quiet, like a dream. Where was I? Slowly it came back. The war had started. Griff and I had been on a mission up north. My inflated life raft was floating on the empty desert sea in front of me and to my left, my chute had collapsed neatly. A sudden chill reminded me that I was likely to go into shock and that I must fight it. I took a long drink of water and wrapped my chute around me to get warm."

Griffith: "After I hit, I released my parachute and immediately realized how loud it was down there with all the guns going off. I knew I had to get a survival kit and get out of there. We had two kits, a big one and a small one—the latter called a "dash pack." It had the minimum essential stuff and you can cut it off and carry it when you need to haul ass. I was cutting it off when somebody comes over and drops bombs about four hundred yards away. I felt the blast and my first thought was that I had jumped out of an airplane and made it to the ground, but was now going to get killed by somebody from my own squadron. I was frightened and I took the dash pack and tried to get away from all the shooting. I wanted to get as far away from the target area as I could."

Eberly: "Suddenly, I heard the sound of a truck and saw its lights. Expecting the worst—soldiers and dogs—I scrambled to hide behind the base of a large power line stanchion some fifty feet away. Luckily, I had landed just short of these high-voltage power lines. The truck stopped and a lone soldier got out, listened, looked, and smoked a cigarette. As I lay there trying to quiet the loud pounding of my heart, my eyes were fixated on the red-orange glow of his cigarette. Then he drove off. Time and circumstance had dramatically changed our roles. Now, I was the hunted, not the hunter. I gathered my parachute around me, and using the power line as a reference, I began walking, my mind flooded with the words of the Twenty-third Psalm. Those words were now my comfort."

Griffith: "When the shooting stopped, I sat down like they tell you to do, and got my bearings. Also, I tried calling on the radio. There was nothing. I decided then that I should head northwest toward Syria. There was no way I could make it back to Saudi. I got out the compass, tried to get 330 [degrees] under the lubber line—we have a fluorescent ring for use at night—then saw a truck coming toward me. I had a .38-caliber government-issue revolver but was basically defenseless. I moved away from where I was—the terrain was similar to some of New Mexico and Arizona—not a lot of shrubs and bushes, but lots of little ridgelines. I kept going, trying to keep a ridge between myself and the truck, which was no factor after awhile. I kept walking and called on the radio at the times we were supposed to call. The only person I raised after about two hours of calling was Dave Eberly. We were only about five hundred yards apart. We soon got together and I still had it in my mind that we should keep walking in the direction of Syria. After awhile, though, he said he had to sit down and rest—that he had cut his neck and had lost some blood. We sat down, rested for a bit, and after it started to get light outside, I looked at his neck and saw that he was cut pretty good. He had his parachute with him, but nothing else. I tried to make a bandage out of it to keep his cut from bleeding too much. Then we started walking again. When it got daylight, I took out the escape map I had in my G-suit and, with the Form 70 from our mission showing the turn points, we more or less figured out where we were. After that, I buried all flight planning stuff so if we were caught the enemy wouldn't have that. Then we saw a hill that was sticking out of flat terrain about a quarter mile away. There wasn't good cover anywhere so we decided to go up on that hill and hide there until rescued. The hill allowed us to see around us and it gave us better range on our survival radio. It was clear and cold all day— it probably never got above 40 degrees. We were a little hungry but our big concern was water. I had a couple of pint-size bottles in my G-suit, but the main supply of water was in the big survival pack and we did not dare try to go back and get it. We stayed on that hill all day. We watched trucks going down the road, but they all appeared to be commercial. After we were on the hill, we decided to sit tight, thinking that we would get rescued that night. We didn't think rescue assets would come looking for us during the day."

Before the war the aircrews heard repeated promises from visiting Search and Rescue (SAR) personnel that they were never to worry if they had to go down in enemy territory. "We WILL be there; we can even go into downtown Baghdad to get you." Such were the promises. And why not believe them? This generation of airmen had grown up hearing the hero stories out of Vietnam—of how SAR personnel repeatedly risked their lives to retrieve downed airmen.

Twenty years later, with much more sophisticated assets available for SARs, the Strike Eagles launched on their dangerous missions brimming with confidence, knowing that powerful forces were waiting, poised to rescue them if they could somehow manage to evade the enemy for a short time after "punching out." Col. Dave Eberly and Maj. Tom Griffith, sitting on a knoll in western Iraq, were now waiting for these vaunted rescuers to do as they had promised.

Just after they disappeared, AWACS was notified and the message was passed on to the Joint Rescue Coordination Center (JRCC) that had responsibility for all SAR efforts in the theater. At that time any of the crewmen in Corvette flight (Eberly and Griffith were Corvette 03) could have given JRCC a twenty-mile diameter area where the airplane most probably went down. A-10 Warthogs, which had been positioned at an airfield in western Saudi Arabia for Scud hunting, could have been sent into that area the next morning. Signals from Eberly or Griffith's radio would have been picked up by an A-10's automatic direction finder (ADF), causing the needle of the instrument to point to the bearing of the signal. Through a series of transmissions from the ground, with the pilot flying the direction the ADF needle is pointing, an A-10 could have flown directly over them. (The A-10 pilot would have known when he passed them because the ADF needle would reverse directions on the next ground transmission.) With the downed pilots located, A-10s, with their awesome armament, could have escorted helicopters and protected them while the airmen were picked up.[3]

None of this happened. And at Al Kharj, Col. Hal Hornburg, the 4th Wing commander, was in agony. Said Hornburg, "I called Riyadh throughout the day—I don't remember now how many times. All I kept hearing them say was, 'Well, let's wait awhile to make sure they haven't diverted.' Then it was, 'Well, we really can't do anything till we get some solid facts.' The real problem, of course, was that SAR was not under our air boss, General Horner. He would have had planes up there immediately if he had been in control."

The next night, the Strike Eagles were sent to western Iraq again, tasked to hit suspected Scud launching sites. It was an eight-ship package, call-sign Chevy, that was to attack roughly the same targets that had been struck the night before. As the pilots turned in to the IP and the WSOs were making their maps, the triple-A erupted and

---

[3]This exact thing happened not long after Eberly and Griffith went down. A pair of A-10s patrolling in western Iraq were recruited by AWACS to help find downed U.S. Navy lieutenant Devon Jones. Using their ADF they found him, returned south of the border, escorted helicopters deep into Iraq, north of the Amman-Baghdad highway, and fought off Iraqis about to capture Jones while a helicopter picked him up.

soon the air was full of SAMs. On this night, however, there were Weasels along and some of the SAM radars were blown away.

Capt. John Croghan and Maj. Gary Cole were Chevy Zero-Six that night, and were sweating out the triple-A that was bursting around them. Said Cole, "The triple-A seemed to be everywhere. There was no place to go and I remember thinking to myself that there was absolutely nothing we could do. If we moved to the right and got shot down, we are going to say, 'Damn, we never should have moved to the right.' I'm watching the bombs from the guys ahead of us going off. We were carrying CBU and I could see all the stuff going off all over the ground, and some secondary explosions. Then I made my map and designated the target, and just about the time I'm going outside I hear a voice in the background. Then it suddenly registers; that sounds like Tom Griffith. Then I hear it again and this time Crog [Croghan] and I both go, 'It's Griff! It's Griff!' We're right over the target now. We drop the bombs and come off and I switch the aux radio over to the emergency frequency we were using. He had said, 'Allied aircraft in the wadi area, this is Corvette Zero-Three.' I made a call back, 'Corvette Zero-Three, this is Chevy Zero-Six, we read you loud and clear, over.' Then I heard him make another call and I came back and I said, "Zero-Three, this is us. Hang tight. We'll get somebody looking for you.

"By this time Steep [Turner], who was leading the mission, had tried to check everybody in and, since we were off frequency trying to talk to Griff, we didn't come up on the check. When we came back up, he was just saying, 'Is anybody hurt?' and then we check in. I didn't want to come up on the radio and say we had just talked to Griff. We had been told that the Iraqis had some pretty good listening capabilities. We went back to the tanker, then, when we got on the ground at Al Kharj, I told Croghan to go through the maintenance debrief and that I would run our tape in. I get to the squadron and Steep is standing there, a little peeved because we hadn't checked in when he first called. I said, 'Didn't you hear Griff? Griff was on the radio!' Steep was there with a couple of other of the guys in the flight and it was like they had just recovered from amnesia. They had heard Griff but they had been so busy—number Two had turned hard off the target because he was getting shot at and had cut in front of Lead. They had all heard Griff but it hadn't registered. Now, all of a sudden, it is like, their eyes open wide and they go, 'Yeah, it was Griff! God!'

"Turner and I ran over to intel and called direct to the rescue people up at KKMC [King Khalid Military City]—we called all the appropriate people. They asked if we had done any of the recognition things and I said, 'No,' that I hadn't actually made two-way contact with him but I recognized his voice. I said that both of us were dead sure that it was Griff and I had it on tape. Later a colonel from the JRCC called me to just reconfirm that it was Griff. I told him I recognized his voice plain as day, that he didn't sound like he was under duress—that there didn't seem to be any of that kind of stuff, but that I did not establish two-way contact."

Meanwhile Eberly and Griffith are sitting on their little knoll, waiting. They had recognized Gary Cole's voice and thought two-way contact had been established. Said Griffith, "That's the first time they knew we were alive but they could not authenticate us. We were sure then that someone would be coming for us. But we were very cold and we were hungry and sore—I don't know if it was from jumping out of the airplane or from sleeping on the ground. We still had Eberly's parachute so we wrapped it around us and huddled together for warmth. We probably slept some but mostly we were listening for a helicopter when we weren't checking in at the appropriate times on the radio."

Meanwhile, Colonel Hornburg, the wing commander, was boiling mad, although after the war when he was interviewed he only admitted to having had "a high frustration level."[4] Said Hornburg, "It seemed to me that the forces running the SAR wanted a perfect situation. Before they would launch they wanted to know exactly where they [Eberly and Griffith] were, that they had been authenticated and on and on. I mean, when we got the tape I had [Lt. Col.] Slammer Decuir, Griff's roommate and supervisor when they were running Stan-Eval [Standardization and Evaluation], listen to the tape and verify that it was Griff. But those guys at JRCC would not take our word for it. So we fly the tape to Riyadh and they say, finally, 'Yep, now that we have heard the voice, we believe what you heard was in fact true.' I mean it was frustrating beyond belief that we had to prove to others that, yes, there were people out there who needed to be picked up. What frustrated me the most was that I couldn't push the right buttons to get the SAR going. Horner and Glosson, my bosses, would have broken their necks to get up there, but they were running the air campaign and had no control over the SAR effort. The organization was not right; the wiring was wrong and that drove us all crazy."

So Eberly and Griffith were not to hear any helicopters this night. And the next morning they had to make a decision. Said Griffith, "The sun came up and we had to decide whether to stay where we were or to leave. If we left right then, we were pretty strong, we had

---

[4]A major who overheard one of Hornburg's conversations with JRCC said, "I can give you an exact quote of one of Hornburg's outbursts when he was talking to one of the SAR guys. Flat outright he asked this guy, 'Is this incompetence or is this just sheer cowardice!' I mean Hornburg was really angry because they hadn't even launched anything yet."

a little drinking water, and were fairly well hydrated. We figured
that it was about five miles to the Syrian border, and another couple
of miles to a town that was on our map. We figured we could make
it in our present condition. However, we were fairly secure where
we were and if the helicopters came, we would be in an easy place to
find. The risk was that if we stayed on the hill and the helicopters
didn't come in a day or two, we would be to weak to do anything.
Finally, we decided that we would move on at sunset. Partly it was
because we were tired of sitting there, and by moving out there was
at least some chance that we could find some drinking water.

"That day we took Eberly's parachute and ripped part of it up to
stuff in our flight suits for warmth. The rest of it we used to wrap
around ourselves so if we were seen in silhouette we might look like
Bedouins. Also during the day, we heard the A-10s, using Sandy [tra-
ditional SAR] call signs as they were working the Devon Jones rescue. We kept calling them but were too far away.[5] Devon Jones got
picked up that afternoon but we stayed with our decision. We were
going to start walking at sunset."

Back at Al Kharj the whole Strike Eagle community was in a fren-
zy. Said Maj. Richard Crandall, "I mean, you can't believe how
angry we were that they were not going up there looking for those
guys. We were so angry that Al Gale and I actually proposed to take
a vehicle and DRIVE up there to get them. That sounds crazy now,
but we knew the special forces were driving around out in western
Iraq and we felt we could do it, too."

Steep Turner, the Rockets' commander who, even on calm peacetime days is a bundle of nervous energy, was almost a zombie by
now. Said Turner, "There were thirty-six hours after I came back
from that mission where we heard Griff when I literally drove myself
into the ground. I didn't sleep. Bob Gruver [Rockets operations offi-
cer] or I were on the phone constantly. I'm sure we were yelling and
shouting and doing everything we could to get that SAR going. I
know at JRCC I couldn't get any higher than a captain. But I
explained, 'Hey, let us go up there and when they come up on the
radio, we'll take a DF [ADF] cut on them and we'll locate them for
you.' This captain says, 'No, we don't need you. We have aircraft
that can go up there. We've got F-15Cs flying CAP that can do all
that.' Oh, I was hot, Gruver was hot—everybody was just pissed.
After thirty-six hours I was a vegetable. I finally realized that I
couldn't do any more. I had a squadron to run and missions to fly,
so I finally took some time off and got some sleep."

---

[5]F-16s flying over the Al Qaim area heard Griffith and reported it when
they returned from the mission.

In western Iraq the sun was going down and Eberly and Griffith had started walking. Said Griffith, "We started walking northwest. At one point we crossed a major road but with no problems. Then, in the dark, we stumbled into a Bedouin encampment; we didn't see the tents until we were in the midst of them. About ten dogs—they looked like mongrels—started barking and looking like they were going to attack us. They looked mean but we escaped from there. We never heard anybody. We smelled where sheep had been but we never saw any of them.

"We kept walking, trying to keep up on our radio. About two o'clock that morning, after one of our calls, an airplane called us. It was an F-15 [Albino] on CAP and he had been tasked to authenticate us. He asked us how we were. We said that we were together and in good condition. Then he said, 'Stand by and I'll get back to you.' He never did get back to us.

"At that point we didn't know what was going on but we were ready to get the hell out of there. We were tired and thirsty, and then this guy gets our hopes up. We took a break and as we were sitting there, we could see what looked like an abandoned building. We talked about it and, since we were getting desperate for water now, we start thinking that maybe somewhere close there would be a well where we could get some water. Unfortunately, it was not abandoned. It was a guard shack for the Iraqi side of the border. A couple of guys on the roof heard us as we started toward it. They started yelling and shooting off AK-47s, then other guys came running out of the building—about ten of them, all with automatic weapons. All we had were .38s and we had no chance at all against them.

"We made a big mistake. We had been told in survival school never to go near buildings even if they are unoccupied. But we were out of water—we had used up all our water before we left the hill. Our mouths were dry and cottony and our mind was obsessed with water. Thirst saps energy and the thought of water completely dominates your mind.

"So we were captured. They roughed us up a little bit, but not as bad as we expected. Perhaps, also, we were lucky for we found out later that the border between Syria and Iraq, at least in certain places, is seeded with land mines and barricaded with barbed wire. We didn't know that at the time; intel had never briefed us on that. So maybe it was better that we were captured. We'll never know."

Dave Eberly and Tom Griffith were taken from the guard shack in the back of a truck to a similar building where a lieutenant tried, without any knowledge of English, to interrogate them. Then, in another truck they were driven into a town they believe was Al Qaim where a captain, who spoke passable English and said he was a doctor, tended Eberly's neck. "We got water there," said Griffith, "then, after they did an inventory of our survival gear, they wanted us to sign a paper. We said, 'No, we can't do that. We're not going to sign anything.' That surprised them but we never did sign it. Then we were driven to what they called the 'general's house.' There, the general, if he was a general, treated us fairly well. He didn't speak good English but we got the point across that we needed to sleep. He says, 'Okay,' and they handcuffed us to different beds and we went to sleep."

That was the last decent treatment the two men received. They were transported to Baghdad and thrown in a prison where they spent the remainder of the war in solitary confinement. As for their treatment, a secret spy report reached U.S. intelligence saying that Eberly had been beaten to death. Luckily, that did not happen and both survived their ordeal.

But the morale in the Strike Eagle community went down, especially after they saw videotapes of Eberly's face that were soon broadcast by CNN in Baghdad. (Eberly's wife saw his picture on her birthday and considered it a gift that he was alive.)

Epithets of many kinds were heard in the community after that. They were this and they were that—mostly names that are unprintable. And who were "they"? "They" in the epithets were not the Iraqis who had done the capturing. Nor were "they" the helicopter rescue crews whose courage everyone admired. "They" were the bureaucrats who controlled the SAR missions and who had sat on their hands and let Eberly and Griffith be captured.[6] It was they who were the targets of derision. It was they who were the unprintables.

---

[6]About two weeks later F-16 pilots Capt. Scott "Spike" Thomas and Lt. Eric Dodson were coming back from a mission near Baghdad when Thomas's engine swallowed a compressor blade. Losing power, Dodson radioed AWACS and advised them of the problem. When Thomas had to punch out, Dodson radioed first, that Thomas had a good chute, then second, that he had followed him to the ground and confirmed that he was okay. All the while, AWACS acknowledged this information and repeatedly said that helicopters were on the way. They also said there were no other aircraft nearby that could fly cover. Dodson, running low on fuel, called openly on the strike frequency and several nearby airplanes answered and flew to provide protective cover over Thomas. Dodson then went to KKMC for fuel, and when he got to the Special Forces command center, he discovered that AWACS had told them that it had not been confirmed that the pilot was down and safe so helicopters had not been launched. Dodson stirred things up and the helicopters finally took off and reached Thomas just minutes before the Iraqis would have captured him. Said Dodson, "I shudder to think what would have happened to Spike had I not personally told them that he was down and safe. Fortunately, I had audio tapes of everything so AWACS could not deny any of the communications." This is one more example of why aircrews harbored ill feelings about the search and rescue machinery.

11

Smart Bombs

"We were frustrated, we were bored, we were tired; finally we started looking for our own targets."

Maj. Joe Manion

Technically, they are called laser-guided bombs (LGBs), but to the public, and even to many air force personnel, they are simply called "smart bombs." During the Gulf War the smart bombs were the media stars. Smart bombs were shown going down an air shaft, slicing the thin span of a bridge, and flying through the door of a hardened aircraft shelter. For the millions of viewers who followed the Gulf War on television, it was the performance of the smart bombs that confirmed the arrival of a new technological age in air warfare. Prior to this, high-tech weapon systems bore the brunt of antimilitary press coverage. They were high-priced toys built for military brass, but they would never work in real warfare. That message, in one form or another, had created a lot of skeptics. But the smart bombs did an end run around the editors' blue pencils. They did their job as advertised and the video record spoke for itself. So a new story emerged from the war. High-tech can do the job. Technology works.

However, in the case of the smart bombs, that really was not a new story. Smart bombs have been around since the closing days of the Vietnam War. The F-4 had a laser system for the precise guidance of bombs. So did the F-111, which was what the crews used in the Libya raid in 1986. Smart bombs were not known to the public because the dramatic videos of them doing their work were not seen on the nightly news. That all changed during the Gulf War.

127

But what are smart bombs? And how do they work?

The concept is actually very simple, although the term *laser guided* creates confusion. Most people think that the bombs somehow ride a laser beam to the target. This is not true at all. When a smart bomb falls off an airplane, its eyes—a computer guidance system—are closed. In aircrew lingo, it is blind. It is just falling through the air like any dumb bomb.

Meanwhile the WSO has a system that projects a laser beam from the airplane to the ground, like a powerful spotlight with a very narrow beam. Wherever that beam strikes, it creates a spot that the WSO can see on a small television screen in the cockpit. It appears in the center of cross hairs. The WSO can move the cross hairs, which in turn moves the laser beam and the spot on the ground.

The sequence is as follows. The airplane releases a smart bomb; its eyes are closed and it falls through the air like a dumb bomb. Meanwhile the WSO moves the cross hairs on his screen to a target he wants to hit—the door of a hardened aircraft shelter, for example. Then, maybe ten seconds before the bomb hits the ground, the WSO electronically opens the bomb's eyes, and it becomes a smart bomb. When the guidance head on the front of the bomb locates the laser spot on the ground, guidance fins on the front of the bomb are activated and the bomb is automatically steered to the laser spot. If the WSO is good enough to keep the cross hairs on the door of the aircraft shelter (a challenging problem if the pilot is pulling four Gs in a turn) the bomb will guide itself directly to the laser spot—in this case, the aircraft shelter door. Then, in WSO lingo, it is a "shack"; it is a bull's-eye and the shelter is destroyed.

The Strike Eagle with its awesome night capabilities is an ideal platform for the smart bomb. In fact, the Strike Eagle smart bomb combination was arranged when the Strike Eagle was nothing but a set of blueprints on the drafting table. As mentioned before, the Strike Eagle went to war before it was ready. When the airplanes first reached Oman they had only been certified to carry and release two kinds of bombs, both dumb bombs. In the months that followed, quick computer studies by air force engineers allowed the Strike Eagles to carry a few other dumb bombs. But smart bombs? No way. The Strike Eagles would have to go to war and do the best they could with dumb bombs.

Nobody likes to be told "no." It is almost routine human behavior to circumvent this absolute. "What part of no don't you understand?" has become more than a song title; it is an expression that persistent yea-sayers have forced into our modern culture. An example of such a yea-sayer was Maj. Taco Martinez,[1] assistant operations officer of the Chiefs. He was not happy about the Strike Eagle being denied a weapon with such great potential, and he set out to do something about it.

Said Taco, "In order to use the LGB the airplane has to be equipped with a belly-mounted device called a targeting pod. The pod has a mechanism for projecting a powerful laser beam from the airplane to the ground; it has an infrared viewing system that allows the WSO to search for targets on the ground; and it has a video system that records everything that the WSO sees, including the bomb explosion. With the video record from the targeting pod we know exactly where our bombs hit and what damage they have done. We don't know that when we drop dumb bombs. After our dumb bombs are off the airplane, we have turned away and there is no video record of where they hit.

"One of the reasons we weren't certified to drop LGBs was that we did not have enough targeting pods. In October, when we first learned that the Chiefs would be going to the desert, we received two pods. But one broke right away—a hard break that we couldn't get repaired. The other one was off and on. We would fly one sortie and it would work, then it would break on the next sortie.

"In December, when it was definite that we were going to the desert, I started trying to get more pods. Eglin [AFB] had some, Luke [AFB] had some, and Nellis [AFB] had some. I wrote messages to TAC asking for some of those because we were going to war and needed them. That got us nothing. Then I went on a cross-country up to Langley and personally talked with the folks in the shop. That did nothing. I'm not sure why, although I know there was a turf battle going on. Both the F-16 and the F-15E used the same pod—it was that kind of thing. Then Steve Pingel [squadron commander] called Colonel Hornburg in Saudi and, after that, the flow started. The pods started rolling in and when we deployed after Christmas we had twelve of them, including the two that were inop [inoperable], which we brought along for spare parts.

"While we were at Seymour we also dealt with the basic problem of certification. The guys in the 422 [test and evaluation squadron] at Nellis had dropped some LGBs from the F-15E but had some trouble with spin release wires. Their position was that the LGBs should

---

[1]Martinez bristled when he told of another author who refused to use his nickname because the author thought it was demeaning and racist. Said Martinez, "I was called Taco when I was a little boy; I like the name and I resent anybody who thinks I should not be called by that name now."

not be cleared until they had figured out the problems. But now we're taking their targeting pods and they can't do anything. So we went directly to Wright-Pat [Wright-Patterson AFB—the headquarters for U.S. Air Force engineering], to the folks who do the wind tunnel work and we asked them to help us. They did some computer modeling and came back with our flag clearances. This authorized us to load them on the jet and drop them within certain constraints of air speed and G-loading.

"Now we're at Al Kharj and the war is about a week old. Steve [Pingel] and I are sitting in our tent after a mission where we were trying to take out hardened aircraft shelters with dumb bombs. We hadn't done very well and we got to talking about it, saying how much better we could have done with LGBs. Steve had been my instructor in LGBs when I went through weapons school, and I had dropped them when I was a WSO in the F-4. There were also several other guys in the squadron who had dropped them from the F-4 and the F-111. We talked about all this, and then, as the sun was coming up, we agreed that Steve should call Greeno [Maj. Gary Green] the next night down at the TACC and see if we could get something going."

Maj. Gary "Greeno" Green, a gung-ho F-15E pilot who was smarting because of his forced rear echelon role in Riyadh, was itching for action, and Pingel's call, though not as welcome as orders to return to operations, was a challenge that he relished. Said Greeno, "I got this call from Pingel in the middle of the night. He said, 'Talk to me about how we can do LGBs. We're thinking we should be using them.' We talked about it and I got excited. I had already gotten some static from the generals. 'Why weren't we using LGBs?' Well, the problem was that nobody in the 4th Wing was qualified to load them or build them up. They had no tech data, no test equipment, no kits for building them. Well, when I got off the phone I talked to [Col. Dave] Deptula and [Col. Tony] Tolin, then to [Brig. Gen.] Buster Glosson. They were excited about the idea and essentially told me to get things moving.

"I called on the hot line to TAC and talked to the F-15E weapons guru and explained that we were now top priority. In about eight hours we had a message back telling how to wire them, how to build them up, and with all the technical data we needed. The next day, on the shuttle, we had 200 kits delivered, along with the test kits that we needed. Meanwhile I got guys from the F-111s mobilized and in less than twenty-four hours we had two hundred bombs built, all with the correct wires and everything.

"Glosson was following all this closely and when I told him we had the bombs ready, he told me to frag some airplanes to go up to this airfield that had already been hit several times. He wanted F-15Es to try them out in a safe environment. I did that, then I got in trouble. First, Slammer [Lt. Col. Mike Decuir—the Chiefs' operations officer] chewed my ass. Then Taco called and chewed my ass. Then Hornburg called and must have chewed my ass for thirty minutes."

"The problem," said Slammer, "was that Greeno jumped the gun and fragged us when we weren't ready. He did a great job getting the bombs and all that but we weren't ground trained; we didn't have crews who knew how to load them. That's why we were chewing on him. We appreciated what he had done but we weren't ready to go out that night and drop them."

That night some of the Chiefs did go to the airfield where they were fragged, but they dropped dumb bombs. And when they came in and learned that their ground crews had been trained, Greeno got another middle-of-the-night call. However, this time they were nice to him. "We're ready," they said. "Put us in the frag."

They got some important targets this time—targets that fully justified the use of smart bombs. Said Taco, "Saddam had a comm system using fiber optics cables. But one of the main links between Baghdad and the KTO [Kuwait Theater of Operations] was laid right along an oil pipeline. Somebody had been smart enough to realize that we weren't about to bomb the pipeline and spill oil everywhere. So his comm line was safe.

"However, at intervals along the line he had relay stations with a tower, a bunker and a set of eight to ten solar panels. We had hit some of the solar panels earlier but they were just for backup power; they weren't critical. The towers and the bunkers needed to be taken out, but the F-16s had tried and had not been successful. So they fragged us to two different locations. One was a station near Tallil airfield, the other was near As Samawah; both were between Basrah and Baghdad.

"Slammer and I led one of the four-ship flights. We launched and headed up to As Samawah. When we got close to the target, I found it on the radar, mapped and designated it, then looked through the targeting pod, which slews toward the target when we do the mapping procedure. But there was nothing but clouds in sight; it was overcast below us. Slammer centered up our steering and we punched down through the weather, breaking out above a scattered layer at around 14,000 feet. But there were still too many clouds so we went on down and broke out around 9,000 where Slammer released one bomb with a toss-type maneuver. We came off right, and considering that Slammer had never dropped an LGB in his life and had only had a chalkboard session before we launched, he did a good job. I had to have him ease off on the turn, but I centered the base of the tower in the cross hairs, opened the bomb's eyes, and the bomb hit and took the tower down. It was like dropping a tree.

"Colonel Hornburg [with Maj. Larry "Hammer" Coleman] was number Two and if we missed, we were going to buddy lase for him. What that means is that he would drop the bomb and we would fly in such a pattern that I could use our targeting pod to get his bomb on the target. I would lase the target, electronically open the eyes of his bomb, then it would guide the same way as if we had dropped it.[2] That wasn't necessary, of course, so Hornburg pulled off without dropping.

"The other two-ship was led by [Capts.] Tim Bennett and Dan Bakke. Their DMPI was the bunker and they shacked it with the first bomb. The other four-ship had the same result on the Tallil DMPIs. We went out there that night with sixteen bombs, dropped four, took our four targets, and came home. That was pretty spectacular. We sent our films up to Riyadh and I heard General Glosson was ecstatic."

The rest of the story is predictable. With such spectacular success on difficult-to-hit targets, the Chiefs would spend the rest of the war going against all the targets that required pinpoint accuracy. Right?

Wrong. The whole effort backfired on the Chiefs.

The dictionary defines *backfire* as "a result opposite to that planned or expected." Certainly that is an appropriate way to describe what happened next. "You guys have got the targeting pods," said Riyadh. "You can search with those things at night and you can hit any kind of elusive target. So we've got very important tasking for you. You've got twelve targeting pods, right?[3] Well, we want you to take your squadron out to western Iraq every night in two-ship relays, with each ship equipped with a targeting pod. Using those pods to search the roads and wadis, we want you to find and destroy those darned Scuds. Guys, it's an important mission and we know you'll do a great job out there."

"Oh, no! Not that!"

That was the cry of despair that was heard. But it was a cry lost in the desert winds. For the Chiefs' tasking could now be summed up in two words: Scud patrol.

Scud patrol had several variations, but they were variations around a central concept. A two-ship flight, one airplane with a targeting pod, the other with twelve 500-pound dumb bombs, would

---

[2]Buddy lasing works well except when the target has a vertical structure. If the WSO with the targeting pod puts the laser spot on one side of a vertical structure and the bomb is dropped from the other side, the "eyes" of the bomb might not see the laser spot. In WSO speak, this is called the "podium effect."

[3]Martin-Marietta, the company that makes the targeting pods, had technicians at Al Kharj and the broken pods had been repaired.

launch before dark, fly out to western Saudi and tanker, then head up to the area between H-2 airfield and Sam's Town[4] where they would fly at medium altitude, more or less in a racetrack pattern, with the airplane loaded with dumb bombs dropping one at intervals varying from five, ten, fifteen, or twenty minutes.

That is correct. All one of those airplanes was to do was drop a dumb bomb at whatever time interval the ATO specified; it did not matter where the bomb fell. The idea was somewhat like artillery harassment fire; they were to drop a bomb every now and then so, if anybody down there was thinking of loading and launching a Scud, they would be frightened away from the task. Of course, while patrolling the area, if the WSO with the targeting pod happened to see one of the elusive mobile launchers (the fixed launching sites had been destroyed by this time), then that airplane, equipped with smart bombs, could take it out. Also, if a Scud happened to be launched, in theory at least, the Strike Eagle could swoop down on the launcher and destroy it before it could be towed away and hidden.

Each two-ship flight would have enough fuel for about an hour of Scud patrol. When relieved by another two-ship flight, it would fly south, cross the border, take on fuel from a tanker, then head back north and relieve the other two-ship flight, which would then do the same thing. Theoretically, then, the airplane carrying the dumb bombs could drop one bomb every ten minutes and have enough for two hours of Scud patrol.

That was the general concept, and with a Scud patrol commitment that extended fourteen hours, from one-half hour before sunset until one-half hour after sunrise, the aircrews and one whole squadron of Chiefs airplanes were stretched to their maximum.

When they were unable to fulfill the commitment—when planes and systems broke, and when tankers were not in track or were out of fuel—there would be parts of the night when the Strike Eagles were not on patrol.

One might legitimately ask: So what? Especially since the number of Scuds launched toward Israel dropped dramatically after the Scud patrol started.

What a few folks knew, but what many more were to learn quickly, was that Israel was monitoring western Iraq with powerful radars. Presumably, they were quite content when they saw airplanes orbiting over the area from which Scuds had to be launched to reach them. But have pity for those responsible for Scud patrol in Riyadh when the Israelis did not see airplanes patrolling the launch area. Calls were made and the messages went to those at the highest

---

[4]After Eberly and Griff were shot down, the town of Al Qaim and its immediate environs were called Sam's Town.

levels, who then blasted off words of fire toward Al Kharj. And after that, it was, "Yes, sir! It will not happen again, sir! There will ALWAYS be a patrol over the area, sir!"

So while the Rockets went out on the deep interdiction missions, and generally were doing what the Strike Eagles and their crews were trained to do, the Chiefs, with their smart bombs, were wallowing around in the skies over western Iraq on ho-hum political missions that were about to bore their highly talented, highly trained crews to death.

Part of their problem was their depression, caused by just dumping expensive bombs in the desert. Bored out of their minds, they wanted to get the damned war over. They were there to do a job and they wanted to do it; they wanted to destroy Saddam's military power so they would never have to come back there again. Most certainly they did not want to just dump bombs in the desert; they wanted to dump bombs on something that would hurt Saddam and help end the war.

At this time it should be noted that the intelligence community's performance in providing worthwhile targets and targeting information was one of the major disappointments of the Gulf War—a deficiency that was analyzed and reanalyzed by high-level committees when the war ended. The significance for the Strike Eagles when they went on Scud patrol was that there was a dearth of targeting information for those seeking worthwhile targets in western Iraq. For example, information would come down to them to go hit such and such a target if they had bombs left over. The problem was that that target had been hit for three nights in a row and the crews knew that it had been completely destroyed. Yet, Riyadh was telling them to go hit the target again.

Fortunately for the war effort, the Chiefs had two outstanding intel specialists who, on their own initiative, did something about the problem. First Lieutenant Laura Warn, the officer in charge of intel for the Chiefs, was appalled at the targeting information that was coming from Riyadh. She, with her NCO, Staff Sergeant Lori Helms,[5] took it upon themselves to find worthwhile "dump targets"—targets where the airplane carrying dumb bombs could drop and hit something of military value. For hours and hours the two of them studied satellite photos with their magnifiers looking for military targets that had not yet been identified. And, because Saddam Hussein had such an incredible amount of ordnance stored in

---

[5]S/Sgt Lori Helms was named U.S. Air Force NCO Targeteer of the Year for her outstanding work with the Chiefs and, as this book went to press, her photograph was hanging in the Pentagon.

bunkers throughout the area where the Strike Eagles were patrolling, they were able to locate numerous worthwhile targets. After passing along their recommendations to Riyadh and in turn receiving permission to strike those targets, they then rushed this information to whatever crews happened to be heading out for patrol. Lt. Col. Pat O'Connell, their feisty boss, who was the wing IN, also got into the act. Said O'Connell, "There were times when I, myself, ran out to the jet, climbed the ladder, and handed it [targeting information] to the backseater."

There was still some random dumping of bombs, but more and more often, because of the work of Warn and Helms, the crews were systematically blowing up ordnance bunkers with names like Archie Bunker, Edith Bunker, Meathead, and Gloria.[6] (Credit Helms with the creative names.)

But a new problem was emerging. Many of the crews had flown every night since the war started, and some of them had flown brutally demanding double missions, landing after eight or nine hours of tense flying. On the ground, after their missions, they were often hyper because of the adrenaline still in their systems. Some adapted to the new regimen of daytime sleeping better than others, but they were probably a minority. Most of the crewmen fought the sleep battle every day. At first, with a scarf wrapped around their eyes, earplugs in their ears, and a no-go pill in their systems, they were able to sleep, albeit fitfully. But then, as flight surgeon Jack Ingari put it, "Their bodies began crying out for sunshine—for lazing around during the daytime and doing nothing but maybe tossing a frisbee." But that was not to be for many of them. There were more missions than crews throughout the war. And also, to be fair to the commanders, many of the crews did not want a night off. They wanted to fly. They wanted to stay busy so their minds would be occupied. They did not want to have a whole day to think of their wives and children at home. It was too depressing. The war was on. They wanted to get on with it and get it over.

But even with the hard drivers—those who did not want time off—there were problems. Jack Ingari saw it when a crewman would come to him, gaunt, with dark circles under the eyes, complaining that he could not sleep even after taking a no-go pill. "They trusted me," said Ingari. "They knew I wouldn't ground them unless they were a poten-

---

[6]One of the Chiefs who reviewed what the author said about Warn and Helms added the following comment. Said Capt. James "Chainsaw" McCullough, "Yeah, they spent hours and hours looking for targets, but they also spent hours and hours looking for threats such as mobile SAMs, and, because of them, we knew when we launched that we had the best information on threats that was available."

tial hazard to themselves or their wingmen. So I just talked to them and usually they would admit that, yes, they, themselves, should request to get off the flying schedule. I knew a little bit of what they were going through because I deliberately set my hours to coincide with theirs. I know that at the end of thirty days of working nights and trying to sleep in the daytime, I was almost incoherent."

The flight surgeon was monitoring them and so were the senior officers in the squadron, but despite that, dangerous problems were lurking. After being sworn to secrecy, the author listened as a crewman of a two-ship flight confessed that after crossing the border into Saudi after a long mission, all four of them went sound asleep in their airplanes. One knew that he "conked out" for about forty-five minutes and, later, after talking with the others, he thought they were out about that long, too. Luckily, they were flying on autopilot and over a mile apart. But the potential was there for a needless disaster.

Help was clearly needed. The Chiefs were wearing down.

12

Strike Eagles to the Rescue

"It was the most rewarding mission I've ever been on. We got to save someone's life rather than taking it."

Capt. Joe Justice

"After eight or ten days of doing nothing but flying Scud patrol, our guys were pretty well beat." So said Slammer Decuir, the Chiefs' operations officer, after the war. "When Steep Turner started talking to Steve Pingel about some of the Rocket guys getting checked out with the targeting pods, I'm sure Pingel was very agreeable."

Thus, the targeting-pod monopoly ended. After Turner and Pingel had their little chat, the targeting pods, which now numbered about sixteen—there were no more anywhere in the United States and the factory was sending them as fast as they could be produced—were split between the squadrons. "We just saw them putting them on our planes," said Two Dogs McIntyre, the Rockets' seeing-eye WSO.[1] "That's how I first learned we were going into the LGB business."

---

[1]*Seeing-eye WSO* is strictly a term used by captains and majors, for this is a mature, highly experienced WSO whom squadron schedulers send out to fly in the pit with colonels and generals who, because of tradition, are expected to fly sorties whenever they have an operational command. The seeing-eye WSO's responsibility is to keep the senior officer out of trouble. The term is not meant derisively; it is just a fact that senior commanders, because of the burden of their nonflying responsibilities, usually cannot keep their flying skills as sharp as those of the "kids" who are flying every day.

137

That's also how the Rockets had gotten themselves into the Scud patrol business—although, to be accurate, some of the Rockets had been augmenting the Chiefs from time to time, but carrying dumb bombs. Now, some of the Rockets received a formal checkout on the use of the targeting pod. Said Yogi Alred, "One day Slammer and Taco took Steep and Bones [Capt. Mark Wetzel], Polo [Bill Polowitzer], and me, and two other IPs with their WSOs on a four-ship checkout ride. We flew about seventy miles south of Al Kharj and did a simulated attack on an oil well, then flew back and practiced on the hospital and some of the other installations at Al Kharj. And that was it. From that day on, we were considered qualified to carry LGBs."

Two Dogs McIntyre chuckles when Yogi relates that story. Said Two Dogs, "One night Moon Mullins and I were tasked for Scud patrol and it was, oh, by the way, you'll be carrying LGBs tonight. So we get in the airplane and on the way out to the tanker track, I play with the thing [targeting pod]. Moon and I are still playing with it [the pilot can call up the targeting pod image on one of his MPDs] when we get this call from AWACS. 'A Scud has been launched at coordinates such and such!' We've already seen it, of course. It's a huge flame and your first reaction is that it's a SAM and you want to make a defensive reaction. Then you see that it is going straight up. So AWACS is yelling and hollering for us to get on it and we're heading for the coordinates as fast as we could go [in mil power]. It was about twenty-five miles away from us but when we got there, we went up and down the road and all I could find in the targeting pod was a hot spot on the ground. It was no longer than five minutes after the launch when we found the hot spot. Those guys were fast. They were just like cockroaches that disappear when the kitchen light goes on.

"Anyhow, that was our checkout with the targeting pod. It's kind of humorous because back at Seymour they have this heavy-duty, formal, four-ride checkout program. But really, it's a tribute to the design of this airplane—it is so easy to do everything in it."

When the Rockets assumed a share of the Scud patrol work, the time on station was being mandated in their ATO; they would remain over the Scud launching area for one hour and fifteen minutes. The time interval between bomb dropping was still varying; some nights it was ten minutes, some nights it was twenty minutes, and, according to one crew, they were sometimes dropping at thirty-minute intervals. Finding and dropping on legitimate dump targets was still a problem. However, Sgt. Jim Zema, the Rockets' NCO intel specialist, made a mighty effort to locate better targets than were coming out of Riyadh. Capt. Jeff Latas describes one of them: "My favorite dump target was a huge ammo storage area that we called

'Z-man,' because it was a target that Sergeant Zema found for us. It was a great dump target because after this long, boring patrol, we could go over there, drop a couple of dumb bombs, and stuff would start blowing up like big volcanoes. We went back there for about a week straight. We got so we would do a lap [around the Scud patrol course] then drop a couple of bombs, then go do another lap. It broke the monotony and I'll admit it; it was fun."

Knowing there were good dump targets to bomb greatly improved the morale of the Scud hunters as they roamed the night skies over western Iraq. But that was just the start of the good times. Soon they began to receive blind radio calls that led them to glory.

"Any allied aircraft, any allied aircraft, this is Torch One One."

They were soon to hear such calls on their Guard channel; however, during their postwar telling of all this, they would be careful to repronounce "aircraft" for the author. It was "aircroft," pronounced in their best imitation of the British accent. "They were the bloody SAS, mites [mates]; the British snake eaters."

There would be smiles and laughter after this bit of theater, particularly if two or three of the crewmen happened to be together when they related their stories. But then they would get serious and they would tell how much they admired the "Brits," whom they described as being incredibly cool, brave, and resourceful while operating right under the noses of the enemy. Then they went on to describe some of their own best missions.

What they described were their experiences supporting the British Special Air Service (SAS). Before the war, the commander of British forces, Lt. Gen. Peter de la Billiere, a former SAS commander and Britain's most decorated officer, talked General Schwarzkopf into allowing teams of these elite special forces troops to operate in western Iraq. Their purpose was to gather intelligence, make hit-and-run raids on transport and communication assets, and to seek and destroy mobile Scud launchers. Their deployment was top secret because they operated in enemy territory.

But then the Scuds starting hitting Israel and the leaders in Riyadh saw their tenuous Coalition in danger of breaking apart. Said de la Billiere in his memoirs of the war,

> We had quickly found that the Coalition air forces could not deal with mobile Scuds as easily as they had supposed: bad weather was one factor in the enemy's favour, but it also became apparent that the Iraqis were most skilful at concealing launchers. To a pilot flying at ten thousand feet, a missile in its horizontal, travelling attitude looked just like an oil tanker and, if it was parked under a motorway bridge, a favourite hiding place, it could not be seen at all by satellites or surveillance aircraft; yet it could be run out, set up and launched in only twenty min-

utes. Then, even if surveillance satellites pin-pointed its position from
the heat of a launch, its erector-trailer would have disappeared again by
the time an aircraft could be directed on to the spot.

So, from information-gathering, deception and offensive action in
general, we hastily switched the SAS's aim, as Norman [Schwarzkopf]
put it, to 'Scuds, Scuds and Scuds again', so vitally important did it
seem to close down the attacks on Israel. (Peter de la Billiere, *Storm*
Command: A Personal Account of the Gulf War, Harper Collins,
1992)

Some of the SAS teams were inserted by American helicopters
and left to roam the rugged Scud-launching area on foot. Others—it
was the option of each team leader—drove into Iraq in specially
modified Land Rovers and motorcycles. Each option had its trade-
offs. Those on foot were better able to conceal themselves from the
enemy, whereas those with vehicles risked being seen for the advantage of greater mobility.

At first the Strike Eagle crews did not know anything about the
"snake-eaters" being out in western Iraq. Then, one night while on
Scud patrol, Captains Mark Mouw and Radar O'Reilly heard a
transmission on Guard channel, "Any allied aircraft, any allied aircraft." They responded, and were vectored to a mobile Scud launcher, which they bombed. Then they came home and reported to their
ops officer, Slammer Decuir. "We were pissed off when we heard
about it," said Slammer. "We're out there dumping bombs at random; we could have killed some of those guys. I immediately called
Riyadh. I said, 'We know you guys have snake-eaters out there, but
you better let us know where they are or some of them are going to
get killed.' The next morning the SAS sent two guys to Al Kharj and
we told them we needed a way to communicate other than on
Guard, and that we needed to know where they were operating so
we wouldn't drop on them. They went back to Riyadh and two or
three days later authentication procedures and no-drop zones started coming out in the frag."

Then the Strike Eagles began hearing a lot of radio calls from the
ground, "Any allied aircraft, any allied aircraft . . . " and, after going
through an authentication procedure, they began to respond to a
variety of needs by the SAS teams. "We think we have been discovered. There are trucks coming toward us, could you come down and
put a bomb or two on them, please?" This was a typical request, and
it brought the Strike Eagles screaming down out of the night to do
what they could to protect their brothers in arms. And typically, if a
bomb was dropped, they heard the laconic, good-natured voice of
the Brit saying, "Jolly good bomb, you got one of the trucks; but how
about another one for the next truck, mate?"

What started as impromptu teamwork between the SAS and Strike Eagles soon evolved into more formalized procedures. As word reached Riyadh of the increasing ground-air cooperation, SAS teams were asked to radio their needs directly to Riyadh, which, in turn, would pass them on to AWACS so that airborne assets could be better coordinated. Capt. Darryl Roberson describes one of the AWACS-directed missions.

Said Roberson, "Our two-ship had just come off the tanker and as soon as I reported to AWACS, I hear over the radio, 'OBD,[2] push it up.' That was over the radio from AWACS. I am thinking, who in the world knows that I am out here flying, much less calling me by nickname? I didn't recognize the voice. But I push it up. As we start to cross the Iraqi border, I go burner to get up to speed, then kick it back to mil power to sustain it.

"As we are pressing into Iraq, they come, 'Packard Four-Three, this is Hammer [airborne commander] on AWACS; I have a special mission for you: Stand by words.' That is their way of saying, 'Hey, there is more to follow; get ready to copy.' My backseater [Capt. Baxter Sosebee] is getting ready to write all this stuff down—he does that while I fly the airplane.

"They start giving us coordinates and they say, 'We have some special forces that suspect the enemy approaching.' They give us the frequency to use to talk to those guys, then we put the coordinates in the INS and boom, we are hauling butt to try to get up there to get to them. But we were three hundred miles away. It was out in the middle of the desert area between H-2 and Al Muhammadi airfield. The word that we got was that these guys were waiting to be picked up by an American Special Forces helicopter but in the meantime they suspect they have been sighted and that the enemy is coming to get them.

"We get out there and call them on the radio. They are very quiet, and we have no idea of what is going on, but they are talking in very low voices and only every once in awhile. I am talking a lot to get more information, but it is obvious they don't want to talk that much because it might give their position away. Finally, I figured that out after a few tries and decided we had the minimum information we needed. If they needed something more, they would let us know.

"We set up an orbit over these guys, then we get a call from the guy on the ground, 'Hey, we've got a vehicle approaching from the southeast, headlights on; we'd like you to investigate.' I leave number two orbiting high and I drop down to low altitude and make a high-speed pass over the coordinates on a southeasterly heading to

---

[2]From television's "other brother Darryl."

try and find the vehicle. We are down to 3,000 feet—we're not worried about triple-A because we're out in the middle of the desert—and we see a vehicle in our FLIR, and it has its lights on. We confirm with our heat sensors that it is only one vehicle and I doubted that it was the enemy; they were not likely to be driving around with their lights on. I tell the guy that it is only one vehicle but to stand by. But it drove right by them and never stopped—so that situation was taken care of.

"We go back up in orbit and about fifteen minutes later, we get another call that says, 'We suspect personnel approaching from the northeast of our position.' I drop down again and make a pass to try to see these people. I made two low-altitude, high-speed passes and never saw anything. I told them there was no concentration of vehicles or personnel that we could see, then went back up to the orbit.

"We orbit for fifteen more minutes and we are starting to get fuel critical; we need to go back and get some gas. Just as I am telling AWACS that I have to go back to the tanker, the same person who said, 'OBD, push it up,' comes on and says, 'Hey, OBD, I'm bringing the tanker north to meet you closer to the border.' Then he starts vectoring the tanker.

"By this time I figure out who it is; an old buddy of mine from my Wild Weasel days, call-sign Juice—he was my weapons chief when I was in Germany. He must have had a list of the crews and recognized my voice. Anyhow, Juice says the guys on the ground have an immediate problem. There is a mobile command post with a radio antenna sticking out the top of it and they were afraid that when the helicopters come in to pick up the guys, the Iraqis would relay this information. Juice gave me the coordinates and this time I bring my wingman down [Capt. Bill Schaal and Maj. Jerry Oney] with me in case I don't see it right away. I tell AWACS what we're going to do—that we'll drop some bombs on the target but then we are going to press to the tanker. He acknowledges. I am getting real close on fuel right now.

"We drop down to the coordinates and sure enough there is a heat source and I can see it in the FLIR. I tell my wingman, 'Okay, I've got the target; I'm going to drop six of my bombs—half of my bombs—and I don't want you to drop any. Number Two, retain your weapons and then we'll go to the tanker.'

"This time we got a little triple-A—they must have heard us coming. But we dropped six Mark-82s and took out the target—number Two was well behind me and he saw all this. Then we climbed back up to altitude and pressed for the tanker, which had come up to the border of Iraq. It was a good thing; Juice had excellent SA of what was required and I mean, no kidding, the timing was perfect. We got on the boom, then headed back up there.

"In the meantime another two-ship had been vectored to the special forces guys and as we get back up there, they drop down to fly right over the helicopters who are now picking these guys up. So they got out with no casualties and no problems. Later, after the war, I talked to Juice and he said the guys on the ground called and relayed that we had saved them—that the Iraqis had not dared advance on them with fighters around. We were pleased. We were helping people and, personally, this was my best mission; it's what I would like to have done on every mission."

The SAS teams were doing good work, but the full results of their action was not being relayed to Riyadh; this information would come later. In the meantime, the American Special Operations Forces commander, General Wayne Downing, flew into Riyadh and was briefed by the SAS on what they had learned in their first days of operating in enemy territory. "Downing was quick to learn from our successes and failures," said British commander de la Billiere. "He applied the lessons we had learnt to the deployment of his own troops and the result was a first-class example of cooperation between British and American forces."

The pressure was mounting to stop the Scud launches and soon American Special Forces teams were inserted into western Iraq to augment the SAS. However, so as not to conflict with the SAS teams, the Americans operated north of the main highway connecting Baghdad and Amman, Jordan—an area called "Scud Boulevard" —while the SAS stayed south of the highway in what was called "Scud Alley."

The American teams went right to work, but soon they, too, were calling for help. Captains John Norbeck and Keith "Spitter" Johnson happened to be in one of the first Strike Eagles that would dash to their rescue. John Norbeck relates this story:

"We were Firebird Four-One and [Captains] Rob Shores and Bill Millonig were Firebird Four-Two. We didn't have a targeting pod this night—just twelve Mark-82 dumb bombs—and we weren't happy about that; we had been spoiled with the LGBs and were used to getting instant feedback on the things we were hitting. Number Two airplane was carrying gator,[3] which they were going to dump on a Scud launching area to deny its use. As it turned out, they were never to drop this ordnance because we got new tasking.

"We were just coming on to our Scud patrol when we heard the previous two-ship of Rockets talking to AWACS, saying, 'Hey, send the next guys in here; there are some of our people on the ground—

---

[3]Canisters with tiny bomblets that are set off by vibrations or time fuzing; used to seed an area to prevent access, or to surround a friendly outpost to protect it from being overrun.

call sign Papa One-One—who are being chased by Iraqis and need some help.' The Rocket two-ship was out of gas and not able to help them, so we said to AWACS, 'Hey, we're on our way in, ready to go.' AWACS gives us the freq for Papa One-One and we get in there and start talking to him. He said there was a group of Iraqi vehicles chasing them. We authenticate him, then he gives us their coordinates and Spitter does a map. We see what looks like seven vehicles right where Papa One-One says they should be. We tell him they are north of the road and he confirms that and says he is on the other side of the road. So that was our target; if there hadn't been a road, it would have been hard to confirm it because Papa One-One was pretty close.

"He asks us to bomb the vehicles, so we make another map, designate the first vehicle, then get down lower because we don't want to miss. We drop one bomb, but we don't get any feedback because Papa One-One is on the move. He said, 'Yeah, we're moving and I'll get back to you.'

"We pull off—we can't tell anything because it is so dark—and we go out to make our next mapping leg. Spitter makes the map and sure enough, he can see that one of the seven had been destroyed. Then Papa One-One set up station and started being a FAC [forward air controller] for us. He called us in and we made six or seven passes, and each time he would call out, 'Yeah, good strike.'

"Spitter saved the biggest vehicle for the last, and later we found out that it was a mobile Scud. He yelled as we pulled off, 'Did you see the secondaries?' but I wasn't looking. Papa One-One was real happy and as we left, he got real talkative and told us he was an air force ALO [Air Liaison Officer] with a special forces unit.

"The next day Spitter shows up in the squadron first and [Lt.] Colonel Pingel says, 'Spitter, where is Norbs? And what did you guys do last night? Some general called and said a special forces guy called him up and said you guys did a shit hot job last night.'

"Spitter and I were proud of that. It was our most satisfying mission."

A lot of the Strike Eagle crews were now helping the special force teams in western Iraq, and when the author interviewed them, they invariably spoke of those missions as being the most satisfying they flew in the war. However, two of the crewmen—Captains Tim "TB" Bennett and Dan "Chewie" Bakke—were to relate a tale that was more than satisfying; it was the story of a mission that earned them a place in U.S. Air Force history. They were together when they described it for the author.

Bennett: "It was February 13, approximately 0200 and we were on a Scud CAP mission into western Iraq. We were Packard Four-One and leading the two-ship element. Capt. Greg Johnson and Lt.

Karl Von Luhrte were on our wing; they were Packard Four-Two. We had been on station about forty-five minutes when AWACS gave us a call. They said there were some 'troops in contact' and they gave us coordinates where there were some Iraqi helicopters threatening our guys. AWACS couldn't see up there, but what they heard was a burst transmission—an HF [high frequency] transmission—from the guys on the ground saying that they had been discovered."

Bakke: When they called we were in the process of hitting an SA-3 site near Al Qaim. We were mapping the site and starting our attack when AWACS called us with 'priority targeting.' We broke off the attack and sent our wingman to high cover—they had twelve Mark-82s and we had the targeting pod with four GBU-10s [2,000-pound smart bombs]. I plug in the coordinates AWACS gives us and they are in the middle of a no-drop zone—I read that as a zone where special forces are operating. I confirm with AWACS that these coordinates are correct and they are in a no-drop zone. She came back and said, 'Roger, those are the correct coordinates.'"

Bennett: "Her call sign was Cougar."

Bakke: "Yeah, so I continued the conversation with her—this isn't verbatim but close—she said, 'There are three Iraqi helicopters dismounting troops with possible friendlies in contact. Kill all helicopters.'[4] I reconfirmed with her, 'Kill all helicopters?' She came back and said, 'Roger, kill all helicopters.'"

Bennett: "The reason Dan is repeating that is because it is real uncommon to get an order to kill [all helicopters]. You never hear anything like that because you always ID them."

Bakke: "At that point, TB is starting to the coordinates and we aren't saying anything back and forth."

Bennett: "I am talking to my wingman real quick because we were getting into a lot of weather. Since he had dumb bombs there was no reason to bring him down there with us. I wanted him to stay above the weather. Also, once we got below 10,000 feet we couldn't always talk to AWACS. I am telling him to relay whatever we say back to Cougar and we'll let him know what is going on. By now we are dropping down through the weather at mil power. We're moving pretty good when we get down below the weather. There was no doubt in our minds from the radio transmission from AWACS that we had to get there in a hurry. Normally, we would be a little cautious because we were going into the Sam's Town area, but we're in a hurry. If they were in contact up there, time was of the essence.

---

[4]"Kill" is a directive to commit on target with clearance to fire—with no identification required.

There was a lot of stuff up there that wasn't good, but we're ramping over there in mil power going about 600 knots. Then, when we're about fifty miles out, Dan gets contacts on the radar."

Bakke: "On two of the three [helicopters]."

Bennett: "We talked real quick, back and forth, and it was like, well, let's just let a bomb go if we can ID them as helicopters."

Bakke: "I called AWACS and I reconfirmed with them that we have the helicopters. Actually, what we have on radar contact is their rotor spinning."

Bennett: "We aren't getting an air speed readout yet on them. We are pretty sure they are sitting on the ground. [Their IR image is two-dimensional.] We said, 'Okay, let's go in there.' If he [Bakke] can get them on the targeting pod, we'll let a bomb go. That way, if they take off and move, at least we will get their attention and divert it from our guys on the ground. But, if they start moving, we'll come back and shoot them with an AIM-9. Our main goal was to get something on them fast, to let them know we are there. At this time Dan is working with the radar and about the time we are deciding that we are going to drop a bomb, we are going through 10,000 feet. Finally, we break out of the weather at about 3,000 feet—it was not good weather that night. Just as soon as we break out, the triple-A starts coming up. We're about twenty miles from the contacts and then, at around fifteen miles, Dan's got them in the targeting pod."

Bakke: "We didn't make a map; you can cue the targeting pod from the air-to-air radar. You can get a designation just using the pod. I'm looking solely through the pod now. It's infrared and the helicopters are hot and the rotors look like discs. I have two of the three and we're assuming they are on the ground. At this point, we can still hear AWACS talking but it is broken—we're expecting our wingman to pass on anything important. We go in, get a release cue, TB drops a long ball [bomb] and starts a left-hand turn so that I can track the target."

Bennett: "I'm turning toward Syria [hands showing the banked turn]."

Bakke: "I'm doing the laser, putting it on the white spot, waiting. We released the bomb about six miles away and it has over thirty seconds time of flight."

Bennett: "Meanwhile, I'm looking at the radar because he is concentrating [on the image in the pod]. About ten seconds after the bomb comes off, I start seeing an air speed readout on the radar. I'm thinking, this thing is moving; go back into air-to-air and bring up an AIM-9. Meanwhile, Dan is tracking it big time, but I'm thinking, shit, this bomb is never going to make it. I'm starting to jink around—they're firing some triple A—but I can't jink too much—it's hard enough back there keeping the laser on the spot without me giving him any more problems."

Bakke: We jink off to the left and it appears to me that this guy is moving. What in fact happened, according to the guys on the ground, is that the helicopter was at 800 to 1,000 feet when the bomb impacted. It hit just forward of the center of the rotors, right in the cockpit. And I guess, if you've ever seen a James Bond movie where the helicopter—the model they film—just vaporizes and disappears, that is exactly what happened. At this point, we have already figured out that this guy was airborne so TB goes into a hard left-hand turn and calls up an AIM-9. Also, we tell our wingman to come down and drop six Mark-82s on that spot to stop any troops that have been let off."

Bennett: "I called him in because he could see the fireball through his FLIR and there was no danger of hitting our guys. Also, I wanted to keep the Iraqis' heads down until we could get back in and make another pass."

Bakke: "Right at this point, TB and I are ecstatic, although we haven't said anything to each other. [As soon as we get enough altitude] I get on the radio to AWACS and I say, 'Cougar, Packard Four-One, splash one helicopter. Engaging second [with air-to-air ordnance].' Shortly thereafter we get a call from AWACS asking us to confirm that we had ID'd this helicopter as Iraqi. Now there is no doubt in your mind, when AWACS tells you to kill something, they have basically taken away all your responsibility for identification of that aerospace vehicle. However, in our case, whatever levity was in the airplane dissipated immediately. Our spirits went right through the floorboard of that airplane. And I'll tell you, as soon as she said, 'Confirm you ID'd that that helicopter is Iraqi,' I went through the roof. I told her to get off the scope and get us Hammer, who is the person on AWACS with commit authority.

"While I am talking to AWACS, TB is trying to maneuver behind these guys for the AIM-9. I mean, we have a single [helicopter] running northeast and we are just doing circles down the middle of the entire threat area trying to get confirmation on whether we should engage these guys. As it turns out, we push them as far north as we can for the known threats in the area. For our own safety and for lack of fuel, we turn around. And we don't have any friendly words for the AWACS controller at that point. There was silence in the cockpit."

Bennett: "Hammer did get on the horn eventually. The first thing we thought, since we probably had helicopters operating out of Syria, was that we might have hit one of our own that had come over from there. However, the one we got looked like a Hind

[Russian-made helicopter] to me and to Dan, too. But as soon as she asked if we had ID'd it as Iraqi, all that confidence went right out the window.

"Then Hammer gets on and says, 'Yeah, you are okay.' But when I came back around again, they put that same idiot controller back on and I'm running around in the clouds, right over triple-A alley, and I'm saying 'What are we doing?' Hammer gets on again and says, 'You are good to go on those guys,' so we ran back to the north hoping to get the one [helicopter] heading toward Sam's Town."

Bakke: "I never did see the third one. We saw it on radar, but not in the FLIR."

Bennett: "I think the third one sat down somewhere, but we could see this guy running toward Sam's Town on radar and we're going after him when all of a sudden, I see flashes. I think, oh, shit, I've drug us right into a SAM launch. Then I realized that those weren't SAM launches, those are bombs. That AWACS controller had vectored another flight in even though we had told Hammer that we were going down to get this last guy. She had vectored another flight in from another squadron on a different freq and told them to drop on coordinates. We had twenty-four Mark-82s raining down on us. They had no way of knowing we were down there—she didn't tell them.

"After that, I'm thinking we have exhausted about all of our lives tonight so I said, 'Let's get out of here.' We beat it, no kidding, all the way home."

Bakke: "As soon as we got back, I called the special forces liaison up at TACC and talked with him and tried to get confirmation from him that their guys were safe. About six hours later we got a phone call from TACC saying that their guys were safe and they had witnessed the explosion [of the helicopter]. Then, after the war, I was on a briefing team that went to CENTAF, then to the Pentagon, and then to the White House. One of the guys on the briefing team, Warrant Officer Cliff Wolcott,[5] was a U.S. Special Forces helicopter pilot and had been out there hiding that night. He witnessed the whole thing. As it turned out, these were the guys who had originally called in for help. From what he said, I'm convinced that we, in fact, saved some casualties, if not some lives out there that night."

Tim Bennett and Dan Bakke went on after this mission to prevent more casualties among the SAS and U.S. Special Forces. But so did Abbe Reese and Brad Freels, and Stoney Sloan and Joe Justice, and Slammer Decuir and Taco Martinez, and Ken Garrison and Brian

---

[5]Warrant Officer Wolcott was killed in October 1993, flying a Blackhawk in Somalia during a Special Forces operation.

Allen, and Scotty Scott and Larry Bowers, and Skippy Shipman and Rick Henson, as well as several others who did not have the time to share all their stories with the author.

But it is Tim Bennett and Dan Bakke who will go down in U.S. Air Force history, for they did something that had never been done before. They got an air-to-air kill with a bomb that was guided to the target. Quite a feat, that. And certainly enough of an accomplishment for the likes of Raoul Lufbery, Billy Bishop, and the Red Baron—wherever they are—to have drunk a toast to these two intrepid airmen.

13

Kill Saddam

"No threat was too great; I would have gone anywhere, flown through any threat, for the opportunity to put iron on his head."

Unidentified pilot.

"Oh, no! We wouldn't do anything like that."

This is how, in one form or another, high U.S. officials have denied that there was ever any direct effort to kill Saddam Hussein during the Gulf War. However, those who did the fighting over there just shake their heads in wonderment that their country's leaders would say such a thing. After all, Saddam Hussein was not just the political head of Iraq; he was the supreme military commander who controlled every aspect of Iraq's armed forces machinery. He was the generalissimo, and as such the most important and most legitimate of all the military targets. At least, that is how the fighting men and women looked at the matter.

The fighting crewmen who flew the Strike Eagles were even more dismayed at such pious pronouncements from their leaders. They were dismayed because they had gone out on missions where the specific purpose was to kill Saddam Hussein. Of course, these crewmen are not naive. Through their dismay they understand that after the war there had to be a certain amount of covering up—diplomatic gobbledygook. They really did not expect their leaders to stand up before the world's press and say, "Yeah, you're right; we certainly did try to kill that son-of-a-bitch." However, unlike their political leaders and the career diplomats who advise them, those in the military are governed by an honor code, of which "thou shall not lie" is one of the commandments. Therefore, at the risk of censure from their superiors, but with apparent trust in the way the author would use the information, they admitted, when asked, "Hell yes, we tried to kill him. There were three missions that I know of where the guys were tasked specifically for that purpose."

Then, those who participated in those missions freely recounted the details, proud that they were among the elite selected for the job, but disappointed because their shifty-eyed target did not end up under their bombs. However, getting these crewmen to narrate their stories was the easy part. What was difficult was determining how to put their stories into print without jeopardizing their careers and, more important (because most were not worried about their careers), to avoid exposing them to potential fanatics who might murder the infidels who had tried to kill their leader. For the same reason, the names of those who flew on the Libya raid in 1986 have still not been released. Thus, it was decided to let those who participated in missions to kill Saddam Hussein be nameless FIDOs, commanders, pilots, and WSOs.

"That would be appreciated," said the crewmen when they were later consulted on the decision. "Especially by our families," they added.

"I'll gladly accept that tradeoff," said one of the crewmen, unbothered about being destined to anonymity. "Just tell the story," he said.

Here is the story.

It was during the early morning hours of January 23 when one of the Strike Eagle FIDOs in Riyadh had a senior officer come to his desk. "He never did come right out and use the name 'Saddam,' but he came to me with a pop-up mission of the highest priority. 'At these coordinates,' he said, 'there is an individual of extreme military importance whose demise, if we can bring it about, could suddenly end the war.' Those were not his exact words—I'm making some of this up—but he left no doubt in my mind that it was Saddam Hussein he was talking about and he wanted Strike Eagles in the air now! I immediately got on the phone to Al Kharj and gave the tasking information to one of the senior officers there—trying to let him know the importance of the mission without using Saddam's name. Shortly afterward, I got a call from a more senior officer at Al Kharj. 'How the hell am I supposed to do this? All of my best crews are out flying now. And besides, you're sending us into an area almost as heavily defended as Baghdad, but with no time to plan. You're sending us on a suicide mission.' He was angry with me, and I can't blame him. The coordinates were near Kuwait City, a very high-threat area. But I tried to stay calm. I said, 'Sir, I'm just the messenger.' I think he wanted to shoot the messenger."

At Al Kharj, one of the commanders was taxiing in from a 4.6-

hour Scud patrol mission. He was beat, mentally and physically. He had had little sleep during the previous days and nights and now, after this Scud patrol, with his eyes red, his face creased by the imprint of his oxygen mask, and his body crying for sleep, he reported to the squadron tent and got the news.

Said the commander, "I just got in the tent and the ops officer was waiting for me. He said, 'Hey, they want us to go into downtown Kuwait City and they want us there now.' They wanted us to take an eight-ship package into an area with every kind of threat, without any real planning, and I knew that we would get the shit shot out of us. It didn't pass the commonsense test. I started talking to some of the crews as they came in; I wanted my most experienced guys, but I made it strictly voluntary. They all wanted to go but one pilot came up to me and questioned whether he was physically able to do it. I took one look at him and saw that he was out of it. That's when I decided that I should lead the flight. I sent my WSO in to start planning."

One of the pilots who walked in about that time said, "When I heard what was going on, my blood started pumping, the adrenaline started flowing, and I started getting excited. After a boring Scud patrol, as tired as I was, I was ready to go. This is the kind of mission we trained for; this is what we wanted to be doing in this war. Sure, it was a high-threat mission—the leader told us after it was over that he expected to lose at least two airplanes. But we knew that going in. We knew it was going to be tough. But look what would have happened if we had been successful."

Lead gathered his crews; then, as they were about to step to their airplanes, they received a call from Riyadh. The coordinates had been changed. Instead of being south of Kuwait City, the target was now in the north part of the city. Also, the senior officer in Riyadh was possibly going to send in F-111s and B-52s and he didn't want an eight-ship flight of Strike Eagles. Four would be enough.

The leader picked three crews to fly with him, relegating two crews as spares—one to take off and go part way with them, the other to remain in the chocks in case there was a ground abort.

Then they went to their airplanes. However, before the leader could start engines, he received a call on squadron common, the frequency used in two-way communications between the squadron ops desk and their aircraft. "They've changed the coordinates again," the voice said. "Are you ready to copy?"

The leader's wingman picks up the story. "We did what little planning we could for the first coordinates they gave us; then, when they gave us the second coordinates, we didn't have time to check the maps and study the threats in the area. But we decided, 'Well, this is just the way it is; we'll press in there and do the best we can.' But then, when we get in our airplanes and are ready to crank, here comes the message that they're changing the coordinates again. They wanted to be real discreet on the radio. They said, 'We are going to give you three points and we want you to plot these on the map and triangulate. The middle is going to be your target.' I mean, here we are, out in the middle of Saudi, five hundred miles from Iraq, and they didn't want to say the coordinates over the radio—as though someone could intercept that transmission, write all that stuff down, and then call back up to Iraq and warn this guy before we could get there. Well, Lead feels the same way. He gets on the radio and says, 'Give me a break; give me the coordinates.' The guy reluctantly reads them off. Then Lead goes, 'What is it?' The guy comes back—you can tell he doesn't want to say this stuff on the radio—he says, 'It's a railyard.' Lead goes, 'We are after a railyard!'[1] He comes back, 'Well, you know, it's a bunker in the middle of a railyard.' That's the stuff you would like to know if you're going out to bomb it."

Five airplanes took off, and the pilot in the sixth plane, sitting on the ground, was miserable. "I was just about to beat my fists on the panel I was so frustrated," he said. "I wanted to go on that mission!"

The crewmen flying in airplane number Five were also frustrated because it appeared that all four airplanes ahead of them were good to go. Then they got the word from Lead. Go back home. You are not needed.

On the way out of Saudi, Lead's WSO plotted course and determined that the best routing would be to fly out over the Persian Gulf at Khafji, just south of Kuwait, then fly over the water toward Basrah. The railyard and bunker that they were going to strike was just northwest of Basrah, and the "feet wet" ingress route would keep them away from the threats along the shoreline of Kuwait.

They were carrying twelve CBU-87 bombs—canisters full of bomblets—and because they could not safely drop all twelve with their three auxiliary fuel tanks, they agreed to run those dry, then jettison them over the water on the way to the target. But it didn't work out that way.

"I am waiting to burn all my gas," said Lead's wingman, "and Lead starts pulling away from me. He's said to himself, 'I don't need all this gas,' so he has jettisoned his three tanks. I'm still trying to catch him, but by the time he goes into Iraq, I'm ten miles behind.

---

[1]The wingman's WSO remembers Lead asking at this time: "Are we to take it that Saddam is a hobo these days?"

When he gets near Basrah, the triple-A opens up—this is big stuff, 110mm, and it's coming higher than the airplane. They heard Lead coming, now they've got time to start shooting at me. I start climbing higher and higher to get over the stuff, then I have to go into afterburner. My backseater is going, 'Cut out that afterburner; they are going to see us.' I am saying that I can't; if I cut out the afterburner we have to go down [lower]."

Meanwhile, the crewmen in number Four are having problems. Their internal countermeasures system has malfunctioned and, after talking it over among themselves, they made a decision they would later regret. Said the WSO, "I said, 'We have to let Lead know,' so reluctantly my frontseater called him. 'You say your ICS system is out,' Lead says. We go, 'Affirmative.' Lead doesn't hesitate. 'Go home,' he says. We could have gone on in without telling him, but with the threat up there, it would have been foolish. Still, to this day, I feel guilty not going on in."

They had originally tasked eight airplanes for the mission. Now they were down to three. The pilot of number three continues the story.

"After Lead sent number Four home, I reached down to jettison and my centerline tank doesn't come off. I've got the extra drag now and the other two are pulling away from me—we're twelve to thirteen miles behind when the stuff starts coming up at us around Basrah—big stuff. Then we see a big flash out ahead and in the HUD it looks like spiders floating around. It's the B-52s going in in front of us and they dropped a whole load of stuff. A few missiles are coming up at us along with the triple-A but they don't appear to be guiding. We get toward the target and see the flash of Lead and Two's bombs—there is an undercast below us, but the light of the bombs comes through. We're high now, about 30,000, and our plan is to go in at that altitude, roll in at a 30-degree dive, recover at 20,000 and leave. But by the time we roll in it's ugly. All kinds of triple-A is coming up to 25,000 and some of the big shells are exploding at 30,000 to 35,000. We're watching stuff flying by the airplane, then a missile or two go screaming through the sky. But we get our bombs off, make a real hard right turn toward Iran, then head down the waterway. My backseater then checks the TSD [moving map] and we are actually over Iran. We turn back west and pick up the other two airplanes twenty to thirty miles ahead of us.

"Then, simultaneously, all three of us see an SA-2 being fired out of Kuwait City. Lead makes the call, and we are watching it. It climbs up, approaches our altitude, and looks like it is heading in our direction. There is no indication on the RWR but that was no great surprise; sometimes this missile shows up on the RWR, sometimes it does not. But we know it's not going to get jammed with anything in our airplane.[2] Then it disappears as its motor burns out. We're talking about it now. I say, 'What the hell,' and make a hard left descending turn, then make a reverse turn to the right while my backseater is putting out chaff. And just then the missile blows up about 1,500 feet behind the airplane and scares the shit out of us. The motor had burned out but I think the sustainer motor keeps it going, although it doesn't put out a flame, so you can't see it. But what is scary is that I might not have done anything as that missile was guiding. I moved the jet mainly because I thought it made no sense in not doing something."

The pilot of number Two picks up the story.

"We were about ten miles offshore when they shot the SA-2. Everybody thought it was on them; everyone was yelling, 'It is on me, it is on me'—everybody was breaking for it. They always tell you, if you get a SAM shot at you, be patient, watch it maneuvering to see if it is on you. It is like, whoever wrote that obviously never had a SAM shot at them. That patience would come maybe after the hundredth SAM was shot at you. We all thought it was on us and we all broke for it and it ended up missing. They come a lot faster than whoever wrote the book thinks they do. Even at ten miles, from the time my backseater saw it and said, 'Hey, there is a SAM at right three o'clock,' it is only a couple of seconds or so before I end up breaking into it to force it to overshoot. It seemed like it happened really quick."

Two's WSO finishes the story, "I grew up playing football and was used to excitement, but this mission, even with the threats, really had us pumped up. And it was wild in there by the target; it was very hard for me to keep my head down on those scopes with all the stuff coming up around us. But after we egressed and dodged the SA-2, we were feeling good. We didn't know if we got our target or not, but we did our job and got away. And when we were away from all the threats, we got together, looked each other over [for damage], then Three, obviously feeling good and wanting to have some fun, did a barrel roll over us. Of course, we all had to get into the act, and then as we were letting down coming home, my frontseater rolled upside down and we flew that way awhile, checking out the lights of the city. We were happy. We did the job they sent us to do, proving again the flexibility of airpower. And we got everybody in and we got everybody out.

---

[2]At the time of this conflict the SA-2 was considered an obsolete missile used only by Third World countries, where planners did not expect the Strike Eagle to be fighting. The software has since been upgraded.

"Of course, we didn't get Saddam—I've heard a rumor that he left the area a few minutes before the bombs started falling—but he would have had a rough go had he been at that location. We could have gotten him."

It may be awhile before we learn what actually was going on that night. The intel folks, or "spooks," who were masterminding the process from the shadows are not likely to be telling any tales. The government has special rooms reserved for talkative spooks at Fort Leavenworth.

However, we do know what happened next in the "Kill Saddam" saga. The Strike Eagles were launched on the first of two "Winnebago" missions.

It was another dark night at Al Kharj, and a commander and his WSO were already out the door to their jet. They were going on a routine Scud patrol mission out into western Iraq, but the WSO didn't get to his airplane before he was called back by a senior officer. "Here, come with me and take this call on the secure telephone."

The WSO continues the story. "I took the phone and it was a general at the TACC in Riyadh. He gave me coordinates where this very important person was supposed to be. But he was impatient—he wanted bombs on him within an hour and I had to explain that we were at least one and one-half hours away from H-2, which is about where he was sending us. He was also bothered that we didn't have a secure fax and that he had to give all this information over the telephone. He kept saying, 'Now, don't screw this up; I don't want this done half-assed.' When I got away from him, I went to the jet where my boss was already strapped in. When I told him about the general's comments, he got angry—and that is something rare to see. He did not appreciate the general's suggestion that we might screw up the mission."

The commander and his WSO, along with a wingman, took off and headed to western Saudi and their tanker, then crossed the Iraqi border and headed north. They were seeking a Winnebago motor home, which, according to intel sources, Saddam was using for a command post.[3] Said the WSO, "When we got up there, we found a settlement like a line camp, with one large building, several smaller trailers and buildings, and a van-type vehicle surrounded by an earthen revetment. We held our wingman high—he had dumb bombs—and we made a pass and dropped one of our 500-pound

---

[3]An official at Winnebago Industries said that two 27-foot motor homes were sold to the Iraqi embassy in Washington, D.C. They were the "Elandan" model and the retail price for each was about $80,000.

LGBs on the van. It was a shack, but there was a very strong wind down there, which we could see from the smoke, and guiding the bombs was difficult. We made a few more passes, dropping one bomb at a time on the other buildings, then called our wingman down."

The pilot flying on their wing continues the story. "We had no idea what was going on—we had been sitting in the jet when Lead's WSO was getting all the information. We just went along—we knew we had some special tasking, but that was it.[4] Anyhow, it was a dark night—just a little bit of moon—and when we got to the coordinates, I was glad to see that it was out away from H-2 and with no big threats. Lead went down to 2,500 feet to pickle and there was just one 14.5mm gun about four miles to the east. He fired, but we were out of range. Lead told us to drop six bombs, and I could see through the FLIR the hot spot where his bombs had gone off. And what is neat is that Lead's WSO, with the targeting pod, could actually see our dumb bombs when they hit and could score them for us. He would say, 'You're a little long, shorten up your next one.' Eventually we dropped all twelve of our bombs and the last three were perfect shacks—Lead's WSO recorded them on videotape and they were used in a special 'greatest hits' video made after the war.

"Lead made several passes, dropping one bomb at a time, and when we pulled away, there was nothing left of that camp. For that reason, I was a little surprised when we got on the ground and I saw that Lead was angry—you have to understand that he is extremely even tempered. I tried not to eavesdrop on the conversation between Lead and his Ops officers, but everyone knew he was angry because the general suggested that he might screw up the mission."

Angry indeed. By several accounts the commander had to be persuaded not to fly to Riyadh and present the videotape of the mission directly to the general. That did not happen, of course. The videotape went to Riyadh by courier plane and the general got confirmation that his target had been destroyed. Winnebago Number One—if that was, in fact, the vehicle in the revetment—was no longer in the Iraqi inventory, but its owner was still very much alive. Was Saddam there when the bombs fell, or was he even close to the area? No one in the Strike Eagle community would even hazard a guess.

Winnebago mission number two barely deserves mention in Strike Eagle history. A two-ship flight of Strike Eagles, while on Scud patrol, was sent by AWACS to coordinates near Sam's Town to

---

[4]The WSO, who is now out of the air force, read his pilot's comment and said, "There was no doubt in my mind who we were going after. Just from Lead's comments to us, I was definitely sure it was Saddam that we were trying to kill."

take out a caravan of vehicles, one of which, they found out later, was supposed to have been Saddam's Winnebago. The only problem was that a flight of F-111s was closer to the area and, according to the Strike Eagle flight lead, "There was nothing left for us to drop on when we got there. The caravan had been completed destroyed. I think one of the Winnebago doors was the largest piece left—I heard that some of the Special Forces brought it out as a souvenir."

Three attempts, but no prize and no glory. That sums up the Strike Eagles' attempts to kill Saddam. And what if they had been successful? Even General Norman Schwarzkopf, who described Saddam as "an enemy center of gravity"—a Clausewitz term— admitted in his memoirs that "If he had been killed [in a raid on one of his command bunkers] I wouldn't have shed any tears."

The Strike Eagle crews would not have shed any tears, either. They wanted that man dead. They were tired and they wanted to go home.

14

The Shaka Your Shorts Raid

"The triple-A was . . . well, imagine sitting around a big camp-fire at night—one with lots of embers—and then some drunk idiot throws in a big log. The embers go everywhere—that was what the triple-A looked like. As far as I could see there was nothing but tracers. I was scared shitless."
Capt. Jim "Boomer" Henry

Steep Turner was hot. Not temperature hot, but temper hot. He had just returned from the Sam's Town area and seen the most triple-A and SAMs he had seen during the whole war. For awhile, the triple-A and SAM activity had subsided a bit in that region, but the Iraqis had somehow replenished their stocks. Sam's Town and its environs was Danger City again, and Steep Turner, commander of the Rockets, was fed up with sending his crews back into that stuff night after night. He had made a vow that he would take them all home to their families when this war was over. He knew he wasn't going to do that if he had to keep sending them into Sam's Town. He had grimaced at the after-action reports out of there. Now, after seeing it himself, his anger had risen. He had to take action.

He was at the ops desk when he made the call. He was so angry he did not care that those hanging around the desk heard what he was about to say. He was going to call the F-15E FIDO in Riyadh and get something moving. He would start with the captain who would answer the phone, but he would not stop there if he did not get his way.

What follows is a rough approximation of the dialogue that followed.

Voice: "This is the TACC."

Turner: "This is Lt. Col. Turner at Al Kharj."

Voice: "Well, Steve, you old asshole, how the hell are you. This is General Horner." (Horner had been Turner's DO at Seymour Johnson in 1977.)

Turner: (not expecting Horner, but not surprised either because Horner had a reputation for just grabbing the phone on one of the FIDO's desks) "Oh, hello, sir. I'm not too good tonight."

Horner: "What's the problem, Steve? I know your boys have been having it a little rough lately."

Turner: "Sir, we're getting the shit shot out of us up around Al Qaim. We call it Sam's Town and triple-A alley. I called because I am requesting you guys to frag a thirty-ship package to go up there and take out a bunch of that shit. We're going to lose some airplanes if we keep going up there the way it is now. I was just up there myself, sir. They must have resupplied. You can't believe all the crap that they're putting up."

Horner: "Yeah, I hear that it's rough up there."

Turner: "What about sending a thirty-ship package up there, general? Send some Strike Eagles, some Weasels, some B-52s, maybe some A-6s, and just cream that place . . . just concentrate strictly on the threats up there."

Horner: (after a pause) "Ho, ho, well, Steve, I'd like to help you out. What do you say we send a 117 in there tomorrow night?

Turner: (thinking what a pissant a lone Stealth fighter would be against all the threats) General, you can . . . [perform an obscene but physically impossible act]!

Horner: "Ho, ho, ho . . . now Steve."

Turner: "I'm sorry, sir, but two days before the war you said our job as commanders is not to lose anybody. Sir, we're going to lose some people up there if we don't take out some of those threats!"

Horner: "Ho, ho . . . well, Steve, let's see what we can do."

Maj. Brian "BJ" Dillon and Capt. David Castillo were standing by the ops desk listening to one side of the above conversation. Said Turner later, "When I got off the phone with Horner, I think BJ and Castillo thought I was going to vaporize right there on the spot. I know they thought they were going to have a new commander. And, sure, I regretted saying that to General Horner but I was doing what I thought a commander had to do. Also—and I wasn't thinking about this at the time—I've known General Horner since he was my DO. He is so darned intelligent, he can argue any side of an issue.

He was just testing me. He doesn't like yes men around him. Of course, [laughing] I can say all of this now that he didn't fire me."

General Horner did not even reprimand Steep Turner for the outburst. In fact, the next night a thirty-ship package went up to the Sam's Town area and did just what Turner asked. Their target was strictly the threats up there, and when the raid was over, there were a lot of Iraqi guns and missiles out of action.[1]

The war was more than half over when all of the above was going on. Much had been accomplished by then. The once-feared Iraqi air force was out of the threat picture, with its airport runways cratered, its pilots cowering, and its remaining fighter airplanes hidden or dispatched to Iran.

Also, the military's command and control system was largely destroyed, its production centers for nuclear and biological warfare in ruins, and, while there were still plenty of Scuds undestroyed, none of them were likely to reach Israel. In addition, up in the KTO, where three elite Republican Guard divisions were entrenched behind frontline forces on the Kuwait-Saudi border, air force A-10s, F-16s, F-111s, B-52s, as well as Navy A-6s and F/A-18s were, in the language of the fighter pilot, pounding the snot out of the enemy artillery and armor by day and by night. The Strike Eagles, with their targeting pods and smart bombs, were getting involved up there, too, but that story is told in a later chapter.

Now, going into the last half of the war, about twenty-four of the forty-eight Strike Eagles—a complete squadron—were still needed for Scud patrol to continue to fulfill the agreement with Israel. Another dozen or so were about to be sent to the KTO on a regular basis to help attrit the ground forces and prepare for an invasion. This left a varying number, but usually less than twelve, for deep interdiction missions, where critical targets, in high-threat areas, could be hit with precision ordnance. In other words, a few of the Strike Eagles were flying missions and using the airplane for what it was designed to do.

One such mission was the raid on the Shayka Mazhar airfield, which occurred on the night of February 14, and which has since been called the "The Shaka Your Shorts Raid," or, by some, "The Valentine's Day Massacre."

---

[1]That Horner reacted positively to Turner's outburst does not surprise those who have known him throughout his career. Reportedly, he hated sycophantic wimps and admired gutsy officers like Turner. After the war, Horner came to Al Kharj and, during a dinner in his honor, submitted to good-natured ribbing over Turner's outburst. "That just shows you the size of the man," said Colonel (now Brig. Gen.) Hornburg, Turner's wing commander at the time. "He's that kind himself; that's why he got along so well with Schwarzkopf."

Shayka Mazhar is an air base about fifteen miles south southeast of Baghdad, and, according to intel reports, there were fixed-wing, attack aircraft there, along with a bunch of attack helicopters and "other equipment." It was feared that these aircraft and helicopters might be loaded with chemical warfare weapons, and that they would be used during the impending ground war—which everyone was talking about now, and upon which much of the air campaign was now being focused. The threat of chemical warfare was taken very seriously by all the ground commanders because they knew that the Iraqis had used chemicals in the Iran-Iraq War. The aircraft and helicopters at Shayka Mazhar presented a major potential threat that had to be eliminated—and the Strike Eagles were given that job.

On February 11, an eight-ship flight, led by Captains Moon Mullins and Rich Horan, launched for an attack on Shayka Mazhar. But the mission ended up being scrubbed because the tankers they were supposed to meet were 150 miles away from where they should have been; they had not gotten the proper message from the TACC in Riyadh.

Two nights later the eight-ship raid was on again. However, two other captains, Greg "Moose" Barlow and Greg Torba, were tasked to lead the flight. Capt. Steve "Killer" Kwast, a computer whiz and the pilot who would fly on Barlow and Torba's wing, was assigned a major share of the planning. Kwast describes the process.

"In the squadron we had a piece of computer equipment called the Mission Support System, or MSS. I was one of few who knew how to work some of the key functions, so I spent much of the planning time calling up satellite photos of the Shayka Mazhar airfield. Of course, we had some two-year-old photos of the field but they showed just the runway and apron. With the MSS I was able to pull up the area and see things like access roads and intersections, which would help the WSOs during their mapping procedure. We had no current photos showing where the airplanes and helicopters were— they supposedly had those in Riyadh but, throughout the war, that stuff rarely got to us. So all we could do in the planning process was divide the ramp up into eight DMPIs where each airplane, with its twelve CBU-87 bombs, could drop on one DMPI and expect to get some overlapping coverage. Theoretically, if everybody hit their own DMPI, the whole ramp would be covered and we would take out everything on it. This was a high-priority mission for us. I know [Brig. Gen.] Glosson called [Col.] Hornburg stressing its importance. And it was exciting to me that there was some war fighting capability up there that we could take out and prevent being used against our forces."

Despite the high priority, the mission almost got scrubbed. Moose Barlow, the pilot flight lead, explains. "We had a good plan, but there were so many SAM rings up there, we couldn't get to the field without going through them. They were SA-3s, SA-6s, SA-8s, and possibly a couple of Hawks, which were our own missiles that the Iraqis had captured in Kuwait. We definitely needed Weasel and EF-111 support, but when I called the Weasels, they said they had a commitment to support the F-111s that were to be in the KTO. I went to Turner who called the TACC and said that we weren't going without the Weasels. TACC said for us to stand by, to not scrub the mission, so we laid around until they called back. 'The Weasels will be there for a later TOT,' they said, 'and a 117 will go in just ahead of you and take out one of the SA-3 sites.' We were good to go, but we had to wait awhile before we launched.

"On the way up we had to fly through thunderstorms and I didn't know lightning came in so many different colors. But we got our gas with no problems—it was easier now—the tankers were finally using their lights—and we headed toward Baghdad at 24,000, in and out of clouds. Then, when we were a hundred or more miles out, the clouds disappeared and it was clear. We could see the lights of Baghdad, and soon we began seeing triple-A. It was all along our route now, and it was coordinated; they would start shooting out ahead of us, then when we passed, the shooting would stop. Most of it was smaller-caliber stuff—a few 57s—but nothing that was a threat.

"As we got closer we could hear the Weasels and the EF-111s working, but, when we got about five miles from the IP, we found out the EFs were not in their altitude block. Two of them screamed right across our nose. We checked to map the target, and as we turned in, I saw a couple of missiles coming up. They were SA-8s and they petered out at about 22,000—not a factor because we were at 28,000. Then, about thirty seconds from weapons release, a Weasel called, 'Heads up! You have an active three at three-twenty and seven [320 degrees from their position and seven miles away].' My heading was 320 and we were seven miles from the airfield; it was the SA-3 site on the field. I looked and saw two flashes. Torba [his WSO] said he had the target and I told him to hold on a second. I was going to put the missiles on the beam like you are supposed to do. But then I wondered how the hell I was going to put them on the beam when they were right under us. I rolled up left and kicked right rudder to follow them. They were definitely SAMs and definitely coming after us. I pulled into a dive, kicked off our centerline tank, and tried to build some energy for a break. They were still coming right at us. I jinked to the right and reacquired. They were still on us so I kicked bombs off, made a break turn to the left, and saw two fireballs go past. Killer [Kwast] said they went off right behind us.

"I'm low now, almost out of energy, and Torba[2] yells for me to pull up. We're right down in all the triple-A and the gunners are having a field day. I hit the burners, knowing it would light us up, but without our bombs I figured we could make good speed out of there and maybe draw off some of the triple-A from the other guys. I called the flight saying that we had jettisoned our bombs. I felt shitty about that, especially listening to them fighting their way in with their bombs."

Capt. Steve Kwast and Maj. Steve Chilton were coming in behind Barlow and Torba. They pick up the story.

Kwast: "The thing that amazed me going into the target was the way everything was lit up. There were bright lights all over Baghdad. It was like flying into Ohio on a clear night."

Chilton: "The amazing thing was the highways. It looked like huge convoys of trucks moving south, all with their lights on—just like there was not a war on.

Kwast: "We get close, made our map, turned in, and the triple-A is getting heavier and heavier. Chilt is saying, 'I don't know about this, I don't know about this.'"

Chilton: "What was bothering me was that we were going into all this and there was really nothing on the ramp that looked like a viable target. I designated on a couple of small things—they could have been jeeps—that were in the area of our DMPI."

Kwast: "He had designated and we were heading to the target when the missiles started coming up. There was nothing on the RWR, but that didn't mean anything. They have a height-finder radar and, combined with a range finder from another site, they can get pretty good guidance information without using their tracking radar. I saw the two launches at two o'clock, then saw Moose jinking to the left—I didn't know he got rid of his bombs. I'm watching the missiles and Chilt says, 'Let's get the hell out of here.'"

Chilton: "The one missile was heading in our direction and flew a smooth parabolic arc. I wasn't absolutely sure it was guiding but it was pointing its nose at us and it seemed to have leveled off. I made the comment to Killer, 'I think it's about time to do something.'"

Kwast: "I was very new in the airplane and I wouldn't have blamed him if he had taken control. I doubt if I could have sat back there and trusted a guy like me. But I continued to watch the missile, then two more came up on the right. I decided to honor them. They were straight and level, fixed on the canopy, then the boosters disappear. I wait and time it, 'One potato, two potatoes, three pota-

---

[2]Torba said, in response to Barlow's comment, "It was the most triple-A I saw in the war. It was like an umbrella over the field."

toes, four potatoes,' then rolled upside down and pulled straight down. I rolled level, still in a steep dive, screaming to the ground, and Chilt is in the back dispensing chaff. Then I pulled out and bled off a whole shitload of energy. About then I see an explosion behind the tail that is damn close—it probably detonated at our original altitude and position. It might have gotten us. I looked at the explosion and it was amazing how much it looked like a Fourth of July fireworks explosion. It was a round ball, with white and yellow sparks and looked like it was designed to be pretty."

Chilton: "It looked like a star burst. I'm frantically looking around now, while Killer heads for the target."

Kwast: "We're somewhere around 13,000 now, low and slow, and I know Chilt is unhappy with me. I'm looking around and don't see anything else—there are SAMs being launched but they don't look like they are on us. I keep pressing, drive the next eight miles, and have some speed back up so if another one came up, I could defend against it. There are more coming up, but I watch them. I don't want to do the funky chicken.[3] They're not on us and we continue in and get our bombs off. I bank 100 degrees hard left, watching for the bombs, and slicing toward our egress heading. I see them go off; they light up the entire airfield complex."

Capt. Chuck Robinson and Maj. Paul "PB" Burns were number Three in the train. They dodged the two missiles that were launched at Kwast and Chilton. "However," said Burns, "what was more scary was jinking around, not knowing exactly where everybody else was, but knowing they are doing the same thing. Being in the middle of the pack, we could easily have had a mid-air. In fact, it was as close to a miracle as anything I saw in the war—not having a mid-air, that is."

Capt. Randy "R-2" Roberts and Jim "Boomer" Henry were next, just in time for more missiles. Said Roberts and Henry:

Roberts: "I'm looking ahead and see Chuckles [Robinson] and PB [Burns] get their bombs off; then, as Boomer and I start in, I see two SAMs come off the ground and I'm ready to jettison everything."

Henry: "Just as I told R-2 to turn in, he said, 'Hang on just a second.' There was something going on outside—I'm inside the airplane at this point. Then we're turning and dipping and there are

---

[3]All fighter pilots are warned during training not to yank on the stick and needlessly bleed away their energy when they first encounter a SAM. The typical novice, they say, pulls one way, then another, then another, which doesn't really move the airplane very far, but loses energy that might be needed for a last-ditch defensive maneuver. Because of the erratic nature of the movements, pilots use the term *funky chicken*—the name of a loose-jointed, spastic-looking dance movement—to describe it. They are told, "Don't do a funky chicken when you see a SAM."

missiles flying. Finally we get wings level and the bombs start coming off and you could feel clunk, clunk, clunk—there are twelve of them and in the middle of this thing I'm saying, 'Come on, you suckers, get off the jet.' They finally came off and we turned south. Now, we're getting an indication that a Hawk is locked on us. We begin defensive maneuvering, I am dispensing chaff, and then, down on the right side, I see a missile coming up. I call it, 'Missile! Right three o'clock low.' We began to dig into it, decided it wasn't on us, then came back to the left and as we did, R-2 looked over our left shoulder and saw a missile explode right behind us. We were still showing a Hawk on us and I yelled, 'Randy, you have to come out of burner; I can't see behind us; I'm not going to be able to pick up a missile.' It [the Hawk] never came up, thank God. But now we are working ourselves down into the triple-A and we start climbing. Finally, we get out of that. By now my entire flight suit is drenched and stuck to me, and then R-2 and I start laughing—hysterically and maniacally—and could not stop for about two straight minutes. We were letting the stress out, releasing the tension. It was completely crazy."

Captains Mark Stevens and Kevin Thompson were leading the second four-ship flight. Both were enthusiastic about the mission. "It was a big deal to go in there and smack all those helicopters and be heroes," said Thompson. However, when they got in close to the target and Thompson started mapping the area, his enthusiasm dimmed. "There were no helicopters on the map and I don't think there were any." They, too, saw missiles coming up at them. "But they didn't appear to be guiding," said Stevens, "but then one exploded right in front of us. Rich Crandall, who was right behind us, said he thought for sure we had been hit."

Majors Rich Crandall and Al Gale saw several missiles. "But we weren't that much bothered by them," said Crandall. "We could see that they were being launched ballistically—they weren't guided. They [Iraqi missile operators] knew the Weasels were there and they didn't dare turn on their guidance radars. I did see some smaller missiles, Rolands or SA-9s, but they fizzled out about 10,000 feet. Don't get me wrong, our adrenaline was pumping, but the missiles I saw were not a threat to us. Of course, if the Weasels had not been there, it would have been real ugly."

Captains Moon Mullins and Rich Horan were number Seven. Said Mullins, "We were about twenty miles out when the RWR went off. I looked and saw SAMs leaving the ground. I watched them for awhile and maneuvered the airplane once to see if they were going to guide. One did change course; it appeared to be guiding. I started an aggressive maneuver, but I had pulled my mask down for a moment and couldn't communicate."

Horan, in the backseat, wasn't sure what was going on. Said he, "I had my head down, radar mapping, and suddenly there was this hard maneuver, but nothing from Moon. I said, 'What have you got?' but he doesn't answer me. I assume he knows what he is doing and I'm busy anyhow, so I put my head back down and try to keep mapping. I never saw the missile and I guess I was thinking what I can't see won't hurt me."

Number Eight was flown by a new, low-time wingman who had never seen a missile fired. In his pit was the veteran, seeing-eye WSO, Two Dogs McIntyre. Two Dogs tells what happened. "We're still twenty miles behind when I started hearing the guys calling out that they were defending against SAMs. I was preparing the radar to do a map when I noticed the aircraft maneuvering around. That doesn't bother me too much, but I made the comment that we needed to come left to about 310 [degrees]. I hear, 'No, we can't' and I say, 'We have to.' Then I hear, 'No, we can't; we're being shot at.' I look outside; I don't see anything coming up at us; I say, 'Let's come left.' I hear, 'I can't,' the third time. I look and see why; the airspeed is at 200 knots—as he was seeing the SAMs coming up in the general direction, he kept pulling farther and farther away from the ground. Unfortunately, we kept getting slower and slower. I said, 'You're right.' Then I called out that we were out of the package. We had an alternate target, an early-warning site south of Baghdad, so we went over and dropped on that, then headed home. When we got there, we reviewed the videotape of the HUD. There were SAMs everywhere and one of them blew up three or four miles in front of his [the pilot's] HUD. There was also all this triple-A. It was a fairly significant mission for most people; it was his first experience and I understood why he was scared out of his senses."

Some of the veterans will also admit that they were terrified that night. One of them said, "When we came back home and got out of that jet, I wanted not only to kiss the earth; I wanted to wallow on it—and I don't even like that part of the world. But that was the scariest mission I've ever been on."

Another veteran said, "I remember coming back and being jived all night. I called the wife and talked to her for almost an hour at a dollar a minute. I did it just to unwind. I was happy to be alive, and I'm one of those who helped name that mission "The Shaka Your Shorts Raid."

And, for the old-timers who may be reading this account, do not think that these "kids" are not also aware of what their fathers and grandfathers went through. Said one, "You know what all those old farts are always saying—'Well, when I was in Vietnam and was a flight lead da da da, and my wingman got shot down'—then the other one says, 'Yeah, I lost my wingman, too.' Well, after flying as a wingman in this war, I can see why they got shot down. The flight lead goes in, drops, and is halfway home by the time his bombs go off. But as they go off, the wingman is just coming in; the enemy is pissed off now, and they are waiting and ready to shoot the next guy down. Now I know why so many wingmen were lost in that war."

Another crewman reflected upon what it must have been like during the World War II bombing raids. "After that raid [Shayka Mazhar], I couldn't help but think of those B-17 guys on their bombing runs when the flak was so heavy you could walk on it. I can't even imagine how they did that. I used to think, 'Okay, that's what they did.' But now I understand the courage it took. We were able to maneuver. They weren't; they had to just press on ahead. The cost for them was enormous. I don't know how they did it."

15

Strike Eagles Hit the Jackpot

"In the brief they told us not to hit the shrine and we said, 'Okay, we won't.' That was it. It wasn't a concern. The airplane is accurate."

Capt. Mark "Bones" Wetzel

Col. Dave "Bull" Baker is somewhat of a legend in the Strike Eagle community. In 1972, while flying as a forward air controller in Cambodia, he was shot down, captured, wounded two different times while trying to escape, then was the only U.S. Air Force prisoner released from Cambodia after the war. Later, after a tour flying F-15 air-to-air models, he was one of the first to transition to the F-15E, and, because of his leadership in establishing the F-15E training program at Luke Air Force Base, he is considered one of the community's founding fathers.

What cemented his reputation in the community was what he did when he came to Al Kharj to replace Dave Eberly as the wing DO. At that time the crewmen were disappointed with two of the air force's most highly touted assets. One, of course, was the search and rescue force, which had been awesome during the Vietnam era, but which they now considered impotent. The other was their intel service.

Prior to the war, billions had been spent on spy satellites and other sophisticated information-gathering assets, and it seemed reasonable for the crews to expect up-to-date photo imagery of what they were going out to bomb. By their reasoning, if the B-17 crews had photos of their targets during World War II, were they asking too much to expect photos equally as good from the mega-buck systems operated by present-day spooks?

Of course, the answer was, "Yeah, we may have some of that stuff here in Riyadh, but you're not getting it. That stuff is secret and we have to protect it!" Consequently, the crewmen rarely saw target photos before their missions, and they rarely knew, after bombing a target, the results of their effort. Of course, the latter problem was solved when those with targeting pods went on a raid; they brought home videos that showed exactly what they did or did not destroy.

Then Bull Baker entered the picture. It just so happened that he had an identical twin brother, Steve, who was chief of Flag Operations on the U.S. carrier *Teddy Roosevelt*. When Baker was talking to his brother on secure telephone one day, his brother mentioned that some U.S. Navy F-14s on a recon mission had gotten some good photos of about twenty Iraqi aircraft parked on a road north of Tallil airfield. "He was trying to get this target nominated for an attack," said Baker, "but was having no luck. So I said, 'Give me the coordinates and fax me a picture,' which he did. Then I got our intel people involved and also called [Brig. Gen.] Buster Glosson. 'Hey, I've got a goddamn target that needs to go away,' I said. 'It's a bunch of airplanes on the closest base to friendly forces. They've got the capability to hit the good guys.' I also told Glosson that my brother had mentioned some helicopters on the field. They could have strike capability and could be carrying chemical weapons. Then they called back from the TACC. 'You can't do that. That area is hands off. They're right next to a shrine up there.' It was like in Cambodia; you couldn't hit their shrines.

"About a day later I got a call back, and let's just say that somebody up there cared enough about the threat of those airplanes to make a change to the frag after the ATO for the day was on the street. And even though the area was high-threat, with reported SA-3s, SA-6s, and guns up to 85mm, I was told we could have four airplanes, but no assets for SEAD [search and destroy missions to take out threats], no Weasels, and that I had to guarantee we wouldn't hit that shrine. I was worried about those Iraqi assets up there—so close to Kuwait—and I decided right then that we were going to do it."

The shrine everybody was worrying about was a ziggurat, a large brick "temple tower" of the type that was constructed in several cities in ancient Babylonia. This particular ziggurat was constructed in the Babylonian city of Ur, which is thought to be the early home of the Prophet Abraham, and which, for about two thousand years, between the twenty-fourth and fourth centuries B.C., was a thriving city of commerce on the Euphrates River. Then the river course changed, leaving Ur high, dry, and forgotten except by archeologists, who have conducted numerous digs in the area around the ziggurat.

Capt. Chuck Robinson and Maj. Paul "PB" Burns were elected to lead the four-ship flight, while Bull Baker and Capt. Mark "Bones" Wetzel would fly on their wing. Baker was not taking any chances; he did not want any heartburn worrying about bombs accidentally hitting the ziggurat or any of the diggings at Ur. Both airplanes would be equipped with targeting pods and eight, 500-pound GBU laser-guided bombs, and both WSOs, Burns and Wetzel, were considered among the best in the Strike Eagle community.

The other two ships would be crewed by Captains Matt Riehl with Mike Cloutier and Captains Randy "R-2" Roberts with Jim "Boomer" Henry. They would not be carrying targeting pods, and Baker was not taking any chances with "buddy lasing"; he didn't want any bombs dropped that might not be guided. This two-ship element would be carrying CBU-87 bombs and their targets would be carefully defined.

"What we had," said Robinson, the flight lead, "was the Tallil airfield with two east-west runways. Picture the east end of the northernmost runway; about one-half mile north of that was this enclosed area with the shrine and the diggings. Then, just north of that was a road that arced from the southeast and around to the southwest. The airplanes we were after had been towed to this road and covered with some kind of camouflage material. PB and I planned it carefully, so when we made our run-ins, a long or short bomb would not fall toward Ur. We planned for the other guys to drop some of their CBU-87s quite a ways away, at two road intersections, and they would save the rest for the helicopters that were supposed to be on the field.[1]

Paul Burns, the lead WSO, picks up the story. "We got up there and they were shooting at us pretty good. However, we were between 20,000 and 22,000 and what they were shooting was no threat. We didn't see any SAMs, either, so, with number Two, who also had a targeting pod and LGBs, we set up a racetrack pattern around the road where the airplanes were supposed to be parked. On the first pass, I didn't see anything through the targeting pod.

---

[1]During the planning phase, Robinson received a call from an intel person. "He had a photo of Tallil," said Robinson, "and he tried to direct my eyes to one of the helicopters while I'm looking at our own photo. He was saying, 'Do you see the tip of the rotor blade sticking out of that hanger?' I called the bullshit flag on that; here I am with a seven-inch square, faxed photo, and I can barely make out the hangar he's talking about. We were going to look for them, but we didn't have high hopes of finding helicopters up there."

Then, on the second pass, I'm looking just off the road where an airplane should be. This time I could see the silhouette. It was very easy to see, and both of us in the airplane went, 'Holy cow, that's a Fishbed [MiG-21].'"

Bones Wetzel, the WSO in number Two, heard Burns's exclamation. Said Wetzel, "I heard PB say, 'Bingo, I've got a MiG-21.' I said, 'How do you know that?' I'm still trying to find where they're parked and he's calling out what he's hitting. But I had a problem. Looking through the targeting pod isn't always like looking through prescription glasses where the image is clear. Sometimes it will look like somebody sprayed fog all over it and that is as good as it gets. But after I saw where his bombs were hitting, I could figure out exactly what he was going after."

Bull Baker, piloting number Two, was a bit concerned about dropping bombs near the road. The shrine at Ur was only about 200 yards from where PB had dropped. Wetzel, his WSO, was confident—he had promised Baker earlier that they would not drop on the shrine. With trust in his WSO, Baker started dropping and Wetzel started lasing. Soon both airplanes were in a racetrack pattern, lasing a bomb into an airplane at each pass, and exclaiming excitedly as they identified them. "We got a Fishbed! We got a Flogger! We got a Frogfoot! We got an F-1!"[2]

Baker soon became enthusiastic, too. Said he, "What we were doing was pretty damn impressive. We got a direct hit on an F-1 and this thing comes shooting out of the fireball—it was the ejection seat. We hung around about forty minutes and took out eighteen airplanes. We denied them a whole squadron of fighter aircraft. It was a damn good night's work."

The alert reader will wonder how they could have destroyed eighteen airplanes with only sixteen LGBs. Flight lead Robinson explains that mystery, "We had some misses and a couple [of bombs] that didn't guide. When we left, and after reviewing the videotapes, we concluded that we killed nine airplanes. Later, when the army captured the airfield, they found that all of the airplanes except the Frogfoot had been parked nose to nose, so we were sometimes getting two at a time. It was the intel people on the ground who credited us with the eighteen airplanes. There were just three that we did not hit."

It was truly a memorable night for the Strike Eagles. With their laser-guided bombs they systematically destroyed well over $200 million worth of aircraft, and they did it under perhaps the most

---

[2]Fishbed: MiG-21. Flogger: MiG-23. Frogfoot: Sukoi-25—a twin-engine attack airplane somewhat like the A-10. F-1: Mirage—French-built fighter.

restrictive targeting parameters in Air Force history. Of course, everybody in the community was pleased with the results. However, this was just a textbook mission; this was the type of mission the airplane's designers had envisioned, even when it was only a gleam in their eye.

The Strike Eagles were on a roll now, flying incredibly effective missions that even the designers may never have envisioned. But let us not blame the designers for that. The mission called "tank plinking" had not even been in their textbooks.

16

Tank Plinking

"JSTARS, in my mind, was a huge asset. You can't begin to place a value on how much they helped us."

Capt. Jim "Boomer" Henry

About half way through the war, some of the Strike Eagles got new tasking, which they found out when they walked into their squadron tents late one afternoon and looked on the schedule board. "What the hell is tank plinking?" they asked, when they saw what they were going to do. The dialogue may have gone like this:

Scheduler: "Oh, that means you're going up to the KTO and drop some LGBs on tanks up there."

Pilot: "Okay . . . uh, both of us with targeting pods?"

Scheduler: "Negative. You're got the targeting pod and you'll buddy-lase for your wingman."

WSO: "That's about a one and one-half hour mission, right?"

Scheduler: "Yeah, a little more or a little less."

Pilot: "Then we don't have to tank?"

Scheduler: "Correct."

Pilot (looking at his WSO, grinning): "Hell, we're not even going to need our piddle packs."

WSO (looking at his pilot, also grinning): "And we can leave the seat cushions at home."

Another pilot (who has been listening and who is scheduled to go to Sam's Town): "And you don't have to worry about SA-2s and SA-3s and big guns."

Pilot: "Shit hot!"

WSO (looking up): "Thank you, Lord."

In that fashion (given a few creative liberties), the new mission of tank plinking was introduced to the Strike Eagles. Unlike Scud hunting, which was a royal pain, a tank plinking mission brought both relief and pleasure to the crews. It was a relief because they didn't have to coordinate with tankers and Weasels, the threat was low, and the missions were short; a pleasure because they were destroying Iraqi assets that could kill their friends on the ground, and because they would get instant gratification for their work via the targeting pod images.

But, initially, they ran into a slight problem with the name. Capt. Joel Strabala, who was in the TACC in Riyadh, explains, "The tank plinking mission came up when the planners wanted to use precision ordnance to destroy artillery and armor in the KTO. The first missions were flown by the F-111s—they had the most LGB experience in theater. It was one of their guys, Maj. Cliff Smith, who coined the name, *tank plinking*. I thought it was neat so I put it in our frag when, later, we also got the mission. However—and this is the story that came back to me—General Schwarzkopf happened to see or hear about us using the name *tank plinking* and he said, supposedly, 'I've been a tank driver for thirty-plus years and I don't appreciate you guys using that kind of name.' So we were ordered to no longer use *tank plinking* in the frags. Well, you know fighter pilots; they like challenges. So, each day, we started dreaming up new names for the mission: *tank busting, tank popping, tank slam dunk, pave slam dunk*, and so on. We got real creative and never get caught; it was an inside joke."

The story about Schwarzkopf may be apocryphal; he was an infantryman, not a tank driver, and in his memoirs he speaks matter-of-factly about the mission of tank plinking, which helped attrit Iraqi forces in the KTO. However, the Strike Eagle crewmen could have cared less what anybody in Riyadh thought. Tank plinking is what they called it, and tank plinking is what it would forever be.

Maj. Larry "Hammer" Coleman, who would be the first Strike Eagle WSO to drop LGBs on tanks, tells how his life changed with the new mission. "We had been flying those five-hour missions out into western Iraq—one night we flew one over six hours because the Navy guys that were to replace us were late. That's not slamming the Navy; they had a godawful distance to fly to get there. We had also been having troubles with our tanking. Maybe you've seen the cartoon where the fighter pilot is taking a number to get on a tanker. That was us sometimes. Often we would come back across the border and there would be four or five of them in a row . . . it would be like, go to the second tanker, which meant to go around four or five flights [of fighters] to get to it. It was pretty rough, and sometimes it took awhile. Also, it almost took a KC-10 for us because we took so much gas. We would run a KC-135 dry in a heartbeat.

"It was so much easier when they sent us into Kuwait. We would be airborne an hour and a half, maybe an hour and forty-five minutes. I know our first mission up there—Slammer [Lt. Col. Mike Decuir] and I had just come in from a Scud patrol mission and they said, 'Hey, you want to go up to the KTO?' We said, 'Yeah, we'll go.' We beamed off, second sortie of the night, and went out west of Kuwait City. They had threats up there, but they were mostly shoulder-fired SAMs—nothing that was going to touch us up at 20,000 feet.

"As we went in, it was like an interstate [highway] with airplanes going in and out of that place. We could see lights all around us, and when we got in there, we could see the A-10s dropping flares and working under them.

"We were a two-ship—[Capt.] John Hoff was flying on our wing with [Lt. Glenn] Doc Watson in his pit—and when we got up there we started dropping and lasing, then the wingman would drop. I did all the lasing. I would say, 'I've got the target,' and Slammer would say, 'Okay,' and he would drop. Then I would call the dot, 'Spot on,' and say, 'I'm lasing.'

"A lot of times we had the older bombs [built in the early 1970s] that had what they called 'slam guidance.' When the bomb needed to go one way, the fins would slam all the way to one side till it got on course, then they would slam the other way. It was constantly slamming back and forth and if you started lasing early, you could quickly use up the bomb's energy and it would fall short. You had to be careful; you wouldn't dare start lasing until it was at least 75 percent there—about fifteen seconds before impact.

"But we did well with them—I'm not positive whether it was this first night or not, but Slammer and I, with our wingman, hit sixteen pieces of equipment with sixteen bombs—eight off of our jet and eight off of the other. Sometimes we would get secondaries and sometimes we could see the turrets of tanks flying off. Were all sixteen things we hit valuable targets? Maybe, or maybe not. There could have been trucks in some of those revetments and there could have been tanks in there that had been hit before. You just can't tell from 20,000 feet. All you can say when you come back from one of those missions is that you hit something in a revetment. If you didn't see secondaries, you wouldn't know if it had been a good target."

Soon after Riyadh started sending the Strike Eagles into the KTO, they brought in modified Boeing 707s from the United States that had been flying in an experimental program called JSTARS (pronounced "JAY-stars"). These airplanes were equipped with synthetic aperture radars like the Strike Eagles, and their job was to fly over the KTO and locate targets. Capt. Jim "Boomer" Henry describes how this new asset in the theater worked:

"JSTARS came into the picture fairly early up there, and at first we had a little trouble coordinating. But it didn't take them long to begin to understand what kind of information we needed. Quickly, it got to the point where we would be driving north and we would contact them. They would come back with the coordinates for our target. We would punch them in and the guy would give a verbal description. He would say, 'I have a north-south road with an east-west intersection, and there is a large metal building on the northwest corner. You look up from there and you'll see what looks like a horseshoe and six dots. It is an artillery position.'

"Their radar and our radar is very, very compatible. So I would have a piece of paper on my kneeboard and I'd be drawing a picture as they explained it to me. Then, when we got there, I would map and know exactly what they had been describing. In the beginning, it was tough for them to understand the kind of information we needed. Then we began to telephonically debrief with them and we would say, 'We are looking for this; draw a word picture for me.' The guys got exceptionally good at that. You would know exactly what they wanted; you had it right on your leg. After awhile, it was almost as though you had a map of the target."

Boomer Henry's words of praise for JSTARS were echoed by most of the crewmen who described their missions into the KTO. But there was one problem that aggravated them. Maj. Paul "PB" Burns explains, "The problem with working with them was the radio drill we had to go through. Their radios were really bad. Actually, they were terrible. There was lots of static, and often you couldn't even contact them. Sometimes you would have to wait and wait and use different frequencies to get through to them. It was quite a workout, and a large pain in the ass when you're motoring in at 500 knots and needing a target. The challenge was in getting information back and forth in time to use it."

For JSTARS the highest-priority targets in the KTO were the abundant artillery sites. And much of it was heavy artillery, with "tubes" that outranged most of the Coalition's artillery. This gave the Iraqis a deadly advantage. Artillery is a big killer on the battlefield. But, it was not just the explosive power of the weapons that was frightening; these same long-range weapons could be used to launch poisonous gas shells. So the army commanders back in Riyadh were constantly hammering those on the air staff who were selecting targets. "Take out those tubes and, if you have to, leave the tanks for us. We are not afraid of his tanks, but we're sure as hell afraid of his artillery."

The JSTARS targeteers followed orders, of course, and the Strike Eagles, as well as other strike aircraft, expended tons of bombs on artillery sites. But the armor in the KTO—tanks and armored personnel carriers (APCs)—numbered in the thousands, and they were easy to find. Most were semiburied in mounded revetments, which, in the barren desert, caused them to show up clearly on the radar screens. So, during the last weeks of the air campaign, the Strike Eagles went out night after night and brought home tapes showing incredible kill percentages. Often it was 13 for 16, 14 for 16, 15 for 16, and, occasionally, 16 for 16.

"But was everything we hit a tank?" Lt. Col. Taco Martinez asked, rhetorically, during an interview. "I'll be the first to say, no. I'm sure we bombed our share of empty revetments and our share of revetments with trucks or decoys in them. Were we effective? I think so, by virtue of the fact that I could go in with eight bombs and a wingman with eight bombs, and we could completely work over an encampment of tanks. Also, I've got to think that besides taking out their equipment, it had to have been extremely demoralizing to those guys to be under attack for half an hour. With a bomb going off about every two minutes and with them seeing something blow up each time, that had to be demoralizing—especially when it is three o'clock in the morning and all you can hear in between explosions—with us at 20,000 feet—is just a little whine."

What really excited the crews was the discovery of moving armor—"movers" in fighter pilot jargon. When bombing a vehicle in a revetment, there is always some doubt about its being a valid target; maybe it's a burned-out tank or a decoy. When a mover was sighted, there were no doubts; they knew that if they destroyed it, they were eliminating a deadly threat. So when they heard JSTARS say "mover," their adrenaline started pumping.

Several of the Strike Eagles found movers and destroyed them, but Capt. Darryl "OBD" Roberson and Maj. Dave Wells probably set the record. Said Roberson, "We went up into the KTO for a tank plinking mission, and when we contacted JSTARS, they said they had a convoy of vehicles on this road where a division of the Republican Guard was positioned. They give us the coordinates and, sure enough, they were right where they were supposed to be. We have eight LGBs on the jet and there are eight vehicles, and they are moving. They are APCs, or some kind of tracked vehicle. We target the front guy. We hit him and he blows up. The second guy in the convoy goes hauling butt off the road and tries to run away. Three, four, five, six, seven, and eight stop, and you can see the men pouring out of these vehicles. These were the smart ones. We target the second guy who was trying to get away and hit him. Now we had two. Then we went right down the line and got them all. Just Dave and me—we had a two-ship but it would have been difficult to buddy lase under the circumstances. It was like shooting ducks, and it was 100 percent rewarding to know they wouldn't be around when our guys went in on the ground."

For those who stayed in the squadron, it was easy to tell the crews that had been up into the KTO. They did not look as tired, and usually they were smiling and eager for their commanders to see their videos. And the videos were, for the most part, spectacular. First, you would see the cross hairs, then you would see the cross hairs move and center over the target. Along the edge of the video was a digital countdown in seconds, and when the WSO started lasing, a display would start blinking. Then, suddenly a missile—the bomb— would come into view and streak downward.[1] An instant later the target would vanish in an explosion.

This was great stuff and everybody loved to watch these videos, including the senior officers in Riyadh. It was great stuff for the public affairs folks, too; when released to the media and broadcast to the world, it was awe-inspiring vindication for the U.S. Air Force, which had suffered years of high-tech bashing. The dramatic shots of laser-guided bombs slamming into buildings, bridges, and tanks were hot news and the media appetite for the footage was insatiable. There was only one little problem, so far as the Strike Eagles were concerned. The F-117 Stealth fighter was given most, if not all, of the credit, when many of those videos were Strike Eagle or F-111 footage. The author never heard anyone knocking the F-117; to the contrary, all comments about the airplane were positive. But there was grumbling in the Strike Eagle community (and reportedly in the F-111 community, too) because the media was not giving their airplane the credit it deserved.

However, the commanders at Al Kharj were too busy to be worrying about "media pukes," as representatives of the media are called. What they were worrying about was their crews. They were all experienced now. They were combat veterans who had survived some very dangerous skies. But Iraq was getting beat to a pulp. Some nights the crews would strike targets where the triple-A had been awesome; now, when striking targets in the same vicinity, the triple-A might be negligible. Were the Iraqis out of ammo? Were they tired of the war? Or, were they laying back, trying to lull the strike aircraft into complacency, and perhaps even lure them down into their guns? This latter possibility frightened the commanders. Veteran crews could get cocky, especially after flying a week or more without

---

[1]The bomb would be traveling about nine hundred feet per second—the speed of a .38-Special bullet.

any substantial threats launched against them. Their spectacular success in the KTO was just more fuel to fire their overconfidence, especially because the threats up there were being discounted.

Then it happened—not a fatal shootdown, but a near-fatal shootdown. It was enough to cause the caution flag to be raised, at least among the Chiefs—it was one of their crews that were the near-victims. Capt. Tim Bennett tells the story.

"We're up in the KTO on a tank plinking mission and we're bebopping along, looking down on the A-10s dropping under their flares, thinking what a hellhole that was down there. I'm just looking around, relaxed, when all of a sudden I see this missile flame and its, woosh! I mean it's coming fast, and I'm thinking, oh, shit! I just have time to break into it to give it as many angle problems as I can. About this time the RWR goes off. It's an SA-8, and I'm saying, 'Thanks a lot RWR for all the warning.' In the meantime, Dan [Bakke] has his head stuck down working on a scope, trying to target and he's saying, 'Steady out, steady out.' He doesn't know what's going on and I haven't had time to tell him. All he knows is that I have his head pinned down in a 6-G turn. Then I yell, 'Chaff!' and he starts dumping. Then the missile streaks by and blows up. It just missed us. The SA-8 is a mobile SAM and it must have been down there among the tanks. I'll tell you, it is fast. It was on us in a heartbeat."

"They were on us in a heartbeat." That would have been a good line for the Iraqis who were down on the ground shooting at Bennett and Bakke, had they been using American expressions. Why? Because the Coalition ground offensive, faster even than the famed German blitzkrieg, was just beginning.

17

The Four-Day Rout

"We were all thinking, 'Hey, we will bomb the hell out of those guys for another year if that is what it takes to save our ground buds.' We were perfectly willing to do that."

Maj. Jerry "One-Y" Oney

"When the ground war kicked off there was no question that I wanted to get even with them. They dragged me eight thousand miles away from my wife and kids and I wanted to make them pay. If they would have let me fly five times a night, I would have flown five times a night."

Capt. Bill "Bruno" Millonig

None of the crewmen knew when the ground war would start. But most of them had ideas on what was going to happen. And those ideas covered the spectrum.

At one end of the spectrum were those who argued that the war would be relatively short—no more than three or four weeks long. Those who took this position cited the weeks of punishment that the Iraqi ground forces had suffered. Then there was the starvation factor; it was believed that most supplies to the KTO had been choked off and that the troops on the ground were physically debilitated from lack of food and water. Also, they cited the morale factor; how could anybody be in a fighting mood after being pounded around the clock for weeks on end. "They will surrender in mass the first time they get the chance," said those who expected a short ground war.

On the pessimistic end of the spectrum were those like Capt. Steve Kwast, who hoped it would only last a month, but who feared it could go on for six months. Said Kwast, "I felt in my heart that they had been pounded pretty damn good, but what we did not know was how tenacious they would be. We had read all these books on the Arab countries. In most of them there are descriptions of people so fanatical that they will commit suicide just to inflict harm on Satan's people. That was us; we were the infidels. So would they dig in in their foxholes and fight to the last man like the Japanese did on those islands in World War II? Anybody thoughtful had to recognize that as a possibility. The war would get ugly if that happened, and I felt it could have gone on for several months, at least."

Some of the other crewmen thought like Jerry Oney, whose quote introduced this chapter. Why even start the ground war? Why not just keep on pounding them—just keep raining bombs down on anything the Iraqis could ever use to make war? The threats against air attacks were diminishing, and would be nil after ten or twenty-thousand more sorties. Why quit and leave Saddam with all those valuable military assets? They will surely be used against somebody, someday. And why quit bombing the KTO and take a chance that our buds on the ground will get bloodied? Just let our guys continue hunkering down in Saudi until we pound the bad guys so hard they will have no capability to fight.

But the ground guys in Saudi were impatient. And they were also angry. They had been dragged away from their wives and children and forced to live for weeks in the open desert, amid hordes of flies, and in an almost constant swirl of talcum powder-like sand that ground in their teeth and reddened their eyes. They were like a woman in her last hours of pregnancy. They felt miserable, and they knew that the only way they were going to be relieved of the misery was to endure a lot more pain. But they were ready and willing to do that; most of them didn't want to hunker down and wait for the air jocks to continue pounding the Iraqi troops. Their attitude was, sure more bombing would make it easier for them. But man, we are in misery. We want this thing over. Quit screwing around. Let's get on with it.

The ground forces finally got their wish on the morning of February 24—thirty-eight days after the air campaign had begun. Said Capt. Kent Johnson, a fighter pilot working as an air liaison officer with the 101st Airborne Division, "Out of the entire 220 days that I spent over there, February 24 was the happiest day of them all—and I think it was for most of the guys I was with. Before then you never knew what the future held. Would they start negotiations and keep us over there for six more months, or a year? You just didn't know. Then, suddenly, on February 24, the uncertainty was over. We had some definite parameters in our life now. We knew we would be going home soon. My own guess was that the war would last a week and I predicted that to Andy Glass, a skeptical Cox Publications reporter, just before it kicked off. I was with an aviation brigade and I knew the attack plans. There was no way the Iraqis could have stood up against the massive assault that was planned."

In Al Kharj, after the first day of the ground war, the Strike Eagles launched their normal allotment of sorties for Scud patrol. They had also briefed tank plinking missions up to the KTO. Because there were so many aircraft hitting that area at this time, each flight was tasked to specific "kill boxes"—thirty nautical mile square areas that they were to enter and leave on a specific time schedule. If they entered the kill box early, they could conflict with aircraft already in the box. If they were late getting out, they could be in danger from incoming aircraft. Included in the attack aircraft were B-52s that dropped from very high altitudes. Other aircraft scheduled for the kill boxes had a high respect for their schedules; nobody wanted to be in a kill box under B-52s when they dropped their huge loads of bombs.

"The only problem with this tasking up to the kill boxes," said Capt. Boomer Henry, "was that the army was moving too damn fast. We would get the tasking, then brief, but when we were ready to step, somebody would come running out saying, 'Your TOT has been canceled; there are friendlies in your kill box.' Sometimes we would launch, then take alternate tasking from JSTARS, and sometimes we would just go back in the squadron and wait for an alternate target. After awhile, it really got to be crazy. I came in the second night and Lieutenant Del Toro, our intel officer, went up to the board where they had the plastic markers for the army units—all the groups and battalions. I saw him clean off this huge portion of the board in five minutes. It was the northwest area of the KTO. He just pulled stickers left and right, and I said, 'What in the hell are you doing?' He said, 'These guys are gone; they have been overrun. They have surrendered, or been captured.' Standing there looking at that board, you could just see the gigantic thing going on."

That same night several of the Strike Eagles were hitting targets north of Kuwait. Some were attacking armor and artillery in the northern kill boxes; others were doing what they called "road recce" and "river recce"—they flew over assigned roads and rivers and were cleared to drop on all traffic and temporary bridges. These recce missions had a twofold purpose. First was to cut off supplies heading to Kuwait; second, to keep Iraqi armor from escaping to a sanctuary north of the KTO. It was clear by now that the ground offensive was going to be a rout. And with the Iraqis in full retreat, it also seemed likely that Saddam Hussein would do everything he could to save his armor for another day's fight. Nobody in the TACC at Riyadh wanted that to happen.

The third night of the ground war was the most memorable for the Strike Eagles. Colonel Hornburg, the wing commander, explains, "Sometime during the night I got this call from Buster Glosson. He said the Iraqis were in a massive retreat out of Kuwait City, heading north with all their assets. The weather was terrible up in that region; there were heavy clouds and embedded thunderstorms. Glosson said that the other flights he had sent in had to return because of the weather. He said that he was calling on the Strike Eagles because we were the only people who could get in there and drop bombs through the weather and choke off the roads. I immediately called Turner and Pingel and told them to start waking up whatever guys we had who weren't out flying. I said, 'Take a look at them; if they look good, send them up; if they don't look good, send them back to bed.'"

Col. Bull Baker, Hornburg's DO, was also contacted by Glosson. Said Baker, "He flat out told me that this was an emergency situation and that he had sent three different sets of air in and they couldn't get through the weather. The clouds were at 1,500 feet solid to 25 or 30 [thousand] with massive thunderstorms embedded in the clouds. The A-6s and F-111s couldn't get down through the weather to bomb and the F-16s had to drop on coordinates. What was worrying Glosson was that those guys could have escaped across the Euphrates, then dispersed, and the war could drag on for another two weeks.

"We woke up guys in crew rest and gathered some who were coming in from missions. We got them together and I said, 'It's time now, guys, to put some heat on this son-of-a-bitch. Now I know you have to penetrate some pretty heavy weather, and if you do get down, you're going to be in range of some of those shoulder-fired SAMs. I know some of you guys may not be coming back, but now is the time to stop them before they get across the river. Three different platforms [airplanes] went in and failed; now is the time for you guys to get up there and kick ass and show the whole world and the bad guys what the F-15E is all about.'

"There were some lieutenants and young captains in the audience who had more combat time than regular time in the aircraft—some real nuggets. But in the month they had flown, they had matured quickly, and I knew they were ready."

Prior to Bull Baker's speech to the crews, Captain Merrick Krause and Major Joe Seidl had been called to the telephone. The call came as they were stepping to their jet for a mission into the KTO. "The call was from Riyadh," said Krause. "This guy said he was standing next to General Glosson, and that he had an extremely important mission for us. He wanted us to go to Kuwait, get down through the weather, and, if there were convoys moving on the roads to Basrah, hit them as hard as we could. He said that we were to do it at all costs, and to get back and report as soon as possible.

"Joe and Bull Baker were standing near me while I took the call. When I hung up, Baker said, 'Guys, I just got a report that a Scud has hit a barracks in Dhahran and that sixty of our boys have been killed. Remember that when you go after Saddam Hussein's troops up there on that road. Put some hate in your heart, and I'll be here when you get back.' Then he winked and patted me on the back, and as we walked out, I told Joe that that man went up ten notches in my book.

"We launched, with Captains John Flanagan and Tim Wilson on our wing, and headed up to Kuwait. On the radar we could see these huge thunderstorms, so we went feet wet and skirted Kuwait City on the east, then dove through the weather, and broke out near Bubiyan Island. We were below 12,000 feet, under a ragged ceiling that sloped downward toward the land, and it had been socked in all the way up to 30,000 feet. I sent our wingman to the north to hold over a highway intersection, and then we started a recce over the roads. There were two of them—one was the coastal road that ran along the bay—the other was a big, divided highway that ran straight north. Both were loaded with traffic; we could see hundreds of head-lights."

Krause and Seidl tell the rest of the story together:

Seidl: "I'm looking down on this road and it was like the rush hour on the Dan Ryan Expressway in Chicago. There were trucks lined up bumper to bumper. You couldn't see the road for all the traffic. We went to the intersection just outside Al Jahra, where the two highways split. We figured we would bottle them up at this intersection. We rolled in on the first pass, dropped three bombs, saw them hit, saw a couple of secondary explosions, then lots of triple-A started coming up. This was like going after a cornered ani-mal; they were pissed and the triple-A got really heavy. We went out in a circular pattern, set up a base, and, because they've now turned off their lights, I'm in the targeting pod trying to find them again."

Krause: "Actually, I could see the vehicles by the reflections from the oil fires that had been set; I could see the orange glow reflecting off them. Also, for some reason, they turned their lights back on again. I rolled in and made our second pass using a visual delivery. I put the pipper on the highest concentration of vehicles and dropped diagonally across the road to get the maximum coverage. We were down to 8,000 now and the triple-A was getting worse."

Seidl: "About then we called our wingman and they hadn't gotten any bombs off. We said, 'Okay, make a pass and get rid of your bombs and beat feet out over the water. We're going back in.' The triple-A was getting heavy now; it was getting real toasty down there."

Krause: "When we made the third pass, we were down to 6,000 feet, and as I was circling, getting ready for the fourth pass, I called out triple-A at twelve [o'clock] and three [o'clock], and Joe yells about the same time, 'We've got a missile at six [o'clock]!' I did a break turn, giving up altitude, and went in for the fourth pass at 3,000 feet."

Seidl: "We make our fourth pass—Merrick's having a great time— this is the first time he's had a chance to do visual deliveries. We get our last bombs off and there are fires in the intersection. It is ugly down there. Now we're beating feet out over the water and we get launched on by another missile—an SA-8. We're doing the beam and chaff stuff, and it finally goes away. It either stopped guiding or it ran out of gas. It was kind of a fall-away shot on our tail."

Krause: "We egressed over the water and when we got into the squadron, Bull Baker was standing at the door waiting for us just like he had promised. We gave the tapes to him and he called Glosson with our verbal report. Then we watched our tapes, and in the note I later made in my journal, I said that he watched them 'INTENTLY,' with the word in capital letters. The tapes were dramatic. You could see the burning vehicles. Also, you could see the tracers coming up at us—that was the first time I had seen that on tape. However, Joe and I were both nervous as we watched the tape. Before we went in, we had talked, and we were both afraid that we might be grounded for the rest of the war. We had been told over and over not to fly low and risk losing a jet. However, we had also been told to do the mission at all costs. Fortunately, there was no worry after Baker saw the tapes. He knew we got down to 3,000 feet but he didn't bat an eye. He just said, 'Good job,' and patted us on the back as he took our tape and left the squadron. Joe and I were pleased; this was our best mission of the entire war."

Lt. Col. Mike "Slammer" Decuir, the ops officer of the Chiefs, along with Maj. Larry "Hammer" Coleman as WSO, and Capt. John Hoff and Lt. Glenn Watson as wingmen, may have been the next to take off on Glosson's mission. Together, they tell what happened:

Decuir: "There was a huge thunderstorm just south of Basrah and north of Kuwait City. It was right over the main drag where those guys were running north. At first I thought I could skirt the west edge of it, then turn in from the north. But when we got up there, I could see that there was no way that could be done. So I said, 'Okay, we're going in,' and, boom, we turned right and went into the worst thunderstorm I have ever seen in my life."

Coleman: "I will admit it; I was very concerned. It was a vicious storm. The lightning was so white and dazzling it was almost blinding. Then it would be so black you couldn't see anything. I've got the coordinates for where those guys are running and I'm trying to map but there is no use."

Decuir: "I was yelling at Larry, 'Give me a map, give me a map,' and he is saying, 'I can't map the ground.' That is how thick the rain and the thunderstorm was; the radar returns were bouncing off and we couldn't map the ground."

Coleman: "That was part of it—the other part was the turbulence. It was beating us around and it was hard moving your hands to all the different switches."

Decuir: "Finally, we went in and dropped our CBU-87 on the INS coordinates that had been passed to us by AWACS. About that time the lightning was severe and I can remember thinking, 'Geez, I hope this lightning doesn't hit us while we still have this stuff on board.' And then, as soon as I pickled it off, I remember thinking, 'I hope it doesn't hit any of that stuff until it gets away from us.' My wingman called up and said, 'Hey, I'm not liking this.' And I said, 'I'm not liking it either; just drop your bombs and let's get out of here.' That was the most lightning I have ever seen. It was scary."

Captains Tom Plumb and Two Dogs McIntyre were in one of the two four-ship flights of Rockets that had been launched that night. McIntyre's description is memorable. Said he, "Going up there we talked it over in the flight [Captains Moon Mullins and Rich Horan were leading] and decided to try and stay above the thunderstorms. Then, when we got to the target, we would dive down and make our delivery at medium altitude, through the weather.

"We got up there and had to fly in min afterburner to stay above 300 knots cal [calibrated air speed—as indicated, not true air speed] at about 35,000 feet. There was heavy lightning in the clouds under us and I was wondering whether all those flashes were God's flashes or flashes from Iraqi guns. We're cruising along now, a little bit out of the storm, and we're looking in the radar and we take pictures. Then, it appeared that our radars were malfunctioning. There was just too much metal down there. The [radar] returns didn't look right. It shocked us all when we realized that, yes, what you see is actually what is down there. I'm saying, 'There are thousands and thousands of vehicles down there,' and the rest of the guys in the flight are saying, 'Are you sure?' I said, 'I'm not sure; that's just what it looks like to me.' Then we split up; two ships went north and two ships went about ten miles south. Each of us dropped a string of twelve CBU-87s about two thousand feet long, right straight down the highway. Right after that, another four-ship of Rockets dropped a string—that's ninety-six canisters from our squadron alone. I know the Chiefs also sent up eight ships with the same load, so that is a significant amount of ordnance dropped on that highway."

When the crews returned, they rushed their tapes to the intel shop where Bull Baker and a number of other senior officers were waiting to see the results. Said Baker, "We played the tapes and it showed them descending down into the weather to drop on this endless stream of vehicles. I mean, through the FLIRs, it looked like a gigantic parking lot down there on the highway. There were people scrambling and running around down on the ground—you could actually see them—and about that time this lieutenant colonel, who was standing there watching this, said, 'Good God, that's murder!' Everybody turned around; then I looked at him hard and said, 'Listen, you son-of-a-bitch, that's not murder, that's called war. You're seeing war and all the horrors that go with it.'"

A major who heard Baker's violent outburst said, later, "The press made a big thing out of the bombing of that highway—they called it the 'Highway of Death.' Well, I'm sorry, but they did not evoke any sympathy from me. A lot of those guys down there that night had looted everything they could carry; they had stereos, lamps . . . you name it, they had it. And they were in vehicles that they had stolen from the Kuwaitis. They were not soldiers trying to retreat from a battlefield, and we knew that. We would not have dropped on retreating foot soldiers; none of us would. They were a bunch of criminals escaping in stolen cars. They were rapists, murderers, and thieves, and as far as I was concerned, they deserved what they got."

It would be easy to categorize the major quoted above as bloodthirsty. However, according to those who know him, that is not true. In fact, on an earlier mission, he, his WSO, and their wingmen risked their careers by not carrying out tasking that could have killed innocent civilians. The following is the mission summary from the WSO's log:

> 7 Feb 91 19th mission, 2.2 hrs, TOT approx. 2400. Bullshit mission. Radar road recce. Mission was to look for convoys backed up or parked along a 50 mile stretch of highway about 100 miles SE of Baghdad. Dumb idea. How do you tell the difference between a used car dealership and a group of parked APCs with a radar? Didn't want to kill civilians. Bombed a highway overpass by a railyard since we didn't "see" any military formations. . . . Dropped 12 MK-82 w 904/905. [four names withheld]

The last night of the war was an anticlimax for all the Strike Eagles. Many were sent to western Iraq and told to be extra alert in case Saddam launched a last-ditch Scud raid on Israel. That did not happen and the last crews flew home in daylight after having learned from AWACS that the cease-fire had gone into effect at 0800 hours that morning.

The crews tasked to the KTO the last night were equally frustrated. There were vicious sandstorms in the Al Kharj area and many of their missions were scrubbed. Those who did launch and got to the KTO were told, for the most part, to hold and wait till they were needed. There were hundreds of Coalition airplanes in the area, all wanting to do what they could to end the war, but the ground forces had simply moved too fast. Some in the Strike Eagles got to watch spectacular, last-ditch firefights between Coalition forces and stubborn Iraqi pockets of resistance. But for the most part, the Strike Eagles in the KTO spent their time droning around in a boring racetrack orbit, waiting for tasking that never materialized.

Then they came home. There were smiles and backslapping on the flight line and even some sentimental high-fives between crew chiefs and crews. However, said Maj. Rich Crandall, "This was not the end of a tight football game, where the score had been tied and a last-second touchdown had won the game for the old high school. I mean there was no shouting and dancing in the streets. The guys didn't go wild. It was more like after the old high school has just won a 70-0 blowout against a nothing team. We knew we were going to win. There was never any doubt. What we all did experience was a great sense of relief, knowing that it was over, and knowing that we were going to be going back to our families. There was joy; don't get me wrong. But, from my perspective, it was the joy of relief."

It was also a letdown for many. Said Capt. Steve Kwast, "I observed a lot of little politicians emerging, and there were several who were bitterly disappointed that we did not go after the stuff that had escaped. I know a lot of tanks escaped through the city of Basrah and, because of the danger of civilian casualties, they were not touched. Also, quite a few were disappointed that Saddam, himself, had escaped. We knew, of course, that our mandate did not allow us to continue on into Baghdad. We knew also, that such an action would have turned our Arab allies against us. We knew all of that. But, for several of the guys, there was an unsatisfied feeling, a kind of nagging feeling—a feeling that, yes, we did a good job while we were fighting, but we did not finish what we should have done."

What they did finish that day was much of the Jeremiah Weed that had been stashed for the occasion. Jeremiah Weed! That sounds like something that should be smoked, but it is not. It is the legendary beverage that two dusty and thirsty F-4 drivers were given by a bartender in an old, remote Nevada tavern, after they had been forced to punch out of their airplane. Reportedly, it was, "Thank you, sir!" and "We won't forget this, sir!" and the dusty, thirsty crewmen made a vow to keep their word. Jeremiah Weed became the official, ceremonial drink in the F-4 community, and the heritage has passed on to the Strike Eagles.

So, on that last day of the war, with the amber fluid they had smuggled in for the occasion, many of the crewmen toasted their role in the most massive air campaign in the history of warfare. They were highly pleased with themselves and with their airplanes, and they drank to both. Then they had another toast, a solemn toast to their fallen comrades: Pete and Boo Boo, Teek and Donnie. And then the last one, which was for something they wanted more than anything else: "Guys, here's to going home."

18

The Sad Aftermath

"It was the most disgusting thing I have ever seen in my life."
Maj. Larry "Hammer" Coleman

Nobody flew the night after the cease-fire. Most partied in some fashion, with what resources they had, then went into a long, sound, well-earned sleep. And the next day they lazed around outside, soaking up sunshine, listening to music, and relegating the violence of the past forty-two days into a distant corner of their minds. The peace seemed secure enough, even though there had not been a formal cease-fire agreement. The Iraqis were whipped, and whipped good, and the Coalition had eighty thousand prisoners to prove it. The war was over. There were no doubts about that.

There were doubts, however, about the most important thing on their minds.[1] Their thoughts were of going home to their families, but nobody in high places was saying anything about when that would happen. Would they get to go home immediately? That is what they hoped, but realistically they knew better. In their minds the Strike Eagle had proven itself the most valuable airplane in the Air Force inventory. But they realized that their efforts to prove that to the military brass could backfire on them. "Saddam is still alive

---

[1]"Yeah, going home was heavy on our minds," said Slammer Decuir after reviewing this chapter, "but a lot of us were also concerned about our POWs, Eberly and Griff. Were they going to be released right away, or were they going to play games with them like the Vietnamese did? The war really wasn't over for a lot of us until Eberly and Griff were released."

and, with his weapons, he could still be a threat in the region. If you're so valuable, what makes you think we should let you go home?" Nobody said it in those exact words, but that was the message they expected, but did not want to hear. They were proud to be the best, or what they believed to be the best, but there was nobody else to take their place. They could not even say, "Let the crews go home and leave the airplanes here," because they were about the only ones who could fly the Strike Eagles. They tried not to think about all this, of course, but there was this unpleasant, nagging feeling that would not go away—a feeling that they had become victims of their own success.

The leadership was aware of the letdown that would infect the community after the forty-two days of intensive warfare. They also knew that anxiety about going home would cut deeply into the emotional stamina of the community. They could not do anything about the latter; decisions about going home were above the pay grade of the colonels at Al Kharj. But they could lobby for tasking so their taut, well-oiled combat machine could, for awhile at least, stave off the entropic forces that were like soaring buzzards hovering over the community. Keep them busy; that way they will not have time to think about home. And most important of all: Keep the aviators flying. The tonic of being airborne, in command of flight, is a medicine with enormous efficacy.

Out of some necessity, but perhaps also to stave off a bit of entropy, the Riyadh generals soon put the Strike Eagles back into the air. Day and night they went out to western Iraq to guard against surreptitious Scud launchings against Israel. For the night crews, little had changed, except that there was no opportunity to relieve the boredom by aiding special forces units, or by dropping bombs on juicy ammo dumps. For the day crews, flying out west was another experience. They flew low when they felt like it, looking at whatever they wanted, and they satisfied their curiosity by examining all the targets and SAM sites that had terrorized them. "Hell, it's not big at all," they said after seeing Al Qaim in daylight. "It's just a dirty little town; from all the triple-A that came out of there, I thought it would be a much bigger place."

March 3, 1991, was a big day for a few of the Strike Eagles. That was the day when, in Safwan, Iraq, General Schwarzkopf and key Coalition officers met in a tent with Iraqi general Ahmad and hammered out the formal cease-fire agreement. Before, during, and after the ceremony, someone—nobody wants to accept responsibility now—tasked a flight of Strike Eagles to make low passes over the area. Said one of the pilots, "We were to go in as a two-ship at thirty-minute intervals, with the burner lit to make us louder, and fly by at

300 feet. It was a little bit of psychological warfare just to remind the Iraqis who was boss. I did that a couple times and there were several guys who went quite a bit lower."

"Yeah, quite a bit lower," confessed another pilot who did that. "It may not have been at the surrender ceremony, but at other places, I know we got down to where we would have ripped off our landing gear if it had been down."

The next few days were air show days. Released from the tight discipline of combat flying, many of the crews blew off emotional energy by making low passes everywhere. They wince at the term *buzz*—somehow that connotes irresponsible flying—but buzz is what they did. They buzzed airfields, curious about the damage that had been inflicted, but also to show those on the ground who had won the war. They also buzzed caravans and towns, and, in one case, under orders from a Riyadh general, they buzzed Saddam Hussein's statue in downtown Baghdad while going supersonic in afterburner. "Let'm know down there who really won the war," the general is reported to have said.

All this was great fun, but not without risks. Said one pilot, who swore the author to secrecy, "We were up by K-2, which is the equivalent of our Air Force Academy. I wanted to put on a real show for those guys. So we made a low pass and they came outside and waved—just like all the Iraqis did when we made low passes—they loved it. Then I came back around and lit the burner and went screaming right in front of them. There are about twenty guys standing outside this hangar and they are all waving at me, enjoying the air show. Then I looked out in front and there are telephone wires right in my face. I pulled six and one-half Gs and stood it on its tail. Somehow, I missed the wires; I don't like to think about what would have happened if I had not seen those wires."

Another pilot had a thing about the Coalition ground troops, especially the Americans. "I thought it was the proper thing to do to get down low and salute those guys. They were bored and they loved it. I figured I was helping out their morale. For example, I remember one night coming out of Iraq and seeing a big column of our guys heading south, leaving Iraq. I thought, 'Hey, they need to know that somebody appreciates what they did, right?' So we dived down, flew offset from them at about 300 feet, then, with full blower, I pulled straight up in front of them. In case you haven't seen a Strike Eagle in blower at night, it looks like a comet with that trail of fire coming out of it.

"Another time we were out over the western border of Kuwait— I mean, it is desolate out there. We were motoring along and looked down and there were a bunch of M-1 tanks and Bradleys in a laager;[2] they were in a square, with guns pointed outward, and with their tents inside. Now that is a lonely outpost, right? Well, we decided to help their morale, so we put on a little air show for them. Then we noticed that there was a single M-1 tank out all by itself—an outpost, so we felt sorry for those guys and we gave them a show, too. Several times later, as we would come back from night patrol, we would look for those guys, and sure enough, they would be there. We always made a pass over the outpost tank. It would always be at sunrise, and they would be outside every morning to wave; it was their sunrise ritual. I know it had to be lonely and miserable out there. We could barely get an IR signature off the tank, so it had to be cold. This went on for one solid week, then one morning, as we passed over, the guys at the outpost tank were holding a big banner. We couldn't read it and never ever talked to them, but I'm sure we helped out their morale a lot."

Besides keeping the community busy and the aviators flying, the leadership also realized that everybody needed a break. Soon, small groups were allowed to take a squadron van to Bahrain for a few nights on the town, and later, with the help of an outstanding USO lady (whose name, unfortunately, nobody can remember), they were catching C-130 flights to Dubai, one of the United Arab Emirates, where, for a very reasonable rate, they stayed in a five-star hotel with a pristine beach. (Some were anointed with a special privilege; they were allowed to remain for ten days as a tour guide.)

But even the local area became a little more attractive. Shortly after the formal cease-fire, a dozen or more would cram into a squadron van and go into the neighboring town of Al Kharj. Said Maj. Lee Lewis, "We would pack in as many as the van would hold, then head down this dirt road that paralleled a brand new four-lane highway—we couldn't use it because it hadn't been properly named or dedicated, or whatever. It was about twenty miles into town, and when we would get there, we would go straight to Hervey's Drive Inn. It was a lot like a Hardy's, with orange motif, except that one side was walled off for families—I guess they didn't want their women and girls to be viewed by just anybody. Then, we would go through the, no kidding, Saturday Night Live routine. We would order a big cheeseburger and the waiter would yell at the cook, 'Onea bigga cheese.' Then we would order a big fry. 'Onea bigga fry.' Then a chocolate shake. 'Onea chocolate shakea.' It was funny. And I'm sure we ate some goat burgers and drank goat-milk shakes, but who cared?"

---

[2] A South African term for an encampment, especially with wagons in a circle for protection.

They also got a chance to have a laugh on base. Said one of the WSOs, "General Glosson came for a visit, and of course everybody was talking about the promise he made before the war to bring us beer. Well, he arrives, but of course he doesn't bring any beer. But while he is here, he gives a brief in the wing conference room and I am going to attend. So, in grease pencil, in big letters, I write on this 8-1/2 x 14 legal-size sheet of paper, 'WHERE'S THE BEER?' and tape the sheet to the table opposite where he is sitting. He saw it during the meeting; I know he did. It probably embarrassed him, but he didn't say anything. We didn't get the beer, but at least we got a good laugh."

Then, finally, it happened; the Rockets, because they had been in theater since the previous August, were notified that they were going home. Now there was genuine shouting, dancing, hugging, enthusiastic excitement. From the time they received their orders, they packed and were airborne in less than forty-eight hours.

And when they got home, they received the true heroes' welcome, with brass bands, clutching friends and family, and, to their surprise, fawning media folks with the apparent desire to say something positive for a change about their deeds in the war. After a few days with their families, they then went out on the speaking circuit, talking to service clubs and classrooms of third-graders.

They also did another important task. They unpacked their mascot, the stuffed puffin, Binky, and placed him in the squadron bar. Then they waited, hoping to spring their rehearsed outrage upon an unsuspecting snacko.[3] Just as soon as one of them happened to be heard bragging about anything they had done in the airplane, the old-timer in the squadron would grab Binky, shove it in the young aviator's face, and, with outrage, shout, "You don't know what the hell you are talking about; even this puffin has more combat hours than you!" (Binky was taken on one four and one-half hour combat mission by the unnamed aviator who planned this farce.)

So, the Rockets were happy again, and the Chiefs, with their twenty-four airplanes, were left in the theater to do whatever tasks were needed. That is how they happened to get tasked for what most now describe as the most frustrating, disgusting, and sickening missions they have ever flown.

It all started at Safwan, where General Ahmad and General Schwarzkopf hammered out the agreement that formalized the cease-fire. One of Schwarzkopf's demands was that the Iraqis could not fly any of their aircraft. General Ahmad pleaded mercy, saying

---

[3]The "snacko" is the lowest-ranking aviator in the squadron, whose job it is to keep the squadron bar stocked with beverages and popcorn, and to manage the inventory of squadron paraphernalia such as cups and T-shirts.

(according to Schwarzkopf in his memoirs), "You know the situation of our roads and bridges and communications. We would like to fly helicopters to carry officials of our government in areas where roads and bridges are out. This has nothing to do with the front line. This is inside Iraq."

Schwarzkopf comments on that request in his book. "It appeared to me to be a legitimate request," said Schwarzkopf. "And given that the Iraqis had agreed to all our requests, I didn't feel it was unreasonable to grant one of theirs. 'As long as it is not over the part we are in, that is absolutely no problem. So we will let the helicopters fly. That is a very important point, and I want to make sure it's recorded, that military helicopters can fly over Iraq. Not fighters, not bombers.'"

Three paragraphs later, Schwarzkopf calls Ahmad a son-of-a-bitch. That language is mild. From those who were to fly the Strike Eagles over Iraq in the next few weeks, the descriptions of the "helicopter agreement" are scathing, obscene, and unprintable.

What follows is a synthesized account of what happened, based upon interviews with more than twenty crewmen who witnessed the sad aftermath, but who wish to remain anonymous for reasons that will be obvious.

"We were a two-ship, flying CAP over northern Iraq, enforcing the no-fly restriction in the cease-fire agreement. We were up above Kirkuk, and over the winding mountain road to the village of Chamchamal. The road was jammed, with maybe 450 to 600 civilian vehicles, and with hundreds of civilians walking or leading burros. They were Kurds, fleeing the Iraqis, trying to get into the mountains and into Turkey. Then we look down and there are waves of helicopters that have come off Al Fathah. They are Hinds, Russian gunships, carrying machine guns and rockets, and while we're looking down there in horror, they begin flying in a circle over those people, firing directly into them. We called AWACS and told them what was happening and requested permission to attack the helicopters. 'We'll get back to you,' they said. I mean, it is so bad down there, you don't even want to look. It is carnage; they are firing into innocent civilians—women and children. Finally, after what seemed like hours, AWACS comes back, 'Negative on your request. You cannot fire upon helicopters unless they deliberately fire upon you.'

"We are both angry and sick, and as Lead, I finally decided to try and do something. I tell my wingman to hold above us, then we dive on one of the helicopters from behind and hot-nose him—we slide underneath him and pull up sharply in front of him, hoping that the wake turbulence [a vicious vortex off the wingtips] would snap a rotor blade. That got their attention; they went into a defensive wheel, with one's nose behind the other, and then we did it again, flying just under the wheel. That stopped them; they went over and landed. We climbed back up to altitude, and while we were there, they did not take off again."

That is the general account; that is what many of the Strike Eagle crews did when they saw the carnage the helicopter gunships were inflicting. But there were variations. Some dove alongside the gunships; some dove over the top of them (hoping the wake turbulence would settle); and some, who had heard of the Russians doing it, tried to fire their lasers at the gunship pilots hoping to blind them. Finally, in desperation, one Strike Eagle crew flew close to the stream of machine-gun fire coming out of one of the gunships. After that, one of them made a plea to AWACS: "Hey, they are shooting at me now; the bullets just went by our canopy. Are we cleared to return fire?"

After a few moments came a reply from a wise, but probably sympathetic senior officer—a reply they did not want to hear. "Understand you are being fired upon. Are they actually pointing their guns at you?"

Into the intercom: "Shit!" To AWACS: "Negative."

"Then you cannot fire at them. Acknowledge."

"Roger; understand we cannot fire unless they point their guns at us."

Pilot: "Expletive unprintable!"

WSO: "Expletive unprintable!"

Pilot: "Let's go down again. Do we have enough gas?"

WSO: "We do if you don't use the burner."

Pilot: "Tally ho!"

They dove again and screamed just inches over the top of one of the gunships that was firing. The pilot, in a hard break: "What do you see back there?"

WSO: "Keep your turn."

Pilot: "Can you see it?"

WSO (excited): "It's going down! I think it's autorotating! It hit the ground and dust is flying!"

Pilot: "Shit hot!"

WSO: "Come on, let's head for home or we're going to need a tanker."

So what happened to this gunship, and to others that were subjected to similar treatment? There were all kinds of smiles around the squadron ops desk when the author asked that question.

Pilot: "Let's just say that we kept going up there for several weeks and the helicopter had not moved."

Author: "Then you did get some of them?"

Pilot (smiling): "As long as you quote us as saying that we heard rumors to that effect, I guess you could say that."

Author: "Okay, I can do that. But tell me, did your efforts deter them?"

Pilot (frowning): "Nope. They learned that we weren't going to shoot them, so when we dived on them, they just landed and waited until we pulled away."

Author: "But your efforts did help, correct?"

Pilot: "Only for awhile."

Author: "What happened?"

Pilot (grimly): "We got caught."

The pilot and his friends then went on to explain what happened, after a senior officer in Riyadh heard what they were doing.

"Are your guys up there buzzing Iraqi helicopters?"

"Our guys? They know better than that. Why, I can't imagine such a thing."

"Well, just in case they get the urge, you are officially being ordered to cease and desist. You WILL NOT dive on helicopters; in fact, when you are capping up there, you will not go below 10,000 feet unless you see a fixed-wing airplane. Understood?"

Everybody saluted smartly as the word was passed—so the story goes. But, among themselves, they grew frustrated and depressed just watching the carnage. And it wasn't only attacks on refugee caravans on the roads. They also witnessed small villages being obliterated by rockets and shell fire.

Some, of course, tried to make sense of it all. But in their anguish, they kept coming back to a fundamental question: What difference does it make if a bomb or bullet comes from a fixed-wing fighter or a helicopter gunship?

Even the philosophers among them did not have an answer for that. In fact, after witnessing, or even hearing about those atrocities, many of the Strike Eagle crews grew cynical. Said one of the pilots:

"After the war, while I was waiting to come home, I wrote several letters to kids in Texas who had written me. I told them that what we had done in that war might sound great, but it was just a Band-Aid approach. Try to realize that we were just temporary actors on the stage in a never-ending play. We didn't stop anything. The fighting and bloodshed over there is never ending. It will go on, and on, and on. . . . "

And on and on is how it has been since the war. A squadron of Strike Eagles has remained stationed in the theater, with crews— including those with combat experience in the war—rotated on a regular basis. And nobody in the Strike Eagle community thinks the situation is likely to change. "They have fought for centuries, and they are going to keep right on fighting," said a WSO. "My kids will probably be flying Strike Eagles in the same damn desert."

The only thing the author will say to that is, "Well, at least they will be flying a damned good airplane."

Glossary

ADI	Instrument showing attitude of airplane relative to horizon
AGL	Height above ground level
AIM-7	Radar-guided air-to-air missile; also called a "Sparrow"
AIM-9	Infrared-guided air-to-air missile; also called a "Sidewinder"
Albino	Nickname for lighter-colored air-to-air model of F-15
APC	Armored personnel carrier
ATO	Air tasking order; complete mission data; also called a "frag"
AWACS	Airborne command and control aircraft; capable of wide-area radar coverage
Bag	Slang term for auxiliary fuel tank
Bandit	Confirmed enemy aircraft
Barrage fire	Antiaircraft fire that covers an area rather than attempting to track aircraft
Blower	Slang term for afterburner; also called "burner"
Bogie	Unknown aircraft
BVR	Beyond visual range
CAP	Combat air patrol; protective cover flown by fighters
CAS	Close air support
Castle switch	Switch shaped like a castle turret; has distinct feel; used to scroll "layers" on multipurpose displays
CBU	Cluster bomb unit; a canister munition containing bomblets
CENTAF	Central Command Air Force; Air Force headquarters in Riyadh
Chaff	Aluminized Mylar strips of various lengths used to decoy enemy radar

DO	Director of operations; officer under wing commander in charge of all flight operations
E&E	Escape and evasion
EF-111	Radar-jamming aircraft; called "Raven" or "Sparkvaark"
DMPI	Desired mean point of impact; the place where the bombs should impact
FAC	Forward air controller
FIDO	Fighter duty officer; in Riyadh, a crewman who represented his fighter community at air force headquarters
FLIR	Forward-looking infrared; a pod carried on aircraft that contains infrared sensors; allows crew to have visual capability at night
Flogger	Soviet-built MiG-23 fighter
Fulcrum	Soviet-built MiG-29 fighter
Gator	Canister containing numerous mines, which, when spread over the ground, may be triggered by pressure or by time-sensing devices; used to deny enemy access to an area
GBU	Guided bomb unit; a smart bomb
Gorilla package	Slang term for a large group of aircraft
Guard	Emergency radio frequency monitored by all friendly aircraft; also known as "Navy common"
Hammer	Officer in charge of all decisions on AWACS aircraft
HARM	Missile that guides on radar emissions; used by Weasels to target the radar used by surface-to-air missiles
HSI	Horizontal situation indicator; instrument used for steering information
HUD	Heads-up display; projects vital piloting information on the windscreen
H-2	One of the main airfields in western Iraq
ICS	Internal countermeasures system; used to confuse or jam enemy radar
ID	Identify
IFF	Identification, friend or foe; electronic means for differentiating friends from enemies

IMC	Instrument meteorological conditions; when visual flight is impossible and instruments must be used to maintain flight
IN	Chief intelligence officer
IP	Initial point; the geographic place where aircraft turn toward their target; also, an instructor pilot
IR	Infrared
JRCC	Joint Rescue Coordination Center; place where searches for downed airmen are controlled
JSTARS	During Gulf War a new and untested airborne target location and control center; equipped with same type of radar as F-15E
KKMC	King Khalid Military City; air base relatively close to Kuwait
KTO	Kuwait Theater of Operations; Kuwait and surrounding area where enemy forces were positioned
LANTIRN	Low-altitude navigation and targeting, infrared, for night; pods containing infrared sensors that give crew visual capability, terrain-following radar, and targeting ability in darkness
LGB	Laser-guided bomb; also guided bomb unit (GBU), or smart bomb
Map	See Patch map
Mark-20	Canister containing bomblets with shaped charges; effective against armored targets
Mark-82	Five-hundred-pound general-purpose bomb; not laser guided
Mark-84	Two-thousand-pound general-purpose bomb; not laser guided
Mil power	Maximum power without using afterburner
MPD	Multipurpose display; a cathode-ray tube (CRT) upon which several displays of information may be projected; in the F-15E the pilot has three and the WSO has four; aircraft with MPDs are said to have "glass cockpits"
MR	Mission ready; ready to fly combat missions
MRE	Meal ready to eat; combat food rations
Nugget	New pilot or new WSO

ORE	Operational readiness exercise; very intense practice exercise in which units are evaluated for combat readiness
Pacific Wind	Operation planned (but never carried out) to rescue American embassy personnel in Kuwait
PACS	Programmable armament control set; used for choosing weapon or weapons to feed release computations to computer
Patch map	Radar picture used for targeting
Pickle	Release ordnance; in F-15E gives to the computer consent to release ordnance
Pipper	Visual aiming designator
Rainbow mission	Mission with aircraft from different squadrons; name originated because different squadrons have different colors on tails of the aircraft
Recce	Reconnaissance; "road recce" or "river recce" is armed reconnaissance with aircraft ready to destroy targets on roads or rivers
Rockeye	See Mark-20
ROE	Rules of engagement; rules that limit combat engagement
Roland	French surface-to-air missile; effective at low altitudes
R&R	Rest and relaxation
RTU	Replacement training unit; where crews transition to new airplane
RWR	Radar warning receiver; device that tells direction and type of radar energy striking airplane; pronounced "raw"
SA	Situational awareness; awareness of oneself in relation to time, space, and other aircraft
SA-2	Soviet-designed, radar-guided surface-to-air missile
SA-3	Soviet-designed, radar-guided surface-to-air missile
SA-6	Mobile Soviet-designed, radar-guided surface-to-air missile
SA-8	Mobile Soviet-designed, radar-guided surface-to-air missile
SAM	Surface-to-air missile

Sam ring	Area around a SAM site where its missiles are a threat to aircraft
SAR	Search and rescue
SAS	Special Air Service; British special forces
Scud	Soviet-designed, medium-range ballistic missile modified and used by Iraq
Smart bomb	See LGB
Squawk	Emit IFF signals that can be identified by radar; usually from a transponder-type device
TAC	Tactical Air Command
TACAN	Tactical air navigation; UHF transmitter that provides distance and directional information
TACC	Tactical Air Command and Control Center; Gulf War air campaign command center
TFR	Terrain-following radar; also "TF"
TOT	Time over target
Triple-A	Originally antiaircraft artillery; now any unguided, ground-to-air 12.7mm to 100mm gunfire; also "AAA"
TSD	Tactical situation display; technical name for moving map display
Viper	Nickname for the F-16
Weasel	Complete name: Wild Weasel; in Gulf War, F-4Gs that carried HARM missiles
WSO	Weapon systems officer; pronounced "wizzo"; also "backseater" or "pitter"
Zeus	Nickname for Soviet-designed ZSU-23-4 antiaircraft weapon

Appendix

F-15E STRIKE EAGLE DATA

Designer and Manufacturer

McDonnell Aircraft Company division of McDonnell Douglas Corp., St. Louis, Mo.

First flight

December 11, 1986, St. Louis, Mo.

Powerplants

Two Pratt & Whitney F-100-PW-220 low-bypass turbofan engines with afterburners, each developing 23,450 lbs (106kN) of thrust

Armament (During Gulf War)

Up to four AIM-9L/M infrared-guided Sidewinder missiles

Up to four AIM-7F/M radar-guided Sparrow missiles

One M-61 20mm Gatling gun with 450 rounds

Most conventional bombs and GBU-10 & GBU-12 laser-guided bombs

Avionics

Hughes APG-70 synthetic aperture radar

IBM central computer

Kaiser wide-field-of-view holographic heads-up display

Honeywell ring-laser-gyro inertial navigation system

Seven Sperry multipurpose monochrome and color display screens

Internal countermeasures equipment (Northrop, Loral, Magnavox)

Martin Marietta LANTIRN navigation and targeting pods

Size and Weight

Length: 63.75 ft (19.44m)

Wing span: 42.81 ft (13.05m)

Height: 18.5 ft (5.64m)

Horizontal stabilizer span: 28.5 ft (8.69m)

Main gear span: 9.03 ft (2.75m)

Empty weight: 40,000 lbs (18,181.82 kg)

Max external fuel: three 600-gal tanks

Max ordnance 24,500 lbs (11,113.13 kg)

Max takeoff weight: 81,000 lbs (36,741.36 kg)

Performance

Max speed: mach 2.5

Max range (ferry with conformal tanks and three external tanks): 2,400 miles

Combat ceiling: 35,000 ft

Service ceiling: 50,000 ft

Load factor: -3G to +9G

Index